THE GRAND

ETTEILLA

by Julia Orsini, Mlle Lemarchand
& M.M.d'Odoucet

Translated and edited by
Marius Høgnesen

This book is an English translation of 3 books in French;

Le Grand ETTEILLA, ou l'art de Tirer les Cartes
et de dire la Bonne Aventure
by Julia Orsini
Published from 1838

Les Recreations de la Cartomancie, ou description pittoresque
De chacune des Cartes du Grand Jeu de l'Oracle des Dames
by Mlle Lemarchand
Published in 1867.

Science des Signes, ou Medecine de l'Esprit,
Connue sous le nom d'Art de tirer les Cartes
by M. M. d'Odoucet,
Published around 1806

Etteilla version I card images are from *Theoretischer und Praktischer Unterricht über das Buch Thot* with permission from;
Universitätsbibliothek Johann Christian Senckenberg Frankfurt am Main

Etteilla version II card images are scans from translator´s
own original Julia Orsini booklet from the 1840s.

Etteilla version III card images are scans from translator´s
own original Lemarchand booklet from the 1860s.

Lemarchand version III card images together with version I
have been made into Tarot card illustrations for this book.

Images on the cover are from d'Odoucet´s *Science des Signes*.
Credit: Warburg Institute

Images have been modified, retouched and repaired.

First print September 2021. This is a revised edition from September 2022.

Books available on:
https://www.circleandtriangle.com

ISBN: 978-82-692706-4-8 Paperback
ISBN: 978-82-692706-5-5 eBook

3

THE GRAND

ETTEILLA

or the art of drawing the cards

CONTENTS

1. An introduction recalling the origin of the cards;
2. The meaning of the tarots, that make up the real book of Thot, and how to replace them in case one, could not procure them;
3. A method by which one can easily learn to read one's own destiny, and predict

GOOD FORTUNE

4. An explanation of the 78 Tarot cards or Egyptian cards;
5. A table of synonyms or different meanings of the words which are placed at the top or bottom of each of these cards;
6. A list of the hundred common questions to which it is easy to answer with the appropriate use of the Book of Thot;
7. The rules to several amusing tarot games, etc.

ALL ASSEMBLED AND PUT IN A NEW ORDER

by Julia ORSINI

The Sibyl of Faubourg Saint-Germain
ACCORDING TO THE METHOD PRACTICED
by Mademoiselle LENORMAND

ETTEILLA

Etteilla, image from translator´s Julia Orsini booklet.

9

TRANSLATOR'S NOTE

Although a collector of Tarot books and decks for years, I have found it difficult to find books in English on one rather iconic Tarot; *the Grand Etteilla* or *Etteilla´s Egyptian Tarot.* I am hoping with this book to remedy that, to shed some light on the Tarot-language, which has been attributed to these cards.

Jean-Baptiste Alliette (Etteilla) created his Grand Etteilla deck around 1788, but the earliest published card decks only appeared several years later. There are basically 3 versions of this deck. The *Grand Etteilla I*, the version that resembles the original the most, one of the earliest by Pierre Mongie l'Aine, in 1826, the *Grand Etteilla II* by Simon Blocquel in 1838 and the *Grand Etteilla III* by De La Rue in 1867. There are several reproductions available, such as the ones offered by Lo Scarabeo; the anniversary edition *Etteilla Tarot* with version I cards and the *Book of Thoth*, with version III cards. Grimaud has also long put out their *Grand Etteilla, Egyptian Gypsies Tarot,* with version I cards, and the Biblioteque Nationale in Paris reproduces a version III, the *Tarot Egyptien, Grand Jeu de Oracle des Dames* with a partially English-translated Orsini booklet. Finally, several Etteilla clones also exist, such as; the Anima Antiqua, Cartomanzia Italiana, Dr Moorne´s Tarots Egipcios, Tarocco Egiziano, Esoteric Ancient tarot, Tarot Lenormand and Jeu de la Princesse tarot etc.

The Orsini booklet in French was published from 1838 with version II card illustrations and was intended to serve as a user manual for the Grand Etteilla decks, and is still today a relevant resource in decoding Etteilla's Tarots. Some decades later another booklet by Lemarchand was published, but now with version III card illustrations.

The skeleton of this book is the Orsini booklet translated in its entirety. I have also added the Lemarchand card descriptions for the version III in this book. The cards are presented side by side for easy reference. In addition, I have included the version I, with card descriptions from d'Odoucet, a student and contemporary of Etteilla. The version I illustrations in this book are a later print made by Scheible from 1857, so not those by d'Odoucet from 1806, which do however illustrate the front cover and back of this book. A more up-to-date, modern text on card interpretations is also included. The modern interpretations come mainly from 3 French sources; Collette Sylvestre-Haeberle, Claude Darche and Emmanuel San Emeterio.

Although I am not an expert on Etteilla, I have provided some explanatory foot notes along the way, things that have helped me out and perhaps will you.

Marius Høgnesen

INTRODUCTION

ON THE ORIGINS OF THE CARDS

All the scholars who have published their research on these cards attribute Jacquemin Gringonneur[1], with the introduction of the game of Tarot into France, and history tells us that this painter of these images, in fact, received fifty Parisis sols[2] from Charles Poupart, king Charles VI's banker, for three decks in various colours, made to entertain the monarch during his madness. The name *Gringonneur* is the only name that has survived, but the cards did however, exist before him. They were known during Charles V, who honoured Jéhan de Saintré with his friendship, who himself abstained from playing with cards and dice. Gringonneur therefore transcribed the cards onto paper or parchment, which had before been engraved on gold or silver plates. Those used by fortune tellers were drawn on plates made of ivory.

It is to the ancient Egyptians, that Etteilla attributes the invention of tarot, or the book of Thot; this book consisting of 78 cards made of the purest gold, on which were inscribed hieroglyphs, that is to say, mysterious figures, the explanation of which was made daily, to the community, by their leader. It was, he says, the only book which escaped the fury of Omar, when he sat fire to the famous library of Alexandria.

It was then passed on to the Greeks and the Arabs; these spread it to all the nations, who accepted it as a book of philosophy.

It was at the end of the 14th century, that these cards became a popular amusement in Europe. The Germans

---

[1] Translator: The creator of *Charles VI* tarots.
[2] Translator: Old French coinage; 15 Parisis sol = 1 Livre tournois or 4,13g of gold.

made a considerable trade of it. France hastened to imitate them. The first French factories were established in Colmar, Belfort and Lyon. The manufacturers, who at the time, saw it only as a game, were quick to corrupt its meaning by removing certain symbols and replacing them with others.

It was only after thirty years of research and around the year 1780, that the famous Etteilla restored them to their original state, and explained their secrets in the way of the Egyptians.

This Etteilla, who gathered so much attention at the end of the last century, was he a mind wanderer or simply a cartomancer, or was he both? This question is easy to answer for the one who sees cartomancy only as a simple game, but to the true followers, who want to pay well, to believe even more fervently, have made him into a scholar. We will not speak to that by strength of practice, but in his writings, he did not himself take himself too seriously. His works on the tarots have become rare and much sought after.[3]

Before Etteilla, an author; Court de Gebelin, who had written ten folio volumes, a work entitled; *Le Monde Primitif* expresses himself thus, on the origin of the book of Thot:

If we heard announced, that there exists today, for 3.957 years, a work of the ancient Egyptians, one of their books which escaped the flames, which devoured their superb library and which contains their purest doctrine, on interesting phenomena, everyone would undoubtedly be

---

[3] HERE IS THE TITLE OF THIS WORK:
COLLECTION SUR LES HAUTES SCIENCES, or a theoretical and practical treatise on the wise magic of the ancient peoples, completed in full, in twelve books, which contain everything that (Alliette) Etteilla wrote on hermetic philosophy, the art of drawing the cards ... and in particular the sublime book of Thot.
This work, almost always collected into two volumes, very rarely found, is only retained at a very high price.

eager to know a book so precious, so extraordinary. Yes, we will also add, that this book is much dismissed, in much of Europe; and for a number of centuries, it has been in the hands of everyone, the amazement would surely continue to grow. Would it not reach its heights, when we point out, that no one ever suspected it to be Egyptian? That we have it, as we do not have it; that no one has ever tried to decipher a sheet of it; that the fruit of its exquisite wisdom is regarded as a mass of extravagant figures, which by themselves mean nothing!? Would we not want to tease and play on the credulity of our readers?

The fact is, however, very true. This Egyptian book, the only survivor of their superb library, exists today; it is even in many hands.

Unfortunately, this precious book is not understood by the majority of those, who have copies of it. It would be desirable that a capable man took the lead and clearly explained its contents. We say, we want this to be true, that a scholar take care of this important work, and may he finish it soon!

Etteilla, who had read this passage, therefore undertook to translate this book of Thot, he loved the cards, we cannot doubt it, and as he was nothing short of a millionaire, he had made himself into a Cartomancer, which he succeeded in. His success was immense, he soon had a splendid hotel, where all the beautiful ladies of his time stayed. It is undoubtedly then, that he began to write. It was no longer enough just to be rich, he wanted to be famous. The effects of his ambition went on to posterity, he wrote a lot, so rarely today do we speak of cartomancy, without mentioning his name.

At the time of the Revolution, Etteilla had become all the fashion, but there was no time to waste, in order to achieve success. Everyone was more concerned with public affairs than with their particular future, besides, the future was just a word away. It was only after the appeasement of the revolutionary storm, that cartomancy became a thing again. We could say that it became the golden age, it was during this time, that Mademoiselle Lenormand began to make herself the talk of the town. Etteilla had disappeared, it is not known, whether he left any memoirs, but it is at least certain, that they were never published.

Mademoiselle Lenormand was a bit the second volume, she also took her consultants seriously. It must be mentioned, that they were not insignificant either, but rather important ladies. It was very fashionable to consult her. Her salons were visited, not only by the fairer sex, but by the top brass, the Muscadins[4] and even the most prominent men of the Directory[5]. They went to ask her for oracles, it was indeed good manners to say to someone, when entering a room to converse about the very latest: Have you seen Mademoiselle Lenormand? As this sibyl was very shrewd, she had often successfully turned it to her benefit, which gave her an immense reputation, crowned heads are named, who do not deny calling on her and if the story is true, she received, during the invasions of 1814 and 1815, many visits from foreign princes.

Later, Mademoiselle Lenormand continued to give consultations, but it was no longer in fashion. If one still went to this sibyl, it was only in secret. The oracle had lost its appeal. She did not disclose, like Etteilla, the secrets of her science. Let us add, that she had a method of her own, which acquired a great deal of consideration. This method consisted in giving graceful and flattering interpretations to her predictions, and if she thought she saw something else revealed in the cards, something very serious, or something the consultant himself had revealed, more so than

---

[4] Translator: The Muscadins (*wearing musk perfume)* were wealthy young men, who became an important political group during the French revolution.

[5] Translator: The *Directoire* refers to a political group that headed the French government during a period of the French revolution.

the cards, then it turned into an advice, an advice, certainly not without value. Today the light has shone, the number of people who ask the cards for distractions are still numerous, but most of them do so, just for fun and that has given us a very nice recreation accepted by good society, worth a mention is Patiences.[6] As for those who make the art of drawing cards an entertainment, they will find in our book everything, that may be of interest to them, that is to say, the real explanations, the secrets of the Tarot Cards according to the famous Cartomancer Etteilla, with the application of the method of which we wrote before.

---

[6] This game consists of card combinations put together in any one way and then replaced, according to a given figure, producing a symmetrical arrangement, which then makes a prediction. See the book by Madame J. J. Lambert containing:

LA COLLECTION DES NOUVELLES PATIENCES, 1 volume in fine coloured paper, glossy, price 2 fr. 50 postage by mail.

We cannot ignore a little book, which is currently having much success, its title:

LA VÉRITABLE CARTOMANCIE, 1 volume containing 1,750 words, price 6 fr. and 6 fr. 50 by mail, this volume filled with figures gives all the combinations, one may find in the game of Piquet and its consequences.

We would like to point out to our readers a very nice reprint of the book by NOSTRADAMUS which has just come on sale, here is the title:

Les PROPHETIES de MICHEL NOSTRADAMUS grouped into ten centuries, several of which have not been printed before, with the life of the author, the revelations of Saint Brigite, followed by the Prophecies of Thomas-Joseph Moult. A beautiful volume, printed with the greatest quality, Elzévier typographics, additional paper, price postage by mail: 5 fr.

The prophecies of Nostradamus first appeared in 1550; Enthusiasts, or very learned interpreters, discovered in them the announcements of great historical events, which have since taken place. Nostradamus predicted among other things Saint Barthelemy, which started his reputation. He would later predict the Revolution, the death of Louis XVI, that of Marie-Antoinette, the rise of Napoleon, 1830, 1848, etc., etc.

This book, which has long been missing in commerce, will be much sought after. The prophecies of Nostradamus often resemble riddles and must therefore pique the curiosity of lovers of occult sciences, who will certainly find great pleasure finding in them interpretations relating to the things of the present time.

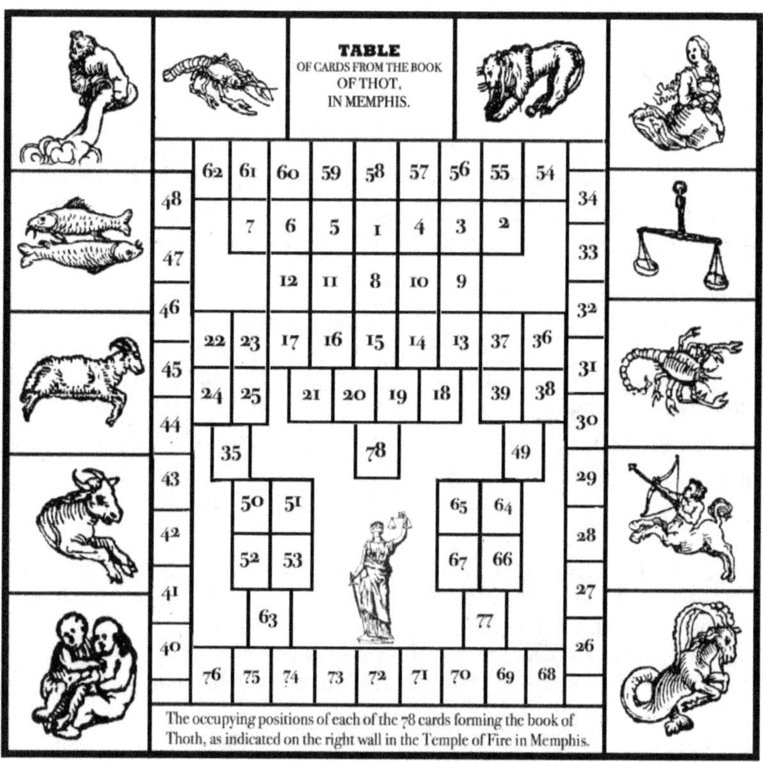

Zodiac images from *www.fromoldbooks.org*

A foldout, representing the Fire Temple of Memphis with the 78 Arcana, where they allegedly first appeared, according to Etteilla. This illustrated the 1838 edition, but was omitted in later editions. This table has been recreated here. –Translator.

INDICATIONS

on the Tarots or the Cards that make up

THE BOOK OF THOT

The book of Thot is made up of 78 tarots or cards, which are distinguished by order of numbers, and by figures appropriate to their meaning. These cards can be divided into series. We notice among them:

4 kings or rulers	No. 22	36	50	64
4 queens or ladies	23	37	51	65
4 knights or jacks	24	38	52	66
4 pages or valets	25	39	53	67
4 ten	26	40	54	68
4 nines	27	41	55	69
4 eights	28	42	56	70
4 sevens	29	43	57	71
4 six	30	44	58	72
4 fives	31	45	59	73
4 fours	32	46	60	74
4 threes	33	47	61	75
4 twos	34	48	62	76
4 aces	35	49	63	77

By removing the 4 knights from the 56 cards we just listed, 52 will remain, which can form an entire deck. Club cards (Baton) will then replace Diamonds (Carreaux); those of Cups (Coupes) will be for the Hearts (Cæurs); those of swords (Epees) will take the place of Spades and those of Coins or Money will appear for Clover (Trefles).

We also notice among the 78 tarots of the book of Thot:
    Etteilla or the male querent no. 1.
    Etteilla or the female querent no. 8.
The six days of creation of the world; Nos. 2, 3, 4, 5, 6 and 7.
    The four cardinal virtues; Nos. 9, 10, 11 and 12.
Finally, ten cards showing significant events in the life of man; Nos. 13, 14 15, 16, 17, 18, 19, 20, 21 and 78.
    It is however necessary to draw the cards yourself, get your hands on the big deck of 78 Egyptian tarots or book of Thot verified by Z. Lismon. 78, cards in a slipcase. Price 6 francs and 6 fr. 50, postage by mail.

OBSERVATIONS

ESSENTIALS ON CHOOSING
A GOOD TAROT DECK

Etteilla in his work on the seven principles of the Philosophy of Hermes[7], page 240 of the manuscript, recommends using only Taros with clear illustrations; he protests against those, which do not depict their main meanings in the top and bottom or whose figures are almost indecipherable.

He in particular points out the German and Italian tarots as being defective and potentially misleading.

The first, he says, are for the most part indecipherable; they can easily be mistaken for one another, as there is such a similarity between those in the same suit. For example, the tarots which should represent Clubs, are hardly distinguishable except by a Roman numeral, very badly made and placed in the opposite direction, etc., etc.

The second (the Italian ones[8]) should not be considered as a tarot deck, as there are really only 26 cards, quite crudely engraved with Egyptian symbols; the other 52 are regular playing cards.

When, he continues, an amateur would want to procure a set of tarot cards, he must; 1. choose it among those coming from French or Arab manufacturers 2. make sure that the 78 cards present each of the figures belonging to the first 21 cards, the first 4 of each series of Clubs, Cups, Swords and Coins, and Folly represented in the 78th card; 3. he must also make sure that, on the others, are depicted the number of Clubs, Cups, etc., which must establish their

---

[7] Translator: The 7 Principles; Mentalism, Correspondence, Vibration, Polarity, Rhythm, Causality and Gender.

[8] Translator: These would be the Italian Tarot de Marseille.

value, and that in addition, their number has been written, as well as their main meaning, either in upright or reverse.

The continuator of Etteilla, strongly urges the cartomancers to use only Tarots made by the factory of Z. Lismon[9], because it has verified their accuracy in all respects.

---

[9] Translator: These are the version II, which illustrated the original Julia Orsini booklet, and are the first card series presented in this book.

METHOD OF DRAWING THE CARDS

OR TAROTS FROM THE BOOK OF THOT AND AN EASY WAY TO ARTICULATE ORACLES

following a shuffle to which these cards will have been subjected

FIRST SERIES OF ORACLES, WITH 42 CARDS

1. Shuffle your deck in both directions and alternate, that is to say, at times placing the cards in the upright, and at times placing them in the reverse.
2. Have the querent cut the deck, make sure he does so with his left hand, which is very important in this operation.
3. Take the first 42 cards from the deck once shuffled, cut and form six piles, each made up of seven cards, and which you will place onto the table in the following order:[10]

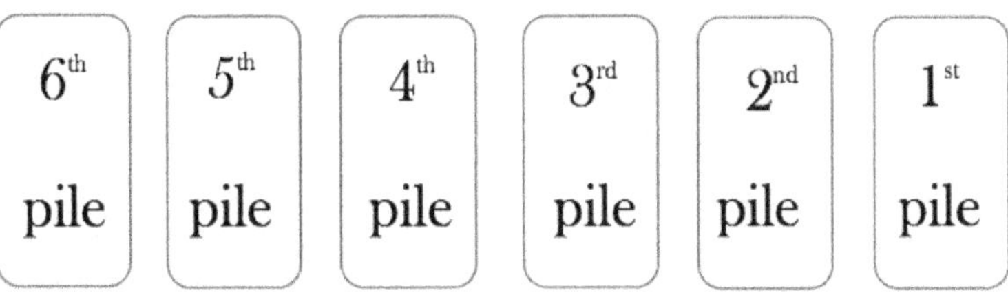

---

[10] Stacked tarot cards must not be turned over; those put in rows, as stated in paragraphs 5, 6 and 7, must face down, so that they can be explained.

4. You will take from each of these piles successively, starting with the first, the cards, which you will spread out in a line, going from right to left, in this way:

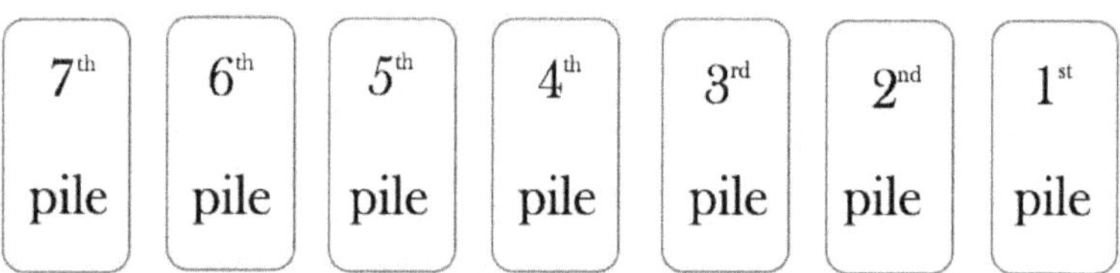

this will result in seven piles of six cards.

5. Take the first card from each of these seven piles, shuffle them together and form a new line, still proceeding from right to left.[11]

6. Then take two cards from each pile, shuffle them and form two more rows of seven, as described above.

7. Pick up the rest of the cards, that being twenty-one; shuffle, and make three additional rows of seven, which you will place below the first three.

---

[11] See the note on the previous page.

Once this operation is finished, your cards will be placed on the table as follows:

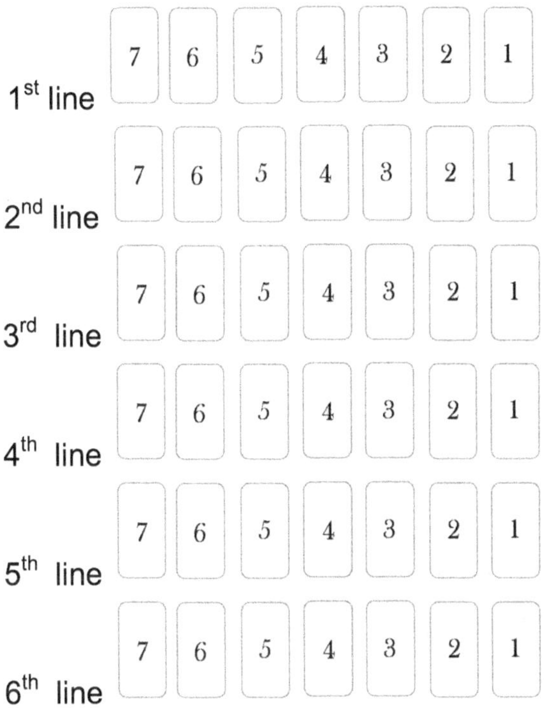

1st line — *(cards numbered)* 7 6 5 4 3 2 1

2nd line — 7 6 5 4 3 2 1

3rd line — 7 6 5 4 3 2 1

4th line — 7 6 5 4 3 2 1

5th line — 7 6 5 4 3 2 1

6th line — 7 6 5 4 3 2 1

Then explain each card as it is given on the pages on the card meanings, taking due care to start with the one on the right, following the method of the Orientals, our masters in cartomancy.

Example: Let's assume you are reading for a young person, and your first line is: No. 63 — 20 — 64 — 77 — 44 — 13 — 42. You take No. 8 from the stack, which represents the querent, and you place it to the right of No. 42, but away from the line, in this way:

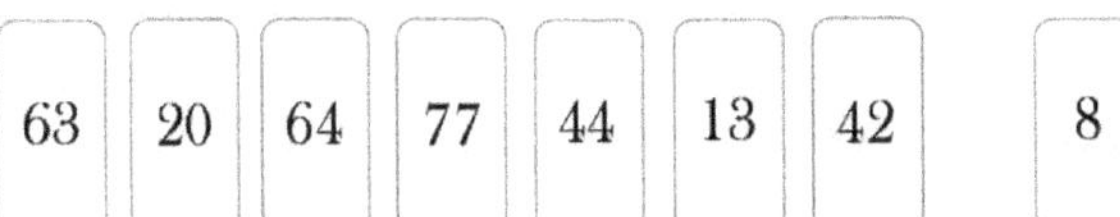

Then you say [8] the Querent

[42] A young blonde girl.

[13] Marriage.

[44] To come.[12]

[77] Happiness.[13]

[64] Brown-haired man.

[20] Fortune.

[63] Pregnancy.[12]

---

[12] These cards are in the reverse.
[13] See the synonyms for this card, which implies perfect contentment, joy, happiness, etc.

Then you articulate your reading (oracle) by saying: The querent, No. 42 is a blonde girl, 13 announces to her a marriage, 44 predicts it will be soon, 77 that she will be happy, 64 that it will be with a dark-haired man, 20 that he will be wealthy, 63 that they will have children.

If the No. 8, which represents the querent, appeared among the cards in a row, you would need to place it at the beginning and away from the first row, take another, at random, from the stack, and put it in its place, so that each row is always seven cards.

Likewise, if you do the reading for a man, it will be the No. 1 card that you would place at the beginning. It should be noted that it is only the card of the querent, that needs to be changed.

If you have not found to form with this first row an assembly that can be explained clearly, for example, if instead of No. 64 which represents a dark-haired man there was the No. 23, a country woman, or another card unrelated to the others, you would proceed to explain the second line and so forth, until you could articulate a reading without any misunderstanding.

The example.

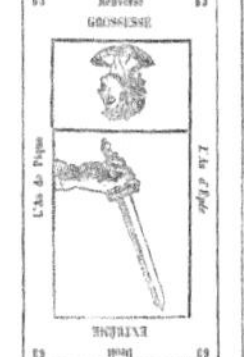    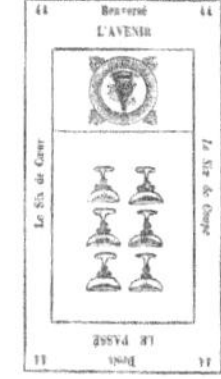  

SECOND SERIES OF ORACLES WITH 35 CARDS

Once the 42 cards on the table have been explained, pick them up and put them aside in a pile, along with the card that represented the questioner (the No. 1 or the No. 8). Then, if you want to continue, take the 35 cards, that have not been used, and proceed with a new series of readings (oracles) as follows: Shuffle and cut these 35 cards as it was explained in point 1 and 2, then divide them into six piles, in the following way:

6th	5th	4th	3rd	2nd	1st
11 cards	2 cards	4 cards	5 cards	6 cards	7 cards

The first will be for the house. - The second for the person who is asking. - The third for what is the outside influence. - The fourth for the surprise. - The fifth, for what may be hoped for, consolation. — The sixth will be irrelevant. You will put down the cards from these piles in separate rows, as you did for the first set of oracles, but observing the numbers shown above for each row, and you will proceed with the explanation in the same way.

OBSERVATIONS

When in a row of the two spreads, we find:

	Upright	Reverse
4 Kings	Great honors.	Haste.
3 Kings	Consultation.	Commerce.
2 Kings	Little advice.	Project.
4 Queens	Big talk.	Bad company.
3 Queens	Women´s deceptions.	Gluttony.
2 Queens	Sincere friends.	Worker.
4 Knights	Serious affairs.	Alliance.
3 Knights	Animated debates.	Duel.
2 Knights	Privacy.	Susceptibility.
4 Pages	Dangerous disease.	Deprivation.
3 Pages	Disputes.	Sloth.
2 Pages	Concerns.	Company.
4 Tens	Contradiction.	Events.
3 Tens	New state.	Disappointment.
2 Tens	Change.	Justified wait.
4 Nines	Good friend.	Usury.
3 Nines	Success.	Imprudence.
2 Nines	Prize.	Small profits.
4 Eights	Setbacks.	Errors.
3 Eights	Marriage.	Show.
2 Eights	New knowledge.	Obstacles.

4 Sevens	Intrigues.	Quarrelsome people.
3 Sevens	Disabilities.	Joy.
2 Sevens	Gossip.	Little women.
4 Six´	Abundance.	Ease.
3 Six´	Success.	Satisfaction.
2 Six´	Irritability.	Fall.
4 Fives	Regularity.	Order.
3 Fives	Determination.	Hesitation.
2 Fives	Vigilance.	Setback.
4 Fours	Next trip.	Walk.
3 Fours	Subjects of reflection.	Worry.
2 Fours	Insomnia.	Dispute.
4 Threes	Progress.	Great success.
3 Threes	Unity.	Serenity.
2 Threes	Calm.	Savings.
4 Twos	Untangled.	Reconciliation.
3 Twos	Security.	Apprehension.
2 Twos	Agreement.	Defiance.
4 Aces	Favorable wins.	Dishonors.
3 Aces	Small Success.	Misconduct.
2 Aces	Deception.	Enemy.

When several Club cards are found in a row, they announce that we will set out somewhere for a time, in proportion to their number; many Cups, that we will attend celebrations; several Coins or Money, that we will make profits, again always in proportion with the number on the cards.

Where the combination cards appear as sets, with the same value, such as Kings, Queens, Knights, etc., or several cards of the same suit, like Clubs, Cups, Swords or Coins, if some are in their upright and some in reverse; when found in equal number in the upright and reverse, their union has no value; but when there is a greater number in one direction over the other, that number alone must count.

For example, if there are three Kings in a row, two of them reversed, it is only the latter two that count.

This way of drawing the cards is the most fun; this is how the Magicians read among the Egyptians; this is how their successors also read. But great care must be taken not to make a mistake in the cut, in the placement and in the explanation, the slightest mistake would tell you things that would not come to pass. *See Note below.*

NOTE.

We will transcribe, what we have read in a book dealing with the subject at hand, so that enthusiasts of the game of tarot can apply the method described, in case they understand it better than we. Here it is:

After having had the deck cut by the questioners left hand, split the cards or tarots into five piles, place them in a row, going from right to left, and only turn over the fifth, when there are at least thirty-three, and at most forty-five, in the row, one after the other.

Count, still going right to left, one, two, three, four, five, six, seven; flip the card and explain what this last card says, proceed in turning over and explain in the same way the fourteenth, the twenty-first card and so on, jumping in sevens.

In the case, where there are 35 or 42 cards or tarots, which amount to five or six time seven, we would have to draw a flipped card, which we would have explained already, which we would add to those already placed on the table, so as not to fall behind in the last card round.

EXPLANATIONS

of 78 TAROTS OR EGYPTIAN CARDS

making up the Book of Thot.

No. 1

Etteilla - The Male Querent
The Chaos

This card[14] represents Chaos, spirit of God, it also represents the one who questions the oracle with the book of Thot.

If you draw the cards for a man, and this one does not come out, you will take it from the deck and put it at the beginning of your row, without making it count among the other cards.

If laid for a lady you will remove it. It would be useless and you will replace it as directed in the chapter *Method of Drawing the cards*.

This tarot signifies discovery, meditation, deep mind.

When this card appears in the Upright and is found near the Nos. 14, 17 or 18 it is an unfortunate sign.

Near No. 76, error; next to No. 71, small loss of money; next to No. 47, lack of success.

It is a good omen, whenever it lies between two favorable cards.

In Reverse, it announces that the querent is a philosopher; it predicts for him glory, immortality. (That is to say, his name will live on, into future posterity).

---

[14] Translator: The Grand Etteilla version II.

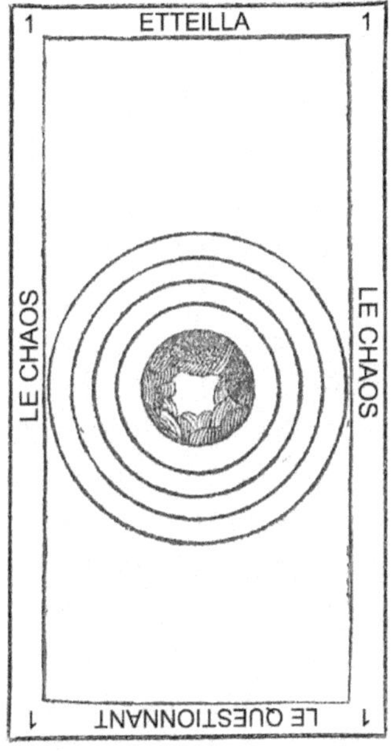

LEMARCHAND

This card[15] represents Chaos. It always represents the one who questions or seeks to obtain an oracle by means of the Tarot. If this card does not appear, one would have to look for it in the deck and place it at the beginning of the row. That would be the case, if the spread was made for a man; while, for a woman, it would have to be discarded and replaced by card No. 8.

This card usually indicates failure, whether it appears in the Upright or not.

However, if it appears among two favorable cards, it can be said to be auspicious.

Between a King and a Queen, it indicates; marriage, greatness, success, fortune.

---

[15] Translator: The Grand Etteilla version III. The images from the Lemarchand booklet have been made into Tarot cards here. Please note that to the first card *Chaos* the booklet assigns the meaning *Le Mond* or the World in the Upright, rather than *Etteilla*.

D'ODOUCET

This first card is the hieroglyph of chaos.[16] It represents an immense vapor, the light pushing back the darkness, set in motion by a central engine. The chaos which is pushed back to make room for the truth, in the moment, the creator manifests his glory and his sovereign goodness to all the creatures of the whole universe, who are scattered within his intelligence.

From the hieroglyphic identity of this card, it implies God in the center of the universe, the spirit of God above the waters, but also the chaos with its numbers and epiths. It follows then, that man is unquestionably the same and often to himself, the most difficult chaos to unravel, the study of man in his physical and moral relations, these being the most complex, since this subject is almost impenetrable.

The chaos is a dark mass impregnated with the formative principle; figuratively it represents the body of the man, whose shape we do not perceive, a dark mass imbued with the animating principle; with the denomination of the querent, the man chained, the Mage thus reading a real chaos, of which he makes out the trajectory using the cards, which he interprets.

---

[16] Translator: The Grand Etteilla version I, printed by Scheible. These have been made into Tarot cards here. Please note, d′Odoucet assigns only the meaning *Consultant* in upright and in reverse for this card. The meanings or keywords assigned here, are as they appeared in the 1890s deck by Grimaud.

This card, with regards to the *Science of Symbols*, represents *the querent*. It represents the male, but also the person, who the female querent is most interested in, and vice versa with card 8.

MODERN INTERPRETATIONS

For this card, the astrological correspondence is Aries. The card has by Grimaud been assigned the keywords IDEAL in the Upright and WISDOM in the reverse.[17]

UPRIGHT: This card personifies the male querent and can be used as the Significator card. If you are female, Chaos can represent an important male in your life, such as a husband or a father, even a soul mate. It is a card which speaks of wisdom and of ideals and usually has no negative implications. It also implies mental strength and moral convictions, which can play in one´s favor. A hope for the future. An urge to apply patience and wisdom in all your dealings. It also implies; honesty, reflection and courage, which again can result in tangible outcomes. This card also implies a new spiritual path, a realignment to self, of deep reflection, of meditations.

REVERSE: In reverse this card also implies wisdom, higher knowledge, philosophy and life experience. It can indicate a visionary and a potential for notoriety in one´s chosen field. The querent has two essential skills; intelligence and talent, as well as resources, which can be put to good use. In relationships, a cautionary card, indicating a need for proper judgement.

---

[17] Translator: The alternative key words Grimaud has assigned to their current version I *the Grand Etteilla Egyptian Gypsies Tarot,* perhaps the most common version I in use today.

No. 2

Enlightenment - Fire
The Light

You see on this card, the fire, the light that illuminates us, its appearance is always favorrable; the two children, who are in the lower panel, announce great posterity.

If you are reading for a man, it implies explanation, resourcefullness, glory, the interpretation of the most secret of things, of rewards.

If you are laying out the cards for a young person, it predicts a forthcoming marriage. For a lady, it predicts children to come.

For a young lady returning, it informs her, soon her qualities will make her be noticed by a man of advanced age, who will come to offer her his heart and his hand, and that accompanied by a great fortune.

Placed near the No. 13, this card announces a marriage made or ready to take place.

Near No. 58, it offers hope for children and near the No. 72, of awards or honors.

In Reverse, it signifies fire, anger, discord; next to the No. 21, betrayal discovered by you, victory over your enemies, invincible obstacles to a much-desired union.

LEMARCHAND

You see the sun, it is natural light. The associations are always favorable with this card. When the querent is a man, it signifies glory, greatness, accomplishments and assured success.

For a young person, this card announces immediate marriage; for a woman, it is an indication, that she will have beautiful children.

Located near the No. 13, it announces to the querent, balls, celebrations, parties of pleasure.

When the reading is performed for a man, it predicts honors and rewards, and if the No. 21 is in the row, it is the indication of a desired union.

This is a card, that can change a lot in a spread, however it is generally advantageous.

Translator: Etteilla assigns a slightly different meaning to each number, than seen traditionally in numerology:

0. The Globe
1. Man, us
2. Vegetation
3. Generation, Reproduction
4. Universe, Pyramid
5. Animation, Universal Spirit
6. Movement, Sphere
7. Life
8. Circulation, Generational
9. Expansion, Effusion
10. Completion, Perfection

D'ODOUCET

This second card is the hieroglyph of fire, the second element. It is the radiant sun, the instrument used by the creator to make life of all beings' bloom. It spreads the light afar by its powerful rays. At the bottom of the card is a pyramid, and at the foot of this pyramid, a pair of twins.

Considering man as a privileged being, we must place him at the top of a new combination by examining him in the relations, in which he finds himself in collaboration with all the other cards of nature. The progressive development of his individual being is the product of true vegetation. Note that the number 2 is the characteristic symbol of stable, permanent vegetation, as it was, is, and will be, as long as the centuries last. But what is this principle of vegetation? A central and permanent fire, creating from the origins of the world.

This fire is indicated to us by the hieroglyph of this card, whose 3rd dimension is *light, enlightenment*, and which is its most natural inscription. Let us observe moreover, that we would have before our eyes only the active principle (fire), if by the number 2, we were not to include, that of the inherent passive or the woman. This, by virtue of its innate quality, should be understood having the same number as man: or to put it better, by its moral parity, almost individually, in pairs, as both are symbolized by 1. Further, because of the competition between these two 1s, we also attribute the number 2 to man, in order not to distinguish him from his other real half. However, it is advisable to apply these various functions properly, to agent and *patient*, especially as the latter in particular highlights, and makes manifest the power of the former.

MODERN INTERPRETATIONS

Astrological correspondence is Taurus. It represents the second element of Fire and the 1st day of creation. This card has by Grimaud been assigned the keywords ENLIGHTENMENT in the Upright and PASSION in the reverse.

UPRIGHT: A card of *road to success*. It provides clarifications to your dealings. The card predicts fertility and expansion in the family. Relationships will be fulfilling and lasting. This is also a card of fair and balanced negotiations, of confidence and friendships. Success in business and the arts. A newfound clarity on challenging situations. It implies brighter days ahead, of joy, love and the end of struggles.

REVERSE: A card of passion and impulsiveness. A card of exacerbated feelings, possessiveness and destructive connections. Also, a card of pride, arrogance, thought-lessness, anger, jealousy and rage. In connection with business, a card that foretells hectic situations, of risks that you take that may end up costing you. Certainly, a card that urges you to compose yourself.

No. 3

Discourse – Water
The Plants

This card represents the moon, water, earth, the night. It implies bad talk, gossip, discourse.

Near the No. 23, it announces news from the countryside.

Next to the No. 21 it predicts dissension, caused by words from two different understandings.

If the questioner is a mariner, it foretells him of distant journeys, unnecessary exploration, waste of time.

For a young person it predicts tears, if this card is preceded by No. 45, it announces to him or her, that his or her tears will cease with the news of an inheritance, and if it is followed by the No. 39, that she will marry a blond and wealthy young man.

Next to the No. 47, it predicts that a celebration will be attended peacefully.

Near No. 67, it warns you that you will have an unpleasant and unexpected visit; but if the No. 3 comes up in Reverse, to you that would imply foiled plans.

If this tarot is in Reverse and next to cards not indicated above, it announces that a friend or that a relative will stand up for you to an influential person. If it is a young person, a house party will be disrupted because of rain, to which she has an invite.

LEMARCHAND

Here is a card which represents many things: plants, water, earth, moon or night. No doubt it would be difficult to interpret, if each thing had to be assigned a different meaning. The proximity to the other cards modify or change this card´s meaning considerably.

Near the No. 23, it indicates you will receive news from the country, romantic interest, a bouquet, flowers.

Near the No. 45, it predicts an inheritance; while next to the No. 47, it implies, you will attend a celebration of significance.

When this card appears in Reverse, it implies news of small annoyances, postponed house parties, gloomy weather. In winter, it always announces excessive cold.

D'ODOUCET

This third card is the hieroglyph of water, the first element. It depicts a silver moon, clouds frame the sky of the image, two towers, at their feet occupying the lower part, a wolf awake and a dog asleep; a body of water, towards which a crayfish directs its march.

The number 3, being the symbol of generation or animal reproduction, it thus has to be preceded by the symbol of vegetation, which in fact occurred just prior, during creation. The hieroglyph of this card, is that of humidity, *water*, which is the first vehicle of the first generation of all the subsequent cards, and so to speak, their primal nature, since they are reduced to it. This card´s third dimension is *discourse*. It implies all the species, good and bad, the only means of propagation, all that relates to science and the ordinary things of life.

MODERN INTERPRETATIONS

Astrological correspondence is Gemini. It represents the first element of Water and the 3rd day of creation. This card has by Grimaud been assigned the keywords DISCUSSION in the Upright and INSTABILITY in the reverse.

UPRIGHT: This is a card of doubt and hesitation, a need for dialogue. You may be the victim of gossip and slander. A card of imagination and creativity too, if in business it implies an important phase, perhaps involving a great deal of skill. You will have increased awareness and sensitivity to the opinions of others, you may be quite emotional too. Trust might be an issue as well. A card that urges you to be careful.

REVERSE: This card predicts, that there will be uncertainty around relationships and finances. You will be required to fight for your interests. The future outlook is dim. A card of sadness and doubt in reverse. There may be disapproval around your situation or work, lies and obstacles in your way. There is trouble ahead, hidden enemies, a need for discretion. A need for persuasive action, and of tact.

No. 4

Desolation – Air
The Sky

The Egyptians took great care in explaining this card, they regarded it as their bad star.

It signifies considerable loss and hypocrisy.

If the querent is a lady, this card tells her, that she has been slandered by one of her best friends. But if she stands up for herself, this slander will soon be brought to light and will ridicule those who have conjured them.

In Reverse, it predicts thunderstorms, frightening noise, presence at a concert, hurricane, shipwreck.

Near the No. 17, it announces a fairly benign disease.

Near the No. 71, it predicts a loss of little importance. If it is between two favorable cards, its prediction will be modified.

Next to No. 20, it warns you that speculators have inclinations towards your fortune, and that you need to be on your guard.

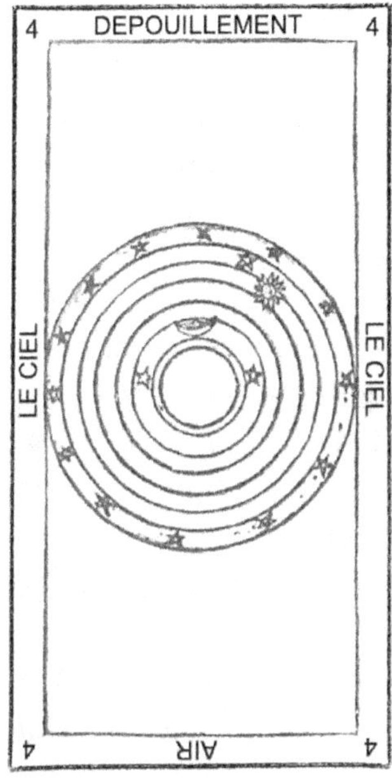

LEMARCHAND

This card has, to cartomancers since antiquity, been an unfavorable omen; but they supposed, in such case, that it appeared in a spread accompanied with unfavorable cards. If it is accompanied by the No. 20, it warns you to mind your fortune and your reputation.

Next to the No. 17, it brings you news from distant lands.

If Reversed, it tells you that you would be caught by the rain, if you persist, in making the trip to the country of which you have recently spoken.

If one reads for a woman, it announces very pleasant surprises for her.

D'ODOUCET

This fourth card is the hieroglyph of air, the third element. Nature is represented here by a kneeling woman, who lets two jugs spill over onto the earth, one from a vessel of gold, and the other from a vessel of silver, heat and humidity. These two fluids merge making a single stream providing mineral nutrition to plants and animals. The governed are represented here by a butterfly, a large tree, a few small plants, and a mineral stone on which this woman, naked and natural, is kneeling. The sky of the image is adorned with planetary signs.

The number 4, symbol or rather the number of the universe; its integral parts are represented by the hieroglyph of this card, the atmospheric fluid that surrounds us, (commonly called air) is in a way the abbreviation of this same universe, but in a way hidden, that is, to say almost deprived of any point of recognition, just naked in form: could this be expressed in any other way than by *desolation,* by the deprivation of accessories? The application can be made to infinite parts of a reading, as well as to particular circumstances in life.

MODERN INTERPRETATIONS

Astrological correspondence is Cancer. It represents the third element of Air and the 2nd day of creation. This card has by Grimaud been assigned the keywords REVELATION in the Upright and BEHAVIOUR in the reverse.

UPRIGHT: This card indicates good and happy news. It implies an easy path forward, an encouragement, what feels right is right, the simplest route is sometimes also the best route. The times ahead are bright, a time of meeting caring people, of meeting potential ideal partners. You will share things with others, things will be reciprocal. Also, a card of soul mates, destiny, and increased psychic awareness. A card of vitality and of good health too. In business, your situation is improving, however, you may invite envy from others. Generally, a very good card.

REVERSE: A card of bad luck in reverse. A card of losses, deprivation, overthinking, of emotional trouble, even break-ups. In business, it may indicate trials and projects delayed. A time of hardship, job loss and bad outcomes. Your life situation needs some work. This card in the reverse is largely negative, but you still have some control of your situation and you are urged to take control, as it is not a time for unnecessary risks.

No. 5

Voyage - Earth
The Man and the Quadrupeds

The naked woman in the middle of the circle indicates that the truth hovers over the earth, an olive branch announces general peace for you, the attributes of the four evangelists who circle the circle of the earth, are signs of wisdom, the pyramids indicate an imminent increase in fortune.

This card brings you happiness, courage, battles won. Next to No. 38, it announces arrival of money.

Next to No. 36, it tells you that you will soon be appointed to a high position.

Preceded by the No. 9, it predicts winning a lawsuit. Followed by No. 77, is a great sign of happiness.

If one of the four Knights accompanies this card, it promises news, that will cause great pleasure for the public.

But if this card appears in the Reverse, it indicates, if not the opposite, at least major modifications in each of the situations indicated above.

LEMARCHAND

This card is the announcement of the greatest success in all possible endeavors. A successful warrior, if the querent serves in the army; great fortune, if he is a trader; invincible courage, if a conscript.

When it is a woman who consults, and if this card is accompanied by a Knight, it predicts, that she will shortly receive news from a friend, who lives far away from her. If this tarot was preceded by a Page, it is a sign of opulence; and when one of the four Kings or one of the four Queens is either before or after, it predicts greatness.

After no. 78, it would not be favorable, but still it would only make you fear an indiscretion.

D'ODOUCET

This fifth card is the hieroglyph of earth, the fourth element. Nature is represented by a standing woman, sparsely covered and with long hair, holding a branch in her right hand, surrounded by seven stars[18], and placed between two pyramids. It all enclosed by a snake biting its tail and forming a circle. Outside the circle are depicted; above an eagle and an angel, below a lion and a bull.

The number 5, a symbol of the universal spirit, surrounding and animating its beings. Its function and movement is indicated by the specific number and by the words *journey and action*, however no action without patience; and what is more relevant but on the globe of the *earth*, which entitles this card to bear this hieroglyph.

---

[18] Translator: Curious, no stars are depicted on this card nor on the card illustrating the original book.

MODERN INTERPRETATIONS

Astrological correspondence is Leo. It represents the fourth element of Earth and the 6th day of creation. This card has by Grimaud been assigned the keywords TRAVEL in the Upright and COUNTRY PROPERTY in the reverse.

UPRIGHT: This is a card of great satisfaction. This may be in connection with a trip with friends, travel is implied with this card. A card of new places, opportunities, exchanges and new experiences too. Opportunities may come from abroad, a lover, most often an earth sign, or travel in connection with work is also implied. In business; a dynamic period, promotion, advantages at work, often in connection with new projects or particular talents. Finances are stable and may increase, a good time to invest or make financial decisions.

REVERSE: In reversed, the card predicts a turn to the worse, often in connection with work, money, or business. Opportunities will not materialize. There is an inability to make changes, perhaps with an attitude of refusal or of fear. A need for grounding, to make things tangible. Finances are at best stagnant, but may deteriorate. Relationships may be stuck in patterns or habits, that are not helpful for future growth. In a relationship, a partner may be withdrawn or bored. A card that urges you to apply yourself, workwise, health-wise, get more balance.

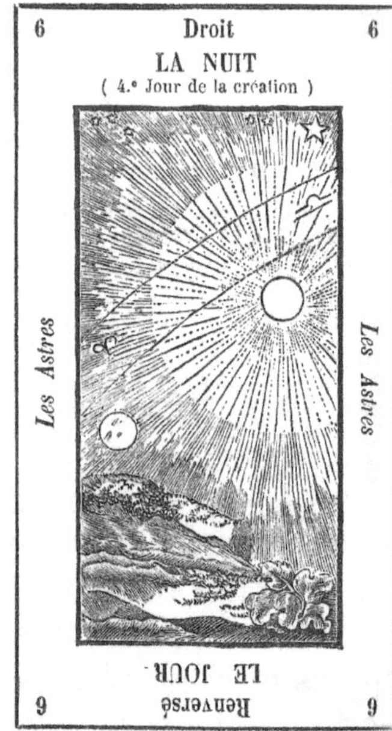

No. 6

The Night – The Day
The Stars

This card represents the sky to you, the sun still shines on the earth, but the pale moonlight will soon replace it. The mystical meaning of this figure is not very difficult to explain.

It means darkness thunderstorms, eclipses and blindness.

If the person for whom we are reading is elderly, this card predicts for him long days. If for a young person, she will experience, many obstacles to a union, which has been planned for a long time.

Near the No. 16, it predicts a supernatural phenomenon; a magician whom you have consulted has told you of many things, which however will not come true.

In the Reverse, it promises clarification in muddled affairs.

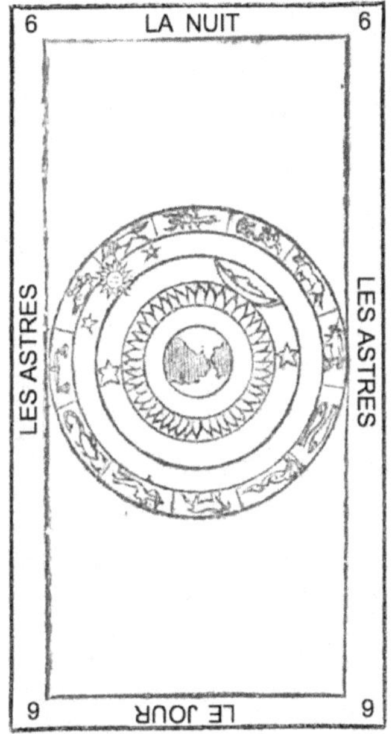

LEMARCHAND

This tarot, which represents the stars, can have no other meaning than the No. 4[19]: however, the sign of the Zodiac adds to the meaning of this card.

In the Upright, it is an indication, that the querent, whether male or female, will endure long days.

In Reverse, it tells you that the light has been shed on a very dark matter, of which you have been very concerned about for some time.

With the No. 16, it only predicts things having to do with natural phenomena, meaning, extraordinary rain, frost, snow and thunder-storms.

On occasions, it announces a pleasant surprise, when the querent is a woman.

---

[19] Translator: Etteilla ties in certain meanings to the numbers, the no. 4 represents the universe, pyramid or fortune.

D'ODOUCET

This sixth card represents a portion of the zodiac, from Aires to Libra; the sun, the moon and a star. Below is the land adorned with just a few plants.

The number 6 exposes to our eyes the terrestrial globe, which an expanding divine spirit animates with the insertion of movement. Without the active presence of this spirit, everything physically is *night* and darkness. Morally without the light of reason, our individuality is only a passive mass (primitive state). Everything changes to the contrary by the presence of the fertile or intelligent principle; everything becomes *manifest*, with day, physically and morally; secondly, the respective states, both in the macrocosm and in the microcosm, when they each have reached a perfect point of reciprocal formation. The inscription is thus in the most direct relation to the hieroglyph of this card.

53

MODERN INTERPRETATIONS

Astrological correspondence is Virgo. It represents the 4th day of creation. This card has by Grimaud been assigned the keywords SECRETS in the Upright and TRUTHS in the reverse.

UPRIGHT: This card in the upright is a card of mystery, secrecy, obstacle and confusion. In relationships, this implies bad feelings. A lack of clarity, anxiety, misunderstandings or obsessing over a person. You may need to step back from a situation until you have more clarity. A relationship may not be reciprocal. In business, your situation will be stagnant, you may feel you are pushing on a string. People may hinder your professional advancement. It is not a time to take advice from others, you should try to be more focused of what you are doing yourself. If you do seek advice, make sure it is from neutral and professional sources.

REVERSE: A card of unresolved issues, but you will begin to see improvements, good conclusions and solutions ahead. You are rediscovering your confidence and radiance, and moving forward, you may need to let go of old relationships and make way for new ones. People around you will notice the change in you and you have opportunities to form new friendships and business partnerships. Your hunch is correct in love. In business, this card predicts help from influential people and you will be able to achieve your business objectives. You could explore new hobbies and interests. Finances will improve.

No. 7

Support - Protection
The Birds and the Fish

The serpent crawls over the earth as a curse, the sea is calm, the birds fly swiftly over the aerial regions to indicate the difficulty in rise.

This card announces the support of a great person with whose support you will attain a much sought-after job.

If the querent is a young lady, this card predicts, that she will marry a rich and famous man.

Next to the No. 68, the card promises great profits in trade.

Near the No. 42, it predicts the loss of a relative, who however will leave you a small inheritance.

Near the No. 71, this tarot announces money that will be sent to you by an old provincial relative.

When this card appears in Reverse, it predicts that your enemies will be thrown into confusion, which will compel them to absolute silence, for a long time.

LEMARCHAND

The true meaning of this card is deep peace. If this card appears in the Reverse, it announces that your enemies will be confused. Next to No. 5, it promises you the support of a great person.

When the querent is a young person, it predicts, she will receive for her birthday, from an older relative, a cage filled with the prettiest island birds.

If it is for a man one reads, this tarot announces for him, that in the countryside, he will do remarkable fishing.

We can also assign it the following interpretation near the No. 71; inheritance from a distant relative.

D'ODOUCET

This seventh card represents vast seas inhabited by monstrous whales, and other aquatic animals. Part of the land is used as a retreat for crocodiles, snakes, and other amphibious animals. Above are depicted flying birds.

The number 7 is the recognized symbol of life in general, this hieroglyph is consistent, it is without opposition, the firmest *support* of the species of animals; it supports those of its kind, which come directly or indirectly from it.

MODERN INTERPRETATIONS

Astrological correspondence is Libra. It represents the 5th day of creation. This card has by Grimaud been assigned the keywords SUPPORT in the Upright and PROTECTION in the reverse.

UPRIGHT: This card implies liberation of trials, and of support. There is an improvement in relations. Although there may be hidden enemies, there is also hidden help around, from your friends. This card implies a happier and easier life. Relationship are good, more family time, there may even be plans to expand the family. Plans and goals in general will succeed quicker than expected. In business, there is a lot of support and finances will improve. This card may predict favorable legal outcomes. Health is good.

REVERSE: This card meaning in the reverse is the same as in upright, albeit to a lesser extent. If you are lonely, the people around you will make you feel better, it may imply a reconciliation with a past love. If you are having financial difficulties, someone may offer their help. Generally, you will feel more optimistic about the future.

No. 8

Etteilla - The Female Querent
Rest

This card is the person for whom we read. If the card does not appear among the cards you have drawn already, and the person for whom you make the spread is a woman, you will retrieve this card from the stack and place it at the beginning of the row, you are going to interpret. If the querent is a man, you will remove it from your row and replace it, as explained previously.

The circles which surround this woman, represent the labyrinths of the future, where her imagination is disorientated; but soon the oracle will have spoken and this future will be known to her.

Next to Nos. 9, 13, 35, it is a good omen. It is a bad omen when it appears next to No. 14, 17 and 18.

If it appears in the Reverse, it urges you to be on your guard, because you are surrounded by traps, that you must try to avoid by all possible means. However, if the No. 50 is next to it, also in Reverse, your enemies will themselves fall victim to these traps, they have set for you.

The ancients have written a great deal about this card, but they were almost all wrong about its real meaning. Etteilla alone has managed to fix its true meaning.

LEMARCHAND

The female querent.[20] If you are laying out the spread for woman, and this card is not among those you have drawn, you must retrieve it from the deck and place it at the beginning of the row. If you read for a man, place the no.1 instead.

The true meaning of tarot 8 is temptation[21]; the querent must therefore be warned that he is surrounded by traps; however, placed near no. 9, 13, 35, it is a favorable omen.

When this card appears in the Reverse and close to Nos. 14, 17, and 18, it only gives obscure predictions; you would need to start over again.

---

[20] Translator: The Lemarchand booklet assigns the meaning *Repos* or Rest in the upright rather than *Etteilla*.

[21] Translator: The day of rest, symbolized by this card, is here depicted by Lemarchand as the fall from grace in the garden of Eden. The rest draws the parallel to the eternal state of Gods mind, of the mind open to intuition (symbolically expressed by the fairer sex), of the mind silenced, the mind at peace, the meditative state, the mind-state of the ancient Egyptians. The traps are the traps of your mind. D´Odoucet draws our attention to the eternity, expressed by perpetual human reproduction but also to nature in general. Nature has an instinct and can be thought of as the intuitive ways of the woman.

D'ODOUCET

This eighth card[22] represents the garden of nature. A woman situated in the middle, standing, encircled by eleven circles, with no other clothing and with beautiful long hair. A river flows, winding through this garden of earth. The number 8 designates the continuity, or circulation of generations; but this circulation is mainly owed to the female gender, who is the vessel of reproduction as in all dominions. The querent and nature are therefore here in their proper place; it is in her, who must perpetuate the species, where this reproductive principle is embodied.

---

[22] Translator: d´Odoucet assigns only *Consultante* in the upright for this card, not *Etteilla*.

MODERN INTERPRETATIONS

Astrological correspondence is Scorpio. It represents the 7th day of rest. This card has by Grimaud been assigned the keywords TENACITY in the Upright and PROGRESS in the reverse.

UPRIGHT: This card personifies the female querent and can be used as a significator card. If you are male, this card can represent a significant female in your life, such as a wife, mother or a friend etc. A card of soulmates too. This is a card of serenity, wisdom and tenacity. It also indicates a fertile time for research, education and the arts. Finally, this card can indicate meditation, psychic abilities or a deeper understanding.

REVERSE: In the reverse this card implies need to reassess your heading. Your judgement may be impaired, you may be reckless and there may be hidden enemies leading you astray. You may be tempted to do something that will turn against you later. In case of a soulmate, it is indicating a delay or an obstruction, which can be of your own making. In business, there may be someone trying to lay a trap for you. A card that urges you to be prudent and cautious.

No. 9

The Justice - The Jurist.[23]
The Justice

King Solomon seated on his throne holds the attributes of righteousness in his hands.

This card tells you, that the lawsuit you have spent huge sums of money on, will soon be judged in your favor, or that a quarrel that has estranged you from a powerful relative or friend, will cease to cause you distress.

If it is for a woman you read, this tarot announces, that slanders sown on her account, will be discovered very soon.

With the No. 28, whether it presents itself in the Upright or in the Reverse, raises the fear of an ambush, where the querent will be hated if he is a man; if a woman, she will be grossly slandered.

If this tarot is near the No. 22, and when in the Upright, it announces dignitaries, titles of nobility; but when in the Reverse, it predicts the loss of a lucrative office, or a sum of money.

---

[23] Justice, says the scholar, means Equity; but this word is only a sound. In order to give us a fair idea of what this harmonious sound contains, because although not arbitrary, it is to the contrary fixed, it is therefore necessary to decompose it, without which, man will pronounce Justice and Equity a hundred thousand times, and it will be no less unjust. Justice implies the positive natural rights of people; right of the fathers of families, of the sovereign, of masters and finally of the superior over the inferior.

In Reverse, this card is still a bad prediction, it implies a fight; wordsmiths will try to disrupt your affairs, but if the No. 71 is to the right; or to the left, it only indicates hassle.

LEMARCHAND

This tarot, which represents justice with its attributes, is for you the announcement of a complete success in a trial, you have undertaken. It has a different meaning when it comes out in the Reverse; but, by the Nos. 9 and 22, it will be much modified, for it implies expected delays.

If the querent has no lawsuit, this card tells him, that he has earned the esteem of honest people; but also, if in Reverse, that he is the target of unfair suspicions. Near Nos. 18 and 27, in whatever heading this card appears, it assures him of unanimous considerations.

If it is for a young person you read, it predicts success.

D'ODOUCET

This ninth card is the hieroglyph of Justice. It presents a seated woman with a scale in her right hand and a sword in her left. This virtue is seen in a yellow dress, lightly covered with a blue cloak. On one end of scale is a black triangle, and within this a small white cube, at the other end of the scale, a white sphere, hanging. This virtue wears a crown and on her belt, is written THOT, a green drape shapes the background of the image and a white and black mosaic makes up the floor.

The 9 is a figure appropriate for the philosophers in generative work, for the reason, that she offers the aspect of a being complete, and whose tools below, seem to pour out the spirit of life. Indeed, is it not divine and human *justice* that gives or perpetuates, that which one receives? Man, or every being, have only fulfilled the task imposed on them by nature, once they reproduce their living image; *true*, by that alone is their expression. The various dimensions of this hieroglyph are united into a perfect correspondence.

MODERN INTERPRETATIONS

Astrological correspondence is Sagittarius. This card has by Grimaud been assigned the keywords JUSTICE in the upright and LAW MAKER in the reverse.

UPRIGHT: This card represents everything relating to legal issues, business with the court system and with people in the legal system, such as lawyers and judges, but also contracts in general. It is also a card of order and balance, of setting things right. Consequences are implied, on a situation or with individuals, often a solution in a dispute with family or friends. In business, a card of things done by the book, reasonably and without imagination. It may imply a rigidity in health, a need to move physically and psychologically.

REVERSED: In the reverse, it may imply injustice or things needing to be resolved in the courts or the need for a person of the law to be involved in your situation somehow. This can also indicate slander or gossip, things unfairly done behind your back.

No. 10

The Temperance - The Priest
The Temperance[24]

This card is one, which embodies the most moral aspect; it warns you, that if you are not frugal, you will soon be ruined. It urges for sobriety in all things.

With the Nos. 45 or 47, this card gives rise to fear of an

---

[24] Temperance signifies or announces, that one must temper oneself in the habits relating to the topic indicated in the following card, either to the physical or to the moral aspect; to the extremes, in either case these are contrary to human reason, and even to the law indicated by wise nature, in general that of movement.

The Egyptians regarded Temperance differently from us, they did not say it exerted more directly onto our passions, than onto all our other vices; below a few lines of what they wrote about it in the book of Thot, this will put it within our understanding.

Temperance is a virtue that governs morals, as well as the physical, it is called the precursor of truth. Without temperance, man brings all the other virtues to a state, which corrupts them. Intemperance from a man who is virtuous makes him, a maniac, an enthusiast, a fool; thus, all the more so, the necessity of temperance, generally, in all our vices, our blind passions, our flaws, our weaknesses, our miseries, our infirmities, and even in the crude things necessary to the physical life of man.

Temperance dominates over; continence, leniency, modesty, study, affability (lenient, gentle, easy, treatable and considerate), mercy, humility, moderation, simplicity, and it masters, ambition, curiosity, luxury, play, drunkenness, self-esteem, indeed all vices, as Prudence prevents them and Strength subdues them.

accident, the result of bad food preparation in the consumption of a meal.

Near the No. 25 it announces a letter, which will give you news of a person you love.

When this tarot is in the Reverse, it predicts, a priest will shortly call on you to lend his ministry for a marriage; but if it is found next to the No. 16, it will be because of illness and in such case, it does not say, whether it is for this or that person, if it is a neighbor or a friend.

Near No. 29 it is a sign of cowardice.

LEMARCHAND

Temperance[25]. Here is a tarot which has only one meaning, temperance. Whichever way it appears, Upright or Reverse, it tells you to temper yourself in all things.

Temperance is a virtue, that only few people possess at all levels; but he who can be master of his own person, easily achieves any superiority.

The old interpreters of tarot always regarded this to be one of the best omens, because it announces, for whom one reads, the most brilliant result.

For a soldier, it indicates great courage and great valor; for a young person, this tarot predicts a partner with the finest qualities.

---

[25] Translator: The Lemarchand booklet assigns the meaning *Le Sage* or the Wise man on this card in the reverse, rather than *Le Pretre* or the Priest.

D'ODOUCET

This tenth card is the hieroglyph of the Temperance. This virtue is represented here by a standing and winged woman, one foot resting on a black triangle and the other on a white sphere. She has in her hands two jugs, one of gold and the other of silver, mixing the liquid contained in them, amalgamating them. This virtue is presented in a purple coat, seems in yellow; Thot is written on her belt; on her forehead rests a sun, her wings are painted with the rich colors of Iris. The top of the card is showing the azure sky; below a terrace in light red, on which the triangle and ball lay.

Here the numbers are combined, made up; their simple meaning reflect better the vicissitudes of life, the implications of which are infinite. The Egyptians wrote their works from right to left, we must therefore also explain the numbers on each of the cards thus.

The 0, the symbol of the terrestrial globe, expresses here its dependency, by the value which it seeks with its first master, the privileged Being, who resides there. It is also the first to pay some homage to it, numerically, since 10 is the first of the combined numbers. But this recognized denomination of man is also particularly the most enlightened, a reminder for him only to use his powers with moderation.

Among the Egyptians, the sciences were understood particularly by the *priestly* class, who enjoyed the advantage of tempering, the deep knowledge of the physical and moral events of which this same globe was the cause or the object.

MODERN INTERPRETATIONS

Astrological correspondence is Aquarius. This card has by Grimaud been assigned the keywords TEMPERANCE in the upright and CONVICTIONS in the reverse.[26]

UPRIGHT: This card indicates friendliness and tenderness in relations. Partnerships deepen, a re-igniting of things. Moving forward, this indicates positivity, a turning point, perhaps slow but steady movement towards your goals. In business, a slower time, but with the certainty of good progression. This card also implies moderation and harmony. Generally, a card of improvements.

REVERSE: This card in reverse indicates sound advice and help needed, thus, it may imply that you have a problem accepting advice. You may also be too self-critical, in a job situation, guidance could be offered, but you would need to be open for that. Finally, a third person could introduce you to partner.

---

[26] Translator: On this card, the reader will notice the triangle and sphere under the angel's feet. Etteilla connects certain geometric shapes to the numbers: *"1, the point; 2, the line; 3, the triangle; 4, the square; 1, the sphere; 3, the cylinder; 4, the pyramid; 6, the cube, are generally the basis of all practical geometry; to which we could add the pentagon, the first of the polygons; which would be easy to think on, by using the 5 on its own; indeed, all figures are in the sphere, like the numbers in a unit."* Manière de se récréer avec le jeu de cartes nommées Tarots, by Etteilla, p. 68 (transl.).

No. 11

The Strength - The Sovereign
The Strength[27]

Complete success in whatever you undertake. The crowning of your labors and honors will come to you from all sides; you and yours will be showered with incalculable riches, especially if this card is found with Nos. 20 or 72.

In the Reverse this card does not bode so well; it announces to you the disgrace or the loss of confidence from an important person, who extended much benevolence towards you.

Next to No. 50, it predicts to you bad news.

---

[27] The Strength offers magnificence, confidence, patience, perseverance. Its traits are; piety, obedience to God in moral and physical virtue. For men, obey and observe, humanitarian, national and provincial laws, which extend themselves over sovereigns, lords, magistrates, but also towards relatives, righteous men, superiors, equals, the benefactors, the friends, the poor, the sick, the weak. Finally the Strength instructs us to have regard and even to obey all that is virtuous, although for a stern man, it may be his personal strength in shaking off his inestimable docility, which would disturb the celestial harmony, the Creator has put between creatures. It requires scrutiny, to be submitted to the truth of divine laws and the laws of men, it dictates to us recognition, respect and true friendship. If man's strength deviates, but for a minute, from the spirit of divine strength, man immediately places himself in the arms of heavenly vengeance, and the secular arm of human justice: the willingness to learn embodies the true spirit of strength.

With No. 18, and always in the Reverse, it predicts loss of employment or of lucrative clients.

If accompanied by the No. 51, expect a present of little importance.

All the learned cartomancers viewed this tarot, when it presented itself in the Upright, as one of the happiest. To warriors, it predicts battles, they will win.

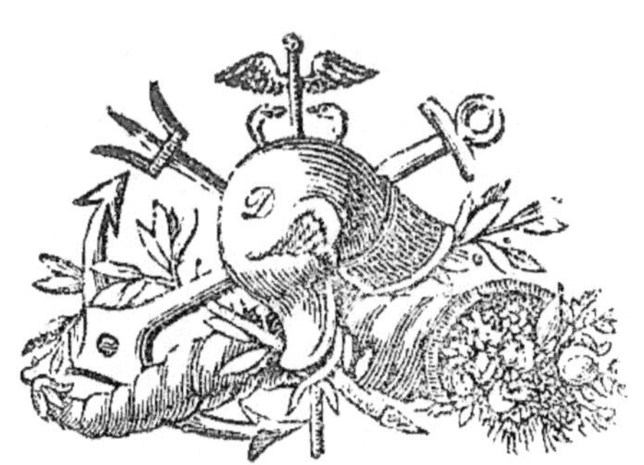

LEMARCHAND

The cartomancers have always given this tarot a happy interpretation. If it appears in the Upright, it announces honors, riches and all the best chances of success.

If this tarot appears in the Reverse, it can mean disgrace; but in such a case, it is necessary, for the tarot to the left or to the right to be of a bad omen.

Accompanied by the No. 51, it predicts that you will receive great gifts or even a magnificent inheritance.

For a lady or for a young person, it predicts great success in a ball or other meetings. For a warrior, advancement, success in battle. For a litigant, winning a lawsuit.

D'ODOUCET

This eleventh card is the hieroglyph of strength. This virtue is represented in this image by a seated woman resting her arm on the head of a lion, who rests on one of her knees. She wears a ruby coat, a golden crown and a belt, on which is written THOT. The seat of this virtue conveys a very suitable trait of solidity. A grey drape forms the background of the image, and a paved pattern in white and black, the flooring. The sovereign is under the immediate domination of this virtue.

Two 1s symbolize the best, an overabundance of *Strength*; untamable by the union of the two strongest beings; the physical and the moral. In the end the man is found to be doubly composed; adding the *Sovereign*; with the powers people entrust in him, effectively doubling his qualities.

MODERN INTERPRETATIONS

Astrological correspondence is Aquarius. This card has also by Grimaud been assigned the keywords STRENGTH in the upright and POWER in the reverse.

UPRIGHT: This is card advices you to have strength and confidence and to encourage confidence in others. You need to stay on course, put in the effort and do not let anything stop you, success is at hand. In relationships, it is card of rising above conflicts and to show affection.

REVERSE: In the reversed this card warns of an abuse of power, like a despot in absolute power. You or someone around you may be domineering, intolerant, prideful, arrogant even violent. It may imply an unhealthy attachment to title and possessions and if not careful may cost you, those you hold dear. In a relationship, this implies a situation of uneven power between partners.

No. 12

The Prudence - The People
The Prudence[28]

You have already behaved wisely in difficult situations, this card urges you to apply the same in the future, because you will have many obstacles to overcome. The serpent is always a sign of temptation, it predicts that you will be seduced by deceitful people, who will lead you astray, if you're not careful.

Next to the No. 64, this card tells you that you will argue with a dark-haired man.

In the Reverse, this tarot does not predict anything particularly interesting for you, news of people, a foreigner, for whom you have some interest, or a country that you have wanted to visit.

When No. 12, still in the Reverse is found, near the No. 15, it announces a popular meeting or a dangerous quarrel; near No. 70, it implies certain loss; next to the No. 19, predicts captivity with short duration.

---

[28] Prudence, wherever this card appears in the spread, is wise advice to operate prudently, recognizing that prejudice and ignorance make us commit the most serious of criminal acts, when people do not understand the steps we take to bring a wicked man into a life of honesty and usefulness to society.

Prudence, in consultation, judgment and command; adherence, memory, intelligence, science, reason, foresight, circumspection, skill. Its wants; honesty, solitude, economics, work, activity, politics, etc.

LEMARCHAND

This tarot warns you to be on your guard on all occasions, as the serpent represents the tempting demon.

But if this tarot arrives in the company of Nos. 9, 10 or 11, it is an approving sign, on the way you have conducted your business.

Next to the No. 64, it is a warning of minor hardship; and the card is modified by the cards that follow; whether in the shape of one of the four Knights or one of the four Pages, because it announces, that you can count on your friends to support you in such situations.

D'ODOUCET

This twelfth card is the hieroglyph of Prudence. This virtue is portrayed here by a woman, who walks with precaution, so as not to disturb a reptile, which is at her feet. She is depicted with the head bare, her hair tied back with a headband. She is dressed in blue, holding a caduceus in one hand while lifting up her long dress with the other. A terrain in various colors, a nape of water and a rock in the distance are the main accessories in this image, the blue of the air make up the sky. *The people* are under the immediate influence of this virtue.

The Vegetation of 2, always stable as it is slow in its march, designates *Prudence*, a virtue, which precisely symbolizes the large and diverse class of people, who nevertheless derive their positive value from the 1, a promoted leader, who directs them, or promotes the produce of others.

MODERN INTERPRETATIONS

Astrological correspondence is Pisces. This card has by Grimaud been assigned the keywords PRUDENCE in the upright and POPULARITY in the reverse.

UPRIGHT: Prudence is needed with this card, a time to be practical, methodical and mindful. Action should only be taken after careful deliberation. There might be outside influences, that trigger you and you may want to say certain things, however here you must apply patience and diplomacy in all your dealings personally as well as professionally.

REVERSE: This card in the reverse is an encouragement for you to step out and socialize, perhaps speak at a public place. Also, you may be placing your trust in the wrong people or situations. It generally implies attention from the wider public, good or bad.

No. 13

Marriage – Union
The High Priest

The Egyptians dwelled much on this hieroglyph, because they regarded marriage as an absolute will of the creator.

If the querent is a young man, this card announces an imminent union with the person he desires; if the querent is married, one of his relatives will get married instead.

If this card is found near No. 18, it is love chilling, if it is near the No. 14, beware of a person, who only makes you look good to deceive you. If it appears next to the No. 70, your present or future marriage will be very happy and your family line will be numerous.

Next to the No. 57, it announces an upcoming reconciliation with a person, that you have not seen for a long time.

When this card is in the Reverse, it only predicts things to the contrary, failed marriages, either for the querent, or for someone he cares about.

LEMARCHAND

If the querent is a young man, this card tells him, he will soon marry the person he wants. This prediction means the same when the querent is a young lady to be married off, that is, she will be united with the young man, she has cast her sights.

But if the querent is married, the card then speaks of a very close relative.

Next to the No. 57, it announces to you a reconciliation with the person, who has recently held out against you.

Near No. 70, it is an announcement of a marriage, where many children will be born.

D'ODOUCET

This thirteenth card is the hieroglyph of marriage. It presents a young man and a young woman, whose union is enforced by a Mage or a priest dressed in green and with an aurora tiara headdress.

The generation, the number 3 expressing itself, needs the intimate union of the 1, its immediate agent, to be brought to its true product, or goal imposed by nature, protected by laws, sanctified by religion, which sanctions it with the name of Marriage, the union inspired by this very nature.

MODERN INTERPRETATIONS

This card has also by Grimaud been assigned the keywords MARRIAGE in the upright and LOVE AFFAIR in the reverse.

UPRIGHT: This card represents contracts, agreements and of course marriage. In relationships, it implies a time of affection and deepening of friendships, which will lead to serious commitment. In business, if a situation has been difficult, this certainly is a sign of improvement and a time of contract signing. Generally, a card of happy relationships and family life.

REVERSE: In the reverse this card does not necessarily imply anything bad, rather just the upright in a lesser degree. However, it can imply a painful relationship, of infidelity, or animosity. This may also imply a delay in plans such as with a marriage or a contract. Also, of being in an unserious or paperless relationship, either voluntarily or involuntarily.

No. 14

Force Majeure - Minor Force
The Devil[29]

An improper joke will cause you some annoyance. You will be led into great mistakes, which will not spare you from unfortunate assumptions, but you can endure, your strength is slowly returning and the mockers are not always on the same side.

This card predicts a small forthcoming indisposition as a result of recklessness. Next to No. 16, it indicates an impossible love.

Next to the No. 60, it tells you, that one of your relatives or friends has ventured too far on a journey faraway.

---

[29] The devil. The Egyptians by this word the Devil or Demon did not read hellish spirits chained up in the abyss, but a man whose science far surpassed that of others. Indeed, who knew more about the occult arts than the Brahmans, the Gymnosophists, the Druids, etc. This hieroglyph signifies force majeure in all matters of human life, minor force in all that concerns the future or life eternal.

countryside.

LEMARCHAND

The interpretation of this tarot can be made in various ways. It demands the greatest attention from the reader; for example, if it comes upright, and accompanies the No. 12, you need not fear anything, because its meaning is modified by its good neighbor.

In the Reverse, it announces that you have resisted the devil, and that you have put more faith in reason than prejudice.

Near No. 78, it indicates that you will soon attend very beautiful festivals in the city or even in the

D'ODOUCET

This fourteenth card[30] is the hieroglyph of the genius of the universe in the midst of men and women. This image presents a demon; his head is equipped with two ram horns and flames; a full beard split into two, and reaching down to his chest and breasts; his arms, his thighs and legs have fur. He is presented standing on a pedestal, holding a torch in his hand. At the foot of the pedestal, chained and held by their collar, a black man and a white woman, both wearing headdresses of horns and flames. The pedestal is planted on green grounds. The blue of air paints the background of the image.

Here the whole universe is at the disposal of its rightful master.[31] His qualities, both hidden and obvious to you,

---

[30] Translator: d´Odoucet assigns only *Force Majeure* in the Upright and in the Reverse for this card.

[31] Translator: A little disturbing conclusion d´Odoucet reaches here for this card. The Age of Enlightenment; renaissance man has eaten from the tree of knowledge, assisted by the devil. This would certainly be one view from this time period. It should also be noticed, that the Priest in card no. 18 is described as a traitor, undoubtedly reflecting the betrayal of the Church felt by many during the French revolution. A more sinister view would be that d´Odoucet is pushing the Luciferian doctrine; that Christianity is an oppressing religion; the priest is suppressing his natural desires etc., and that Lucifer is the light-bearer who brings light and knowledge to mankind. In support of this argument there is an overwhelm of symbolism back to Freemasonry, and Freemasonry is often tied in with Luciferianism. Whatever d´Odoucet´s angle was, I do not think Etteilla was thinking along those lines, I have found Etteilla venerating God in his books.

move with the intelligence of one another, he becomes the force of all force; who can resist it! It is therefore proper, that this card bears the name *force majeure*.

MODERN INTERPRETATIONS

This card has by Grimaud been assigned the keywords VIOLENCE in the upright and WEAKNESS in the reverse.

UPRIGHT: This is card of big energy and charisma. You may have the most ambitious goals, that will work out for you. In business, a very favorable card, of success and profits. Also, a good card for politicians and strategists. This card may imply, that you listen more to your animal instincts than your logic or intuition. In relationships it implies elevated passions, sensuality and fascination, you may be in a domineering role. This card can represent your desire to control and manipulate as well. A card of ego-inflation and a card that magnifies whatever card it lands on.

REVERSE: In reverse, you may find yourself in a marriage where your spouse is cheating on you. You are being dominated by someone or used by someone. This card may indicate, you being a pawn in somebody's game, or that somebody is trying to disrupt your plans. Certainly, a card of huge obstacles in your way.

No. 15

Sickness - Sickness
The Magician or The Juggler

This card indicates a disturbance of the mind in a person you care about, but patience! It is not card No. 78, it implies merely that the person is known to you as such, the No. 1, your perspective, however it may indicate in this case, that the querent is sick, what do you expect, madness has its nuances, madness is a variety, not all madmen can be put into small categories.

If this tarot was near the No. 17, it would imply walking on water, which you would not be doing, without exposing yourself to some danger, after the No. 70, it implies that, the querent is a real carefree type.

There is good reason to modify the meaning of this card when tarot No. 15 appears last, it is only then a small annoyance, like missing out on some fun, being caught by a rainstorm; finally, what you expect to be agreeable, will turn out to be the opposite.

LEMARCHAND

This card announces a significant and unforeseen change in your position. The wand of the magician indicates, that it will only take a short time for this prediction to come true.

Next to No. 17, it warns you of an imminent peril to your fortune; and preceded or followed by the No. 70, it predicts dangers caused by bad information.

If this tarot appears in the Reverse, and it was followed by the No. 78, it would suggest, that you would commit to some folly or some thoughtlessness; but if it was next to the No. 65, you would have to fear unpleasant news, which you did expect, however.

D'ODOUCET

This fifteenth card represents a Mage, standing, holding a wand in his right hand, the left resting on his right chest. In front of the Mage, an ancient altar, in two of the corners, a head of a ram and another of a bull. Placed on the altar are ten golden rings, arranged triangularly in 4s, 3, 2, 1, and a clay cup; and the book of THOT with pages in gold, and behind the Mage, the symbol T.

The universal spirit 5 comes in superabundantly (and therefore), to suppress his creature, who has been provided, with a portion necessary to his way of being. The balance is lost, and the machine suffers. The hieroglyph speaks for itself here, it is Hermes who shows us the constitutive and urgent principles of our micro cosmos of existence; the four elements, the three principles; two properties inherent in matter; fixity and volatility[32]. In addition, a driving principle; requiring from us imperatively to re-establish, as quickly as possible, an essential concordance, if we wish to remain inscribed in the book of life, where an acquired higher knowledge gives us the right to the cards.

---

[32] The four elements; water, fire, air and earth. The 3 principles; physical, mental and spiritual. Everything in nature is change and therefore everything must change, man must adapt or he will suffer the consequences.

MODERN INTERPRETATIONS

This card has by Grimaud been assigned the keywords SORROW in the upright and ILLNESS in the reverse.

UPRIGHT: This card implies bad relationships, conflicts disagreements, depression, worry and doubt. This could manifest into actual health problems, sickness, and disease. You may find yourself misunderstood, or be the person in the wrong place at the wrong time. A situation could escalate, be postponed or delayed. In business, disappointments, promotions will not come through, a situation will worsen. Unexpected expenses and declining finances. You may be associated with friends or groups that are dangerous to you and your reputation. It is a card that encourages you to take the reins, if not stop, then at least take measures to break the fall.

REVERSE: In the reverse, this card represents mental illness. There is trouble in your personal relationships. This card may imply that you are pretending to be something you are not, and that this will blow up in your face. It also indicates in general depression, nervousness and of uncomfortable situations.

No. 16

The Judgement – The Judgement
The last judgement

A lawsuit, will soon reach a conclusion, the consequences of which will be unfortunate for your fortune, you will almost be ruined, your friends will abandon you, fearing of being forced to come to your aid. However, a future inheritance will restore your fortune, it will then turn out to be a payback to your enemies.

Next to the No. 58, it predicts that you will be summoned as a witness in a matter of honor; if it is for a lady, that she will be a witness to a hoax towards a person foreign to her usual relations.

When next to the No. 24, it indicates a matter that leaves the querent worried.

Followed by the No. 68, it predicts a winning case, that will bring in a sum of money, which will help ward off a loss.

The No. 17, accompanying the No. 16, announces tribulation caused by an inheritance.

When this card appears in the Reverse, it does not give a favorable opinion on the querent's projects.

LEMARCHAND

If you have any lawsuits, this tarot announces to you, that it will conclude soon. If you are only experiencing troubles, annoyances, it predicts a resolve in your favor. If you have some plans, that you will soon see them come true according to your wishes. If you are uncertain about the future of a large business, that your worries are well-founded.

In the Reverse, this tarot reveals that the querent's judgment is doubtful and that he must receive advice on deciding on something.

Near the No. 58, it warns you, that you will be called upon to judge a small dispute between relatives; next to the No. 15, that your decision will satisfy everyone.

D'ODOUCET

This card is the hieroglyph of universal judgment. A winged genie surrounded by glory promptly overlooking our earth, awakening the mortals sleeping in the bosom of earth, with the sound of his trumpet. These reach out with beseeching hands towards the sky; some in consternation, others over-whelmed with faith.

The sphere presented with an animating spirit 6, comes to submit its whole to the 1 which must dominate it, it thus awaits the *censorship* of its sovereign, who will know how to *condemn* the heterogeneous, to raise those, who preserve among them the most perfect harmony; the desirable state, which alone can put us in a position to endure the presence of this great judge.

MODERN INTERPRETATIONS

This card has by Grimaud been assigned the keywords OPINION in the upright and ARBITRATION in the reverse.

UPRIGHT: This is card of favorable outcomes after times of trials. A moment of clarity, you will proceed with renewed resolve and obstacles are overcome easily. Relationship issues are cleared up. You may feel called towards something, which will be of consequence. Your professional life will have a restart and you will find support around you. You may have new business and romantic offers. In a lawsuit, the ruling will be in your favor. Also, better health is in this card and health issues in general will quickly be resolved.

REVERSE: This card in reverse indicates unfairness and regrets. You will not be treated fairly by other people and circumstances will turn against you. You may feel defeated in a relationship or in life in general. You are encouraged to apply sound thinking in relationships going forward. Also, a spiritual card, you are heading in the wrong direction, a need to realign yourself with what is meant for you. If you are in a lawsuit, the decision will not be in your favor.

No. 17

Mortality - Nothingness
The Death

You fear losing someone, who has been of great service, stay hopeful, there is nothing to fear.

If this card follows the No. 1, then it tells you that a friend of yours has just escaped great danger.

If the questioner is a lady, this tarot predicts annoyances of all kinds. If it's for a young lady, it's a sign that her marriage plans will be botched.

This card is a bad neighbor to every other card, it must be removed from the row, if it interferes with the interpretation of the spread.

Next to the No. 4, it makes it known, that the querent must refrain from contemplating crossing rivers or embarking on boats, because a danger awaits him.

Side by side with No. 20, it warns you, that you must refrain from approaching certain animals.

Preceded by the No. 35 it announces, that one will experience great emotion in a ceremony or at a celebration.

When this card appears in the Reverse, it announces that hopes, that were held on the success of a project will be squashed.

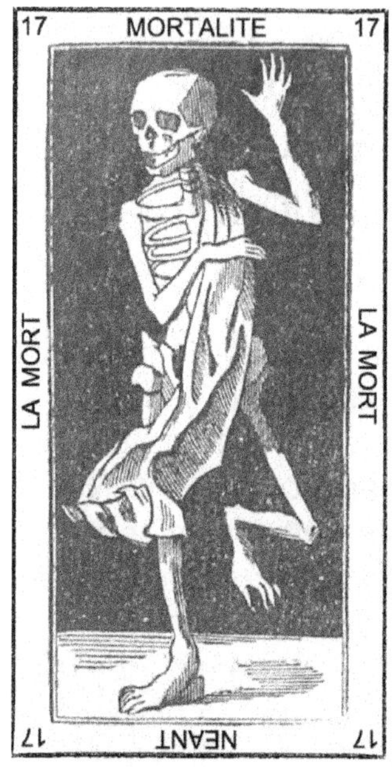

LEMARCHAND

If this tarot[33] is in the Reverse, it tells you that you will be disappointed in your expectations.

After the No. 4, it warns you not to undertake the journey in question, if it is to be done in bad weather. This card warns you to be careful at all times, to avoid werewolves and raging dogs.

Often this tarot is a bad neighbor for the other cards, it prevents the formulation of a reading; if so, you have to remove it from the row. We believe that it is ominous and that nothing obliges the querent to seek to interpret things above that, which comes within the field of recreation.

---

[33] Translator: The Lemarchand booklet assigns the meaning *Fin* or Ending in the upright rather than *Mortalite*.

D'ODOUCET

This seventeenth card is the hieroglyph of death. The end of all things is presented by a human skeleton, wrapped in an ash-grey shroud, holding a scythe in hand, and pointing to the earth, our last dwelling. This specter is depicted in the middle of tombs, and other funeral monuments, which he browses under the flight of a dark and sinister raven, hovering above his head.

Life itself, greedy for generations, assails those whose physical existence is no longer inalterable. Each element claims, what it has entrusted, to enter the circle of a new combination; the primitive form disappears; but nothing can destroy the 1, the inner man; the latter alone, survives this law of fate, which has sway only over the fragile envelope, which the lack of balance or harmony exposes to be broken, destroyed, without a return. This indestructible thing seems to have escaped the material expression, or hieroglyph; however, let us notice that *death* or *nothingness* is always personified by a *skeleton* devoid of all flesh, and which symbolizes with as much precision as possible, the 1, man within, or the interior of man.

MODERN INTERPRETATIONS

This card has by Grimaud been assigned the keywords DEATH in the upright and INCAPACITY in the reverse.

UPRIGHT: This is a card of dying, endings, rupture, cycles, and renewals. The end of something is always the beginning of something else. This card can imply the ending of a relationship, either by a divorce or a separation. The ending is necessary though, since it is not conducive for future growth. In business, a crisis, loss of clients, unfavorable conditions, all of which may cost you your job. There may be a need to pursue other avenues or to reinvent yourself. Finances will not be good. Generally, an unhappy card with dramatic changes, but which you with hard work can turn into something positive.

REVERSE: A bad card in reverse. Whatever hopes you may have had for something to happen, a relationship, a job, a promotion will not materialize. It will be difficult for you to achieve the things you want, opportunities will be lost, a chance meeting will not turn out the way you hoped. You may have difficulty in accepting something is over, but it is nevertheless necessary. This card can represent a life-threatening disease or a death in your social circle.

No. 18

Traitor - Hypocrite
The Capuchin[34]

This card tells you that a deceitful individual will spread slander at your expense, he or she will repent afterwards, but it will be too late.

With the No. 2, it predicts, this impostor will be discovered.

If the querent is an official, this card warns him, that he will be reprimanded soon.

If this tarot is preceded by the No. 66, it announces, that one of your relatives or a friend will become a nun.

If this card is near the No. 19, it announces annoyance as a result of slander.

When it encounters the No. 3, it predicts a falling out with a close relative.

When it is near the No. 24, it predicts, that soon you will be the victim of malice from a man, who will abuse the power which is entrusted to him.

Side by side with No. 16, it raises fears of a setback, that will jeopardize the querent's future.

When in the Reverse, it does not predict anything unpleasant, especially when placed next to the No. 41, also in the Reverse.

---

[34] The Egyptians did not take, as people in Provence say; the *Hood,* before they reached the first degree of Science and Human Wisdom. These Philosophers were, in a way, forced to do so by their contemporaries, and by their disciples, according to the vulgar idea, that the body of the sublime does not exalt itself so freely. Today this hieroglyph indicates a hypocrite, a traitor.

LEMARCHAND

This card[35] warns you, that some nasty jokes have been made at your expense, but that no one believes them; the deceit has been revealed.

This tarot, placed near the No. 66, is favorable to you, because it means that in any event, you will have people who defend you, and that this slander cannot affect you.

The lantern that the figure holds in his hand indicates, that the light should shine on people who doubt the truth; the dog is here the symbol of friendship, since there is no animal more devoted to its master.

Near the No. 20, it announces great satisfactory subjects.

---

[35] Translator: The Lemarchand booklet assigns the meaning *Faussete* or Falsehood on this card in the Reverse, rather than *Faux Devot* or Hypocrite.

D'ODOUCET

This eighteenth card represents a loner turning his back to the light of heaven, and striding away from the temple of wisdom and from true science. A staff in one hand, a lantern in the other, advancing with a lantern towards an isolated altar. This fanatic and deceitful loner is presented in a hermit´s dress, dull and sad in color; he wears a blue mantle and red shoes.

To rule out all the discussions that metempsychosis gave rise to, I will not entertain the question here if the interior of man, surviving his vessel, can live in another. I am satisfied in saying, that the way of generations was designed for the propagation of the species, and we see indeed that the 8, the symbol of progression of the generations, is presented here under the auspices of their principal engine 1. How are these generations currently operating? Always unexpectedly; it is indeed a kind of *treason*. Nature does not let itself be taken in by facts, it acts, it acts resolutely, without our knowing of it; the work appears unexpectedly! What does the *traitor* do? Precisely that of his march. Thus, the lantern deaf by its ambiguous light, manifests the unforeseen moment, which remains hidden.

MODERN INTERPRETATIONS

This card has by Grimaud been assigned the keywords BETRAYAL in the upright and FALSEHOOD in the reverse.

UPRIGHT: This is a card of betrayal. You need to be suspicious about people in your life, who may lack sincerity and honesty. Some may slander you or betray you, in case of partner this may imply infidelity. In business, your goals may be thwarted and people may fall back on their deals. Be mindful of people who offer advice, apply discretion and vigilance.

REVERSE: This card in the reverse indicates a deception being discovered. A time of emotional distress and hurt. Financial advice whether investments or work should not be acted upon. Hard work may result in nothing. With this card in reverse it is a warning to you to be careful where, how and who you spend your time with.

No. 19

Misery - Prison
The Stormed Temple

This card is the symbol of all unforeseen catastrophes; it signifies famine, adversities, torments and disgrace.

Next to the No. 62, if the querent is a man, it predicts a big quarrel with one of his best friends.

Next to the No. 10, this card predicts for the querent persecutions for political writings.

Preceded by the No. 23, this card announces a resounding success in a matter involving religion.

In the Reverse, it is not a favorable omen, it announces an unfair appreciation of your person. When this card is next to No. 59, it is a sign of shipwreck, if the person you are reading for is a navigator.

Next to the No. 15, and in the Reverse, it announces disgraces as a result of theological or religious quarrels, from which you will not emerge with advantage, unless an educated man agrees to lend you the assistance of his skills.

LEMARCHAND

This tarot predicts the advent of extraordinary things, but dreadful only when it comes out in the Upright and accompanied with Nos. 10 and 62. This card is always modified by favorable neighbors. If, for example, it is followed by the King, Queen, Knight or Page of Coins, it predicts that you will soon inherit; if Nos. 36 to 39 were accompanying it, it would be a prediction of an abundant harvest.

In the Reverse, next to no. 59, it announces shipwreck; but this prediction is only relevant, if you are about to embark on a boat. Otherwise you would only need to fear heavy rains in a party out in the country.

D'ODOUCET

This nineteenth card presents a solidly constructed circular building, and in the distance the ruins of a tower struck by lightning. It is called the house of God´s punishment.

We now perceive the 1, up to now dominating, oppressed, inconvenienced in action by the image of the sphere, the very outpouring of which it escapes. It undoubtedly experiences a *famine*, well synonymous with *inconvenience*. Alas! Everything seems united to overwhelm sad humanity! The wrath of heaven is unfolding! The nature of our ills (says M. de S. Pierre) reveals its origin. If man is unhappy, it is because he himself wants to be the arbiter of his happiness. The man is a god in exile, all the old allegories attest to the felicity and decadence of the first man. In this last period, death has already wreaked havoc and is false, but still harvests indiscriminately in the back of the superb palaces, as well as at the door of the humblest hovels. O man, it cries at the same time, to think that your perishable vessel is for you only an obscure *prison*, a constant source of vicissitudes attached to the existence of an imperfect card of which you make a number.

MODERN INTERPRETATIONS

This card[36] has by Grimaud been assigned the keywords POVERTY in the upright and PRISON in the reverse.

UPRIGHT: This card predicts tremendous upheaval. Your foundations will be shaken, professionally and emotionally. Arguments, disagreements, violence, shocks, often mitigated by some special unexpected circumstance. It can also be breakdown of a belief system. A life turned upside-down with difficulty, pain and suffering to follow. This card is never positive. You could lose a great deal of money, lose a job or have things stolen from you. It is card that urges you to compose yourself to take responsibility and to act as prudently as you can in the events that unfold.

REVERSE: This card in reverse although sever is less so than in the upright. Things will not turn to your advantage. A work situations may be difficult with a bad boss or a relationship made difficult with a domineering partner. You may feel trapped in a bad situation, which could also be an actual prison situation or a circumstance of extreme financial hardship. Change is not on the horizon and you must persevere as best you can.

---

[36] Translator: d´Odoucet assigns *Detresse* or Distress in the upright and *Captivite* or Captivity in the reverse for this card.

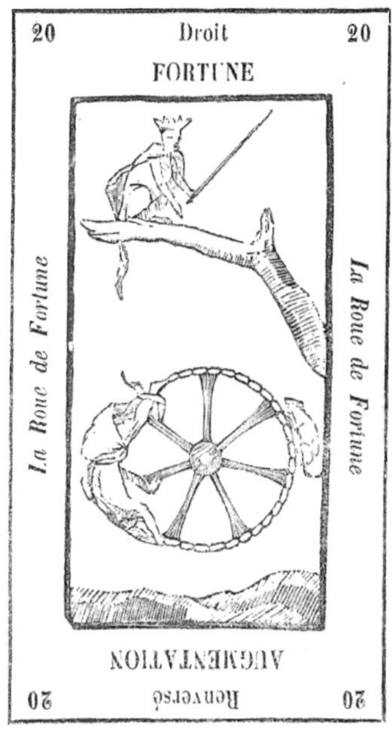

No. 20

Fortune - Increase
The Wheel of Fortune[37]

This card is always very favorable; it is a sign of fortune for the one who does not have one, it announces an elevation of him to a am of opulence.

It alone signifies dignity, elevation and prosperity.

If you are reading the cards for a soldier, this tarot predicts for him, that he will be appointed to a high rank after his next campaign.

Next to all other cards, it adds good onto their predictions.

In the Reverse, it still bodes well. If the querent is a young person, it predicts a military visit.

---

[37] The Wheel of Fortune; this hieroglyph signifies increase and fortune; note, however, whenever it appears in the spread, you must not assume that it is yours; you have to study where it is placed. It is often said to be very mean, and we may go as far as to call it mad, but I believe it to be very wise; since it only takes on the task of tormenting everybody the same.

LEMARCHAND

This tarot is always of a very favorable omen; it predicts fortune to him who has none; a considerable increase to him who has little.

Alone, in the Upright or in the Reverse, it is an omen of elevation, of dignity, of honors.

Next to other cards, it adds to their prediction, for the better, it cancels out the unfortunate meanings of the cards, which precede or follow it; and when it appears with any of the following Nos. 9, 10, 11 and 12, it implies that the querent possesses great moral qualities.

If you are reading for a soldier, it is the announcement of an imminent advancement.

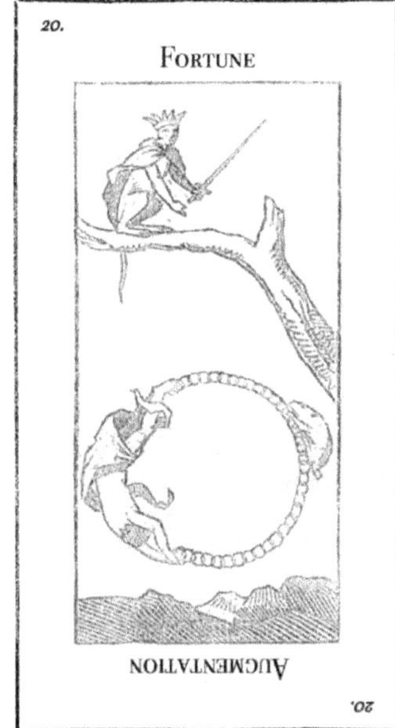

D'ODOUCET

This twentieth card is the hieroglyph of fortune. A crowned monkey, dressed up in a purple cloak, holding in its hand a rod as a scepter. He is gravely seated on a dead branch, which serves as his throne, from where he distributes his favors. Below is a man and a mouse, who cling painfully to the rings of an iron circle; the climbing animal is ascending to the throne, while the man is descending.

Here is the globe of the Earth. 0, receiving its vegetation from the number 2, whose products *increase* the fortune of the cultivator. Let us observe, by the way, that this favorable vegetation is only a continual permutation, the debris of one cooperation of cards in the *amplification* of another. Everything morally and physically is subjected to this common law. The race of the present has replaced the one which served as its cradle, everything follows the other, everything undergoes the evolution formed by the circle of existence. Blind fortune randomly spins its treacherous wheel; it turns, the weak immediately take the place of the dominant; and one thinks one is well established on the frail branch, which however will shatter into pieces with the slightest breath.

MODERN INTERPRETATIONS

This card has by Grimaud been assigned the keywords FORTUNE in the upright and INCREASE in the reverse.

UPRIGHT: This card is a favorable card. With this wheel, there is an increase in luck. If things have been difficult, this card indicates, that everything will be cleared up. This is a beneficial time for new ideas and new projects. You can expect support, rewards, profits, also luck in gambling. If a relationship has been challenging, a renewed tenderness will clear out any misunderstanding. It is a card of enjoyment and vacation as well, perhaps time to make some new purchases with the luck you had at the poker table? This is overall a good card which promises happiness and good health.

REVERSE: This card in the reverse is still a good card, however your progress may be more irregular. An improvement in relationships is implied, with more flow, enthusiasm and support. There may be a promotion or some other type of recognition in business. There may be multiple ways to make your money. Winnings from gambling may come and go with this card in reverse.

No. 21

Dissension - Arrogance
The African Despot

A bad-tempered person will soon be looking for a fight. You will be deceived in an enterprise in which you have interested several of your friends.

If the person for whom you are reading is a lady, this card announces to her a break with her admirers.

Next to No. 17, it announces the loss of an animal, to which one is attached.

Next to No. 67, it urges you not to indulge in any risky speculations.

When this card is next to No. 41, it predicts wasting time, unnecessary work. It is usually a sign of over-confidence.

When you see it in the Reverse, it offers hope that the questioner will soon be released from the abuse of power from a superior.

LEMARCHAND

There are two ways to interpret this card: The first; it can announce to the querent, that he will achieve a high position.

The second meaning predicts, that the querent will come under the thumb of some foreign person, or will experience annoyances, that he will have to endure in all kinds of ways.

If it is for a young man one reads, it indicates that the woman, whom he will marry, will dominate him in all sorts of ways; if it is for a young lady, it predicts to her that the husband she will have, will be superior in fortune.

When laying the cards out for a person in service, this card tells him that he is respected by his superiors.

D'ODOUCET

This twenty-first card represents a conqueror in a chariot drawn by two horses without reins. Here he is depicted in armor, having a gold crown and a scepter made of the same metal.

So, it is done! Man has fallen from his first son! We will only see him reappear under his new reign; dominating the elements and circumstances. We perceive 1 first, with its dependence on vegetation, or reproduction of 2, from which it awaits its subsistence, and even a new being. So, is his experience, the tyranny of imperious needs? What will the result be? Undoubtedly the distinction between yours and mine; then *dissention* rushes in with a crash, *trouble* arises among the offspring; the disputes, which motivate them, turn family members pale: such is the order of things, such is the offer of our day to day lives.

This card[38] has by Grimaud been assigned the keywords LAW SUIT in the upright and LEGAL DISPUTE in the reverse.

UPRIGHT: This is a card of courage and daring, but often reckless or thoughtless too. It implies pride and vanity and a sense of grandeur, which can cause tension with people around you. In relationships, this can cause rupture, poor communication, even aggressive and violent behavior. In business this card indicates achievements, but at what price? Colleagues may be envious and resentful towards you. This may therefore turn out to be a *pride comes before the fall* moment.

REVERSE: This card in reverse implies a change in your situation, this will non-the-less be beneficial to you. In reverse it is still a good card for the ambitious, since achievements are foretold. Often this is instigated by a change in direction, a change in circumstance or a change in perspective. It can indicate more independence and very beneficial financial outcomes. This may also imply you toppling, removing, putting in place a domineering person, in your community or in the work place.

---

[38] Translator: d´Odoucet assigns only *Dissension* in upright and in reverse for this card.

No. 22

Country Man - A Good and Stern man
King of Clubs or Diamonds

An uncle of yours, in a distant country, who has never given you any news, has made a considerable fortune, he has made you his heir, and will soon come and surprise you.

Next to No. 20, this tarot warns you to use your fortune wisely.

Preceded by the No. 47, this card announces good news, which will reach you from the countryside.

Preceded by No. 14, it predicts an advantageous marriage, a royal dowry.

Near the No. 15, this card promises many moments, that will fill your mind with pleasant dreams.

Followed by the No. 77, it gives hope for an honorable and lucrative post.

Accompanied by the No. 78, the luck is a bit contrary to what was announced above.

Next to No. 23, it announces favor, a royal protection. It is always a sign of sincerity.

In the Reverse, this card advices you, that one of your friends will give you some advice, which you should follow.

LEMARCHAND

Here is a tarot[39] whose appearance announces unforeseen success, news of relatives who live in distant countries. If this tarot comes after the No. 20, inheritance from an American uncle or aunt. In the Reverse, it urges you to use your fortune prudently.

Accompanied by the No. 78, it is a less favorable omen; it warns you that your plans will be thwarted by a madman.

But if the No. 12 is among the cards in the spread, it is a prediction to you, that good advice will come to help, in your endeavors and that they will contribute to the success of an issue in question.

When the No. 14 precedes it, it announces an illustrious marriage for the querent.

---

[39] Translator: The Lemarchand booklet assigns only the meaning *Homme Bon* or Good Man on this card in the reverse not *Homme Bon et Severe*.

D'ODOUCET

This twenty-second card represents a country man, crowned and seated, dressed in yellow, holding in his hand a long staff or club, from which he takes support.

This symbol of a useful and permanent vegetation presents itself before our eyes with a double aspect. The vegetative man himself, and the fall from his primitive state of dignity, of independence, his feeling of no longer being self-sufficient, he thus must seek the support of the vegetative principle, in all its forms, which can contribute to his necessities and to his well-being. This man is becoming a competent farmer. The roughness of the path, that this condition entails, makes it *severe*, albeit essentially *good*; because one always will be, as long as one follows the instincts of nature.

MODERN INTERPRETATIONS

This card has by Grimaud been assigned the keywords PROBITY in the upright and INDULGENCE in the reverse.

UPRIGHT: The King of Clubs represents a good, loyal leader. He may be a foreigner, someone not from your circles, but still someone that can provide useful advice, a good ally to have. If he is you, then you would have these qualities.

REVERSE: In the reverse he represents an indulgent, and tolerant man, who may give you financial help. He is also fair, but uncompromising, you can count on his understanding but not his complacency. He may be a friend or a lawyer.

Generally, all the court cards can be read as different people in your life, meaning, i.e. the Page of Clubs in Reverse, who normally indicates some sort of news, may also indicate a young male or a younger person in your life, who in reverse is in some type of disagreement, conflict, a failure to launch etc. with you. The big difference between Etteilla tarots and other tarots is the meaning of the keyword assigned to the cards. In Etteilla, each card has really a range of keywords assigned to it, and therefore can mean several things, and the reverse meaning does not necessarily correlate to the upright. On top of this, the sequential numbering of the cards give a different numerological imprint on each card, than what we normally see in other tarots.

No. 23

Country Woman - Good Woman
Queen of Clubs or Diamonds

The lady in No. 23, is a good woman, thrifty, virtuous, not bigoted, not talkative, not flirtatious, not lazy, not greedy; but a good woman, who in addition has much wit.

When this card shows up in the Upright, it heralds an abundant harvest, predicting, that you will have much fun in the next country party, which you will enjoy with a lot of people.

Followed by the No. 34 it is not particularly favorable.

Preceded or followed by the No. 37, it makes a wait into a great act of generosity; if the No. 37 is in the Reverse, this generosity will be of no use.

Next to the No. 15, it relates to relationships, that are best kept hidden.

When this card is in the Reverse, it announces the good we want to do, but without being able to.

If the number 63 is found next to it in the Reverse, it predicts children for you.

LEMARCHAND

This tarot represents the Queen of Clubs; she is good, virtuous, educated, a spiritual woman, full of merit.

If you are reading for a young man, this will be the announcement that the woman he will marry will be abundant in good qualities; for a young woman, it has a similar meaning.

This card, occurring in the Upright, is a sign of an abundant harvest.

Preceded by the No. 37, it implies a wait in a great act of generosity, however it will not bring in the slightest advantage, when it appears in the Reverse.

If we read for a person of advanced age, this card predicts great satisfaction and a very happy old age.

D'ODOUCET

This twenty-third card presents a country woman crowned and seated, dressed in yellow, holding a long staff or club.

We now see that this benevolent creature is ready to assist the work of the ones she shows compassion. Will the generations increase with the help of the products of vegetation? This is what signifies a *country woman*, supported by the symbol of reproduction. This woman will be *good* in essence, since she tends to perpetuate her species.

MODERN INTERPRETATIONS

This card has by Grimaud been assigned the keywords VIRTUE in the upright and DEVOTION in the reverse.

UPRIGHT: The Queen of Clubs represents a person from the countryside, a peaceful, reserved, discreet, understanding woman, perhaps a mother, wife or a girlfriend, etc. She may not be aware of her own beauty and strength and does not put herself forward. She is a good ally to have on your side.

REVERSE: This card represents a popular female, a member of many associations, who does charitable work and who is devoted to her community. Often, she is in the medical profession, a doctor or a nurse.

No. 24

Departure[40] - Disunity
Knight of Clubs or Diamonds

This card represents a rider for you, its position tells you that something is about to leave. This implies change.

Next to No. 15, it announces an upcoming trip.

When this card is preceded, or followed by the No. 20, it predicts that you will be depending on the fortune of someone you know. If it is next to the querent, it is the protagonist in his spread.

Next to the No. 71, it should serve as advice to the querent, that he should not leave in the hands of a friend, too long, the funds he has entrusted to him.

Near the No. 12, it advises taking legal action to obtain compensation for the harm suffered by the intricacies of a person in whom one had trust.

If you are reading for a young person and this card appears in the Reverse, it announces a marriage in decline.

---

[40] When placed in a row, the word Departure does not apply specifically to this card, but to the one that follows it.

LEMARCHAND

The rider announces news for you; it implies change of position, travel, displacement.

After the No. 71, it is a warning, to be wary of people, you put too much trust in.

Between the Nos. 14 and 16, it indicates, malicious words are circulating about people in whom you have great interest.

If the No. 78 is in the same row, it announces a great reason not to participate in travel plans proposed to you, bearing in mind that a rolling stone gathers no moss. Consequently, to prefer what is certain rather than rely on extraordinary luck, this certainty even being quite modest.

D'ODOUCET

This twenty-fourth card represents a young country man, on horseback, dressed in yellow, holding in his hand a long rod or club.

Our world alone is not bound by the laws of reproduction; all the universal parts of 4, must be susceptible to development; this is why we discover this universe in the sphere of the symbol of 2, of permanent reproduction. But this reproduction takes place only by means of a cart, on whatever *transport* of influence or reproductive germ, what can be better? This is expressed by *disunity*, a *departure* from the main stem; thus, a floret of wheat, beaten under the stick, is broken; and each seed is scattered, very often to different soil, than what produced it.

MODERN INTERPRETATIONS

This card has by Grimaud been assigned the keywords CHANGE in the upright and SEPARATION in the reverse.

UPRIGHT: The Knight of Clubs represents leaving, of motion, change of profession, focus or emotions. A person departing or arriving, who may deliver information to you.

REVERSE: In reversed, it implies quarrel, conflicts, misunderstanding and gossip. This is urging you to clear up any issues, perhaps by a phone call, before it escalates into a bigger ripple between friends and relatives.

No. 25

Good Stranger - News
Page of Clubs or Diamonds

A man who recently left your country will bring you news from your family, which will give you the greatest pleasure.

Next to the No. 5, this tarot predicts, that you will be forced to take a trip.

Preceded by the No. 57, this card is a favorable card for the querent.

Next to the No. 3, it announces the loss of an unimportant object.

Next to the No. 15, it lets you know, that a person who is on the way, is in the business of announcing a marriage to you, which will astonish you.

Next to No. 16, it predicts an acquisition of a built and planted property.

In the Reverse, it announces bad news, unless it is followed by one of the Nos. 17, 39 or 63 also in the Reverse.

In the Reverse, next to No. 18 this card is a sign of revolution in a neighboring state.

LEMARCHAND

This card represents the Page of Clubs; he is also a courier bringing news, but naturally they cannot come from afar.

After the No. 22, this tarot is the indication of goodwill from people in advantageous positions.

Followed by the No. 23, it announces to you, that a lady of high standing is planning an opulent marriage for you.

Following the No. 20, it predicts that you will be interested in an industrial speculation, from which you will derive great profit.

The Page of Clubs is, on every occasion, a fairly favorable card, and it modifies the meaning of opposing cards.

D'ODOUCET

This twenty-fifth card presents a young country man, on foot, in the outfit of a traveler, dressed in yellow, holding a long club or stick in his hand.

The agent, or the universal spirit of 5, still a *stranger* (although of same nature) to the vegetative spirit *specified* in the number, comes here before our eyes, to renew, or rather to restore (if we can use this expression) this constant principle of production.

MODERN INTERPRETATIONS

This card[41] has by Grimaud been assigned the keywords ORIGINALITY in the upright and NEWS in the reverse.

UPRIGHT: The Page of Clubs represents a young person, different, bringing a surprise, happy news, often someone in search of something, perhaps a relationship or a job. A card of new encounters and pleasant meetings.

REVERSE: In reversed, this card indicates messages, letters, phone calls, of movement and visits. Also, of someone who may be trying to interfere with your plans, perhaps a love rival. A card of good news too, perhaps from far away.

---

[41] Translator: d´Odoucet assigns only *Etranger* in upright, not *Bon Etranger*, for this card.

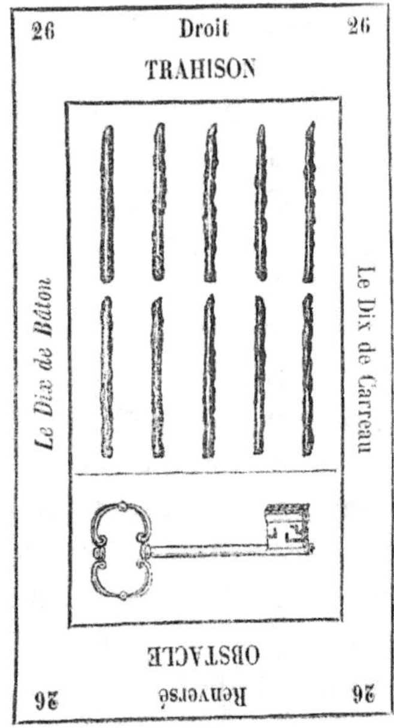

No. 26

Treason - Obstacle[42]
Ten of Clubs or Diamonds

Thunderstorms, earthquakes will strike the area where you live, knights of industry will try to take over your ruin, if you are not careful; the people around you will use cunning to drag you down; but if this card is in the reverse, it indicates that you will foil their nefarious plans after overcoming many obstacles.

When this tarot is found next to a favorable card, it signifies annoyance, surprise and work.

Next to No. 3, it warns you that someone who calls themselves your friend will slander you.

Next to the No. 35, you will overcome obstacles contributing to the success of your projects.

Next to No. 23, this card announces, that the querent will soon suffer a disease, however it will not have long term consequences.

If it is preceded or followed by the No. 50, it gives hope for an inheritance, that will give great relief to the querent.

---

[42] Translator: The figures below on the Club suit cards have been inserted by the publisher Blocquel. In the Reverse this card implies obstruction and blockages. Is that the key to unlock your troubles or the key to your prison cell?

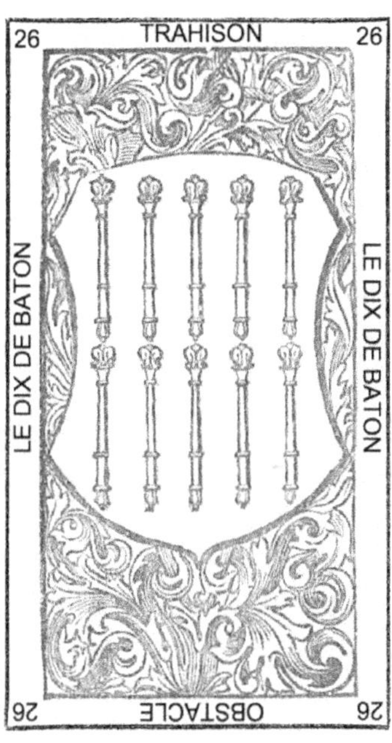

LEMARCHAND

This tarot[43] announces great swings in temperature, thunderstorms and continual rains in the area where you live.

When this appears in the Reverse, it warns you that plans are being made to ruin you, however you will easily outsmart your opponents.

Preceded or followed by the No. 50, it predicts for the querent, that he can hope for a fairly considerable inheritance, especially when it meets a tarot such as the Nos. 40, 54 and 68.

Close to No. 3, it is an indication of slander for you or for a person in whom you have a genuine interest.

Next to a favorable number, it signifies work, accomplishments and success.

---

[43] Translator: The Lemarchand booklet assigns only the meaning *Trahison* or Treason for this card, both in reverse and upright.

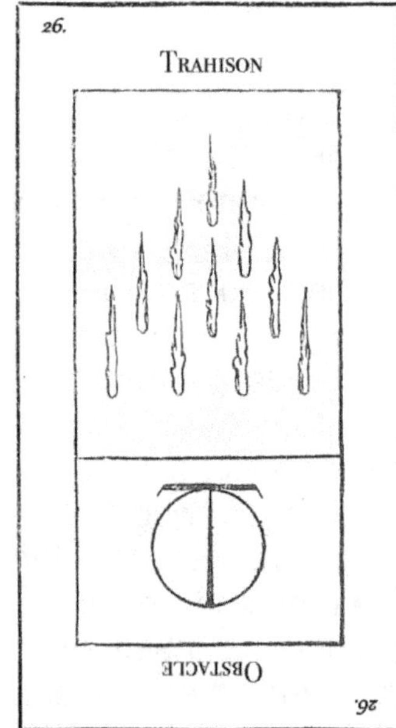

D'ODOUCET

This twenty-sixth card depicts ten sticks or clubs arranged in a pyramid. In the lower part of the card we find the number ten of the Egyptians.

We have said that the 6 represents the terrestrial globe, presented from a general principle of animation, which here is dominated by the vegetative principle of 2, which defines this last aspect. Thus, the generation always operates *incognito*, it is *treasonous*. It results in a vegetative existence, presented before our eyes by ten sticks (number 10 completes the cards), but by this very fact that the card exists, it constitutes an envelope; and every envelope is an obstacle for determined principled actions, be it physical or moral.

MODERN INTERPRETATIONS

This card has by Grimaud been assigned the keywords; LIES in the upright and OBSTACLE in the reverse.

UPRIGHT: The Ten of Clubs is a negative card. In relationships, it implies; jealousy, lies, deception, aggressiveness even violence, which turn you bitter. In business, things will not go your way, malice and slander, people, you thought you could trust, turn against you. Finances may be difficult during this time.

REVERSE: In the reverse, this card is also negative. In relationships, it indicates blockages, a stubborn refusal to listen to the other party, of not making an effort. This is not the right time for achievements workwise, you will have to put in the work still.

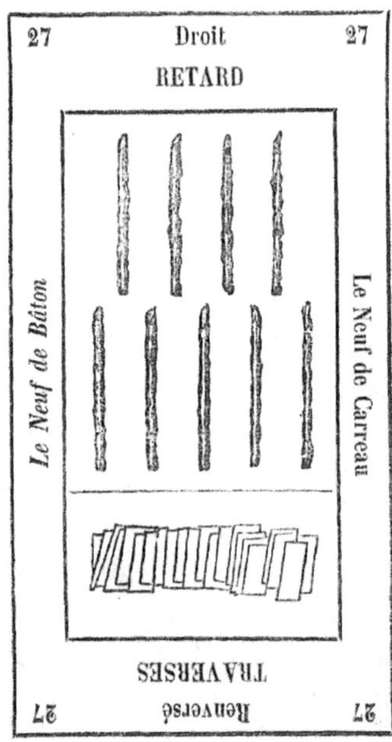

No. 27

Delay - Adversity[44]
Nine of Clubs or Diamonds

This card announces to you a slowness in your commercial affairs; you have an interest in distant expeditions, which will be compromised by your own carelessness.

If the querent is a sailor this tarot predicts bad weather, which will prevent a departure he desires.

Next to the No. 17, it informs you, that you will find an object, which loss caused you great pain.

Next to No. 13, it urges you to take care of your health, fearing that by neglect, you will soon be needing to seek care, however you may avoid this still.

When this tarot is next to the No. 26, it predicts, you will make a fortune in a foreign country.

Near the No. 27 and followed by the No. 30, it announces, that the door of a certain house, where you used to be well received, will be closed to you.

In the Reverse, it gives rise to fear of many nuisances, the consequences of which will be unfortunate for your interests.

---

[44] Translator: This card in the Reverse implies sorrow and misfortune, perhaps the figure below symbolizes someone losing it all in a card game?

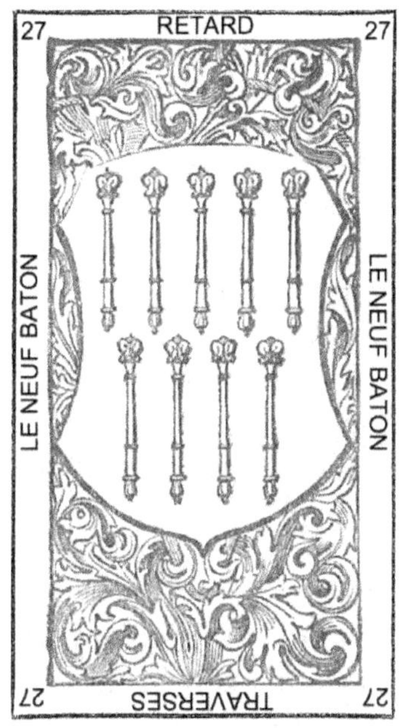

LEMARCHAND

When this tarot appears in the Upright and its neighbors are Nos. 30 and 27, it gives you an unfriendly welcome by people, who usually receive you with cordiality.

Next to the No. 17, it announces, that you will soon find an object whose loss has caused you great grief.

Close to the No. 13, it is a sign of mild illness.

If it is for a sailor, that one reads, this card is the prediction of bad weather and of a great delay in a voyage, which he is about to undertake. If the querent is a soldier, it informs him that he will not be rising in the ranks for some time.

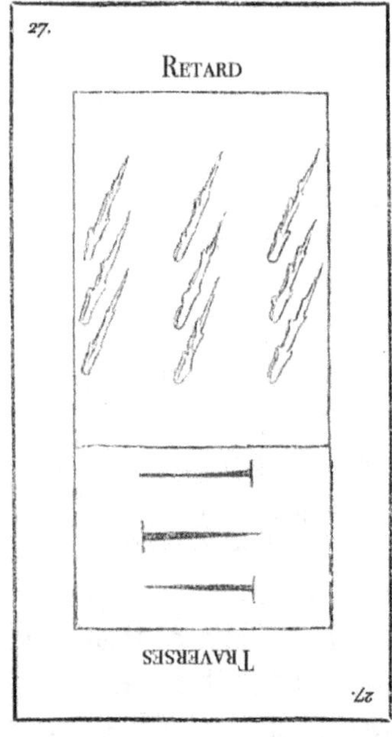

D'ODOUCET

This twenty-seventh card depicts nine sticks or clubs arranged in threes. In the lower part of the card is the number nine of the Egyptians.

7 a specific number of life in general, is presented in the sphere of the symbol of vegetation, from which it needs its physical subsistence. This one *absorbs* going forward the reproductions without which, would multiply ad infinitum, as the 9 of Clubs expresses it, or the 9 sticks, the number implies the world expressing this relationship. This *delay* in multiplication is an effective *obstacle* to the constant and unlimited productions of vegetation.

MODERN INTERPRETATIONS

This card has by Grimaud been assigned the keywords; DELAY in the upright and MISFORTUNE in the reverse.

UPRIGHT: This is not a good card. In relationships, unsuccessful dialogue, misunderstanding and sadness. In business, a card of delays obstacles, complications and setbacks. This card is also associated with natural disasters and bad weather. A time of holding out.

REVERSE: In reverse, this card predicts isolation, loneliness, sorrows and setbacks, which may be instigated and be in the control of strong adversaries. Finances may be hit, but will not wipe you out.

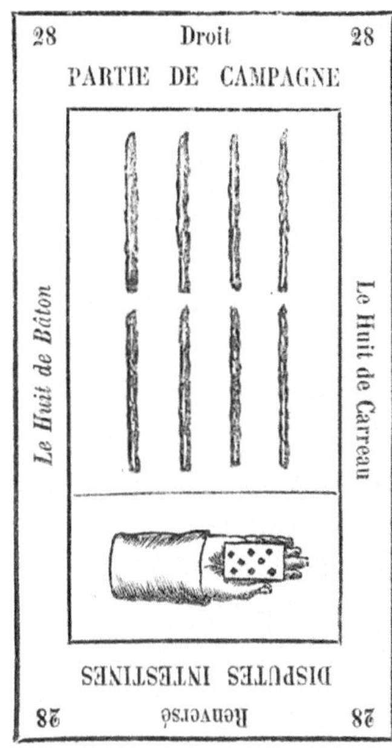

No. 28

Countryside – Internal Disputes[45]
Eight of Clubs or Diamonds

In the Upright, if the querent is unattached, this card announces a house party, which if near one of the Cup cards, will turn out to be very enjoyable. However, if the No. 28 is found with one of the Coin cards, it will turn out uneventful.

If the person is not married, and if the card is accompanied by one of the sword cards, a promenade-walk will be a pleasant one-on-one. The opposite will happen, if with one of the Coins cards appear.

When this card is drawn in the Reverse by a married person, it is a sign of a quarrel, of a household dispute.

In the Reverse and near the No. 42, it predicts quarrels with a young lady; and when followed by the No. 57, it becomes an indication of reconciliation.

In the Reverse, next to No. 76, it announces irritating news, that will cause several members of your family anger.

---

[45] Translator: This card in reverse implies misunderstanding and disputes, perhaps the figure below, the outstretched hand with the 8 of Diamonds, traditionally a card representing caution and work, is not a handshake of friendship, but symbol of more work, of disagreements?

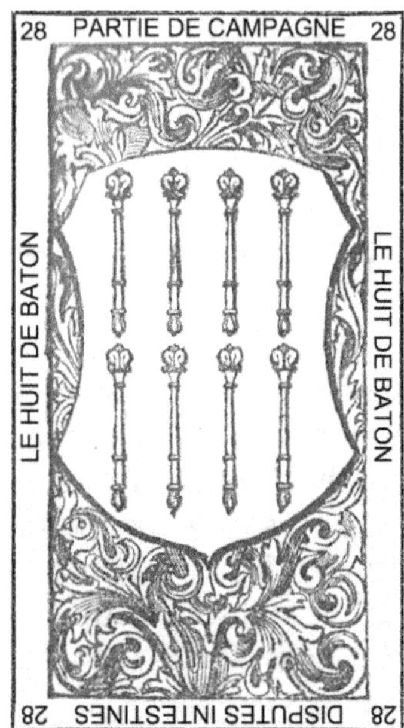

LEMARCHAND

If this tarot[46] appears in the Upright, and we read for an unattached person, it announces a pleasant meeting, a party of pleasure, a matrimonial interview.

When it appears with one of the odd numbered Coin cards, it is a sign of annoyance; with one of the Sword cards, it is a sign of slander, of malicious remarks either of your person or of some very close relative.

Followed by or preceded by the No. 52, it announces an imminent reconciliation with one of your relatives, who did not initially want to consent; but for some reason of interest changed his mind.

---

[46] Translator: The Lemarchand booklet assigns only the word *Disputes* in the reverse, not *Disputes Intestines*.

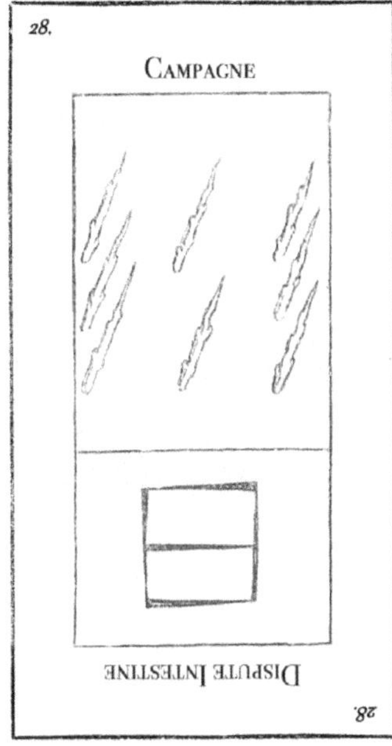

D'ODOUCET

This twenty-eighth card, depicts eight sticks or clubs, in the lower part of the card is the number eight of the Egyptians.

8 a symbol of the progression of generations of all kinds, is here symbolized by the type of plant, *countryside* is the ad hoc attribute; since the multiplicity of reproductions necessarily addresses the surface of the soil, each being competes for the place that suits it, or hastens to seize, to the detriment of the less diligent. Can we offer a more faithful picture of the battle inherent in all these numerous associations?

MODERN INTERPRETATIONS

This card has by Grimaud been assigned the keywords; REJOYCING in the upright and REPENTANCE in the reverse[47].

UPRIGHT: This card predicts harmony in relationships. You will have success and enjoy the pleasures from the good things in life. This may be in connection with a trip, perhaps to the countryside. You may find new interests or hobbies. In business, you are doing things at your own pace, money is not a concern, you may be self-employed. This may also indicate marriages, homes, and children.

REVERSE: This is a card of uncertainty in reverse. It represents a desire to right a past wrong, there may be some sentimental upset, which you are unable to express or to have a dialogue around. In business, a lot of uncertainty and doubt, owning up to things, that leave colleagues unhappy. Finances will suffer, perhaps by poor management.

---

[47] Translator: *Rejoussances – Repentir*, these keywords from Grimaud seem quite different from the original version I; *Campagne – Dispute Intestine* or in d´Odoucet; *Campagne - Irresolution*, however all of these words appear in the list of synonyms for this card.

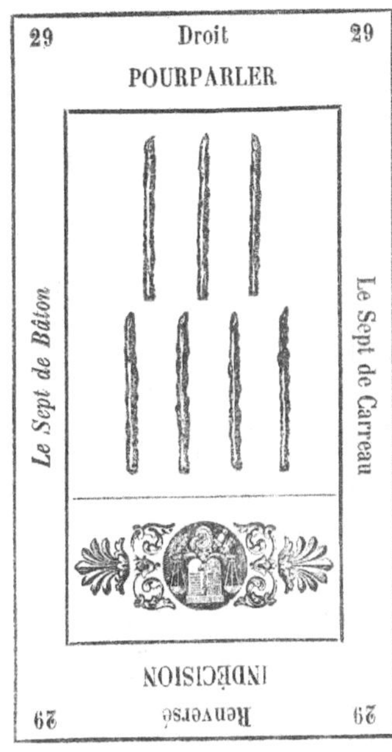

No. 29

Talk - Indecision[48]
Seven of Clubs or Diamonds

This card predicts that your plans are on the verge of success, and that the clumsiness of a friend alone has created obstacles, which however are easily resolved.

For a young person, this tarot is a favorable card, when followed by the No. 13, it announces that an acquaintance of a friend is putting in the effort of finding her a husband.

Next to the No. 22, the No. 29 announces an interview with an influential person, who will respond to your requests by throwing you a full glass of holy water from the courtyard.

When this tarot appears in the Reverse, it implies that the querent is wrong in being indecisive in his plans.

If the person for whom the spread is laid owns combustible objects, and this tarot appears next to the No. 47, he should fear fire.

Next to the No. 18, it announces, that slander has been spread on your account.

---

[48] Translator: This card in reverse implies uncertainty, doubt and perplexity, perhaps the figure below, the 10 commandments, draws the parallel to the unknowable, doubt of faith?

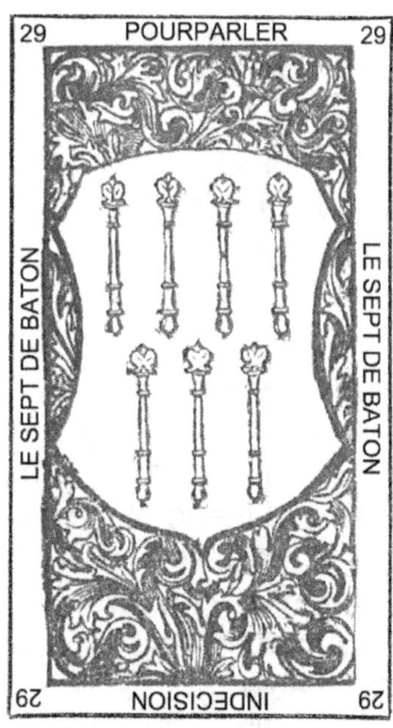

LEMARCHAND

The enterprise which consumes all your thoughts is certain to have the most brilliant result, despite the obvious awkwardness of a person, who could compromise everything.

When it is for a young person that one reads, this tarot announces that several of his friends will take care of his marriage.

Close to No. 22, it warns you that the influential person from whom you expect protection, will promise a lot, but hold little.

If chance makes this tarot appear in the Reverse, it would encourage you to have less indecisions in your projects.

When this card is preceded, or followed by No. 47, it implies fire; meaning fireworks.

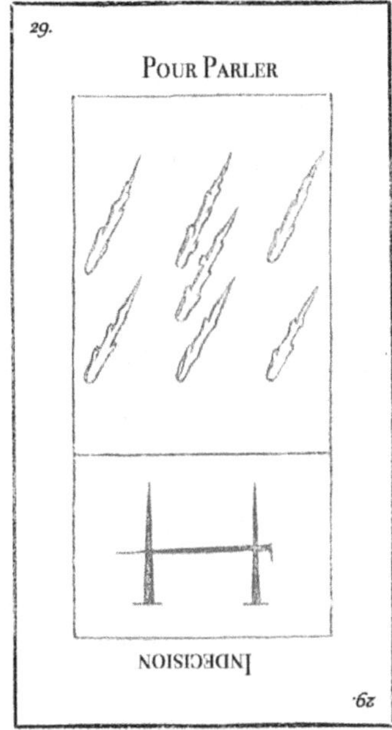

D'ODOUCET

This twenty-ninth card depicts seven clubs or sticks. In the lower part of the card is the number seven of the Egyptians.

The number 9, which we have said represents a prolific world, is here found dominating, determined by the type of plant; the indeterminate profusion as expressed by its form, designating perfectly *talking,* the vague generator of all that matters to us to whatever extent; and this vague or indeterminate outpouring is returned to us in a moment of *indecision,* which could not be better placed. Thus, the 7 of Clubs indicates to us, that the word is the true life of action, communicated through the commerce of society.

MODERN INTERPRETATIONS

This card has by Grimaud been assigned the keywords; NEGOTIATIONS in the upright and INDECISION in the reverse.

UPRIGHT: The Seven of Clubs represents a change in circumstances with the power of conviction and persuasion. It is a time where you are constructive and having success with it, with enthusiasm, resolve and negotiation, both in a private setting and professionally. You can expect an increase in influence or a promotion. Your finances will be well managed.

REVERSE: This card in reverse implies uncertainty. You may not be able to see things clearly, you may be indecisive about what you want. You may question yourself, be uncertain of your feelings. In business you are indecisive, you lack understanding and self-confidence. Finances may be on rocky grounds, if you do not apply yourself.

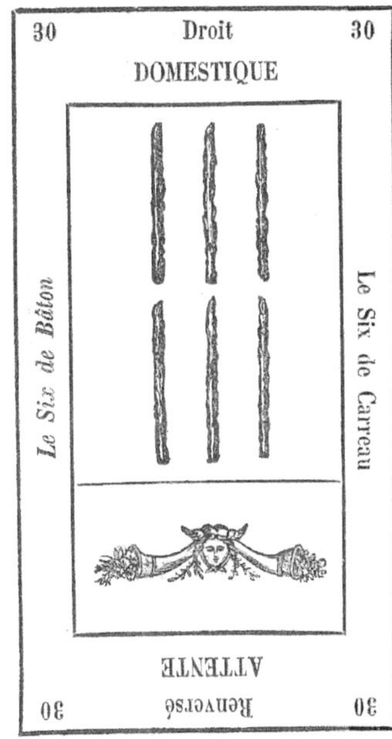

No. 30

Domestic - Wait[49]
Six of Clubs or Diamonds

If this card is near No. 18, be careful not to entrust your correspondence henceforth to the unfaithful courier to whom you have delivered a letter for a very amiable lady.

If the one for whom we read is a servant, the No. 30 makes him fear the loss of the affection of his masters, however if this card is near the No. 42, he will take pleasure in the wickedness of his masters´ enemies.

When this card is next to the No. 45, it tells you that an old relative with whom you had a quarrel, is looking for an opportunity to reconcile with you.

If the spread is for a young lady, this card warns her to beware of an acquaintance, who has made her illegitimate, and who has been trying to deceive her, the last eight days.

If this card appears near the No. 59, it announces that a servant in charge of a message to you, has lost what he was to deliver back to you, which will bring much change in the connections, that you wanted to keep to this servant´s master.

When this tarot is presented in the Reverse, it warns whoever consults, that he will wait a long time for what he

---

[49] Translator: This card in reverse implies hope, wait and trust, perhaps the figure below, that cornucopia or horn of plenty, wants to say all good things come to those who wait?

wants; but if accompanied by the No. 57 in the Upright, that he must not lose hope.

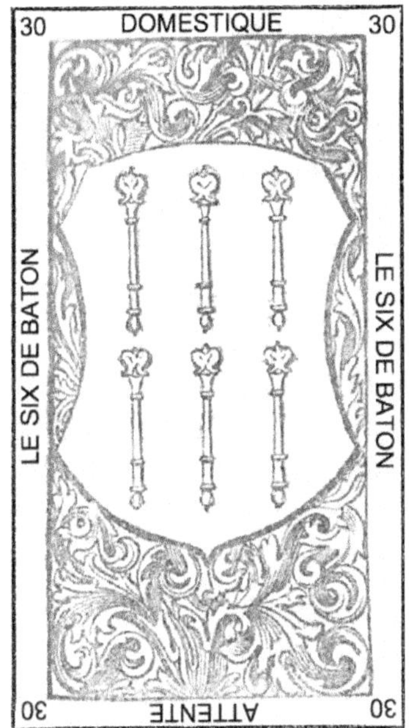

LEMARCHAND

This card warns you, that you have chosen an indiscreet person as your courier, and that the last letter you sent, did not immediately arrive at its destination.

When the querent is a person in service, this tarot warns him to make sure to keep the affection of his masters.

After the No. 42, it promises complete satisfaction and victory over your enemies.

Next to No. 45 it is a sign that you can hope to regain the affection of an old relative with whom you recently have been out of favor.

When reading for a young person, this card warns him, that an acquaintance of his is trying to do him a disservice.

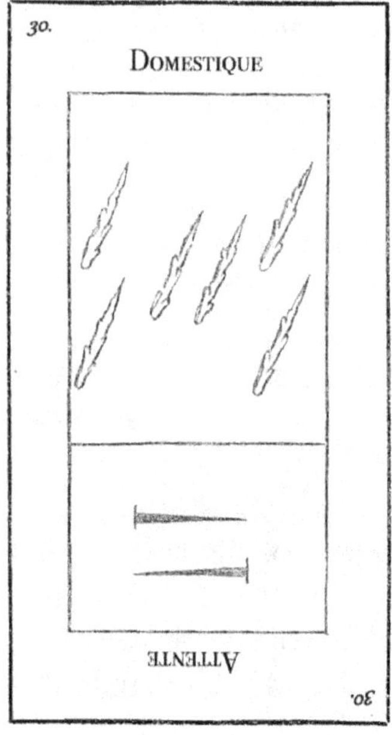

D'ODOUCET

This thirtieth card depicts six sticks or clubs. In the lower part of the card is the number six of the Egyptians.

0, the world, the symbol of our possessions that cooperate with our well-being, needs the support of generations. This does not just appear suddenly; it needs time to develop. The word *Expectation*, is perhaps proper to use in this case. Moreover, the generations operate effectively only with the help of the animating principle, which must be presented to this world; represented by the 6, the number of clubs depicted on this card.

MODERN INTERPRETATIONS

This card has by Grimaud been assigned the keywords; SERVANT in the upright and EXPECTATION in the reverse.

UPRIGHT: The Six of Clubs indicates a time for family, the home environment and the comforts of home life. You may experience an increase in responsibility. The receiving of unexpected presents and flowers are also in this card. In business, it is a time for dialogue, it will benefit you to listen to the perspectives of colleagues. Finances look fine.

REVERSE: In reverse, a card of putting in the effort and reaping the rewards. You may be impatient in seeing something come to fruition. If you have put in the time and effort, and played with open cards, you will be successful, but if you have been carefree and lazy, it will be a fail. This would apply both professionally and in a private setting. Finances may be problematic.

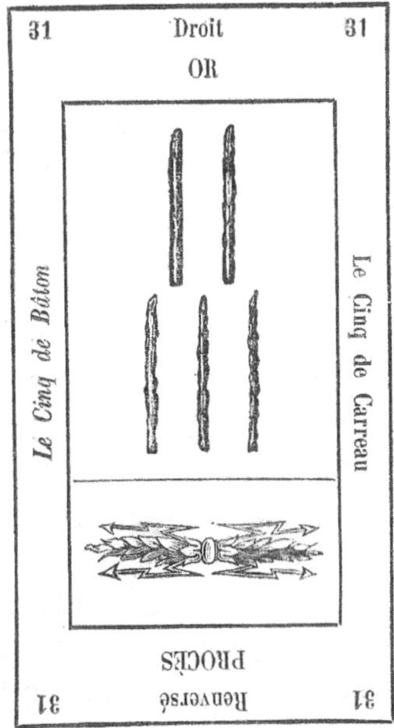

No. 31

Gold - Trial[50]
Five of Clubs or Diamonds

The presence of this card in the Upright suggests sums of money. You will be favored in a financial speculation, if this tarot is found near the No. 32 in the Reverse; but the opposite will happen if the No. 38 accompanies it.

You have already escaped the pitfalls of your enemies; but this tarot warns you, when it is accompanied by the No. 69 in the Reverse, that others will be extended to you, and that you will be robbed, the next time you go to a show or find yourself in a crowd, if you are not careful.

In the Reverse, this card predicts trials, quarrels, but these will conclude to your advantage, when this tarot is found next to the No. 50, in the Upright or in the Reverse.

If the questioner is an adolescent, he will soon have an argument with a lady he has recently gotten to know. Next to No. 49, it announces, that this dispute will take place during a meal.

---

[50] Translator: This card in reverse implies trial, break-up and quarrels, perhaps, not surprisingly, the figure below expresses this with lightning bolts?

LEMARCHAND

Card 31 announces numerous disputes on insignificant issues and during gastronomic encounters.

If this tarot is found near No. 32 in the Reverse, it predicts a very big pecuniary advantage in a matter involving money; however, if the No. 38 appears before or after and in the Reverse, there is uncertainty.

Followed by or preceded by the No. 69, it will be during the next house party, that you will lose your purse, if you are not careful.

After No. 50, it indicates lawsuits and quarrels for one of your relatives; but, followed by the No. 21, it predicts the most brilliant outcome.

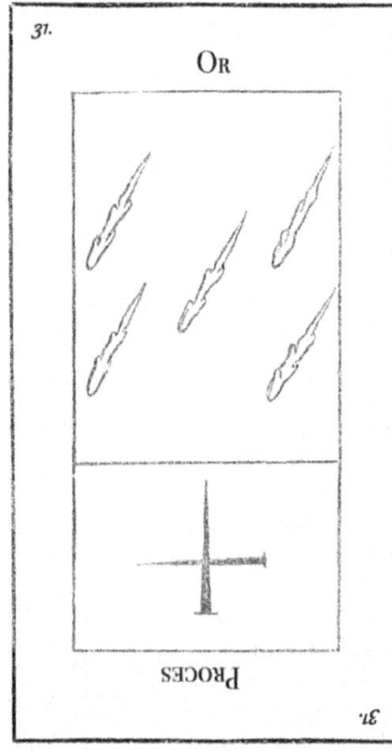

D'ODOUCET

This thirty-first card depicts five sticks or clubs. In the lower part of the card is the number five of the Egyptians.

The no. 1 which symbolizes us, reappears here again in a state of dependency or in a state of reduced presumption. It therefore appears to intercede, to reproduce, to generate 3. It is from it that one hopes, by the multiplicity of forces, by hands, so necessary in agricultural life, to collect the *treasures*, that it only dispenses to the most laborious. Man is answered as soon as he knows how to pray. His family, by increasing, increases its wealth, by the activity it offers to vegetation (indicated by the Five of Clubs), the results? That it becomes manifest, that mediocrity suffices for the happiness of the wise man, since too much abundance, incurs envy, jealousy and sets us up as targets for intrusion, or at least of the *chicanery* of the wicked. They assail us and we escape them only by imitating the sheep, trapped in a hedge of thorns, from which it must pull itself out, always leaving an essential portion of its fleece behind.

MODERN INTERPRETATIONS

This card has by Grimaud been assigned the keywords; OPULANCE in the upright and COURT CASE in the reverse.

UPRIGHT: The Five of Clubs predicts pleasant moments. You will have the love and support from family, a feel of understanding and acceptance. In business, you will be able to concretize, conceptualize the investment needed into what you want to achieve. You may take significant risks, which may pay off. Finances will improve in the long term.

REVERSE: In reverse, it is a card of quarrel, jealousy and discord. In relationships, it may indicate a break-up. In business not much better, a time of trials, testing and dismissal. It implies an ending of something important. A situation may end up in court as well. There may be serious issues with your finances.

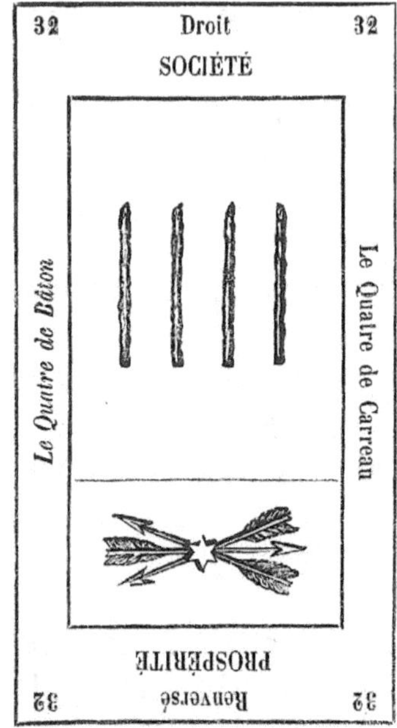

No. 32

Association - Prosperity[51]
Four of Clubs or Diamonds

You will be entertained at a party to which you are invited; an unexpected fortune will come to you; soon the number of your friends will increase.

Whoever you are, this tarot can only be very favorable to you. You will be flattered, pampered, admired; but, you must be careful, every flatterer lives at the expense of his listener; you should be warned that your new friends are only looking to you, because of your generosity.

Next to No. 65, this card predicts a discovery. With the No. 4, it is a bad omen.

If it appears in the Reverse, it announces that your happiness is very much in your hands, but that you must pay the most scrupulous attention to everything around you, because a little nothing can lead to a setback.

When this card is drawn in the Reverse for a married woman, it announces beautiful children for her.

---

[51] Translator: This card in reverse implies advancement, recognition and attention, perhaps like the arrows hitting their target in the figure below?

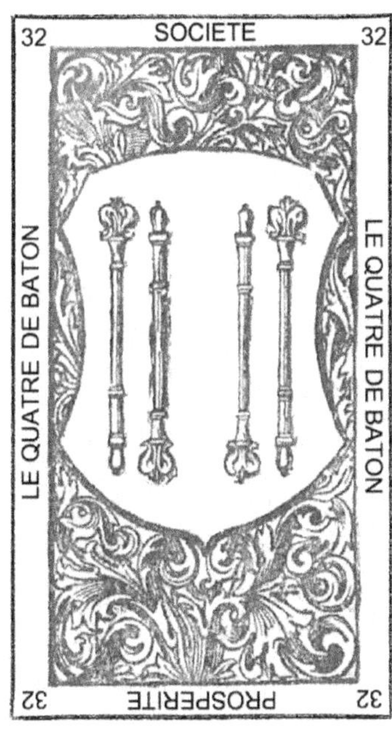

LEMARCHAND

When this tarot is drawn in the Reverse, and the spread is read for a lady, it predicts many children for her.

In the Upright, it announces entertainment, at a house party to which you are invited. It also predicts an immense increase in your fortune, and likewise an increase in the number of friends.

Next to the No. 65, it predicts a find; but with the No. 4, it does not bode well.

In the Reverse, it wants to warn you, that you need to be very careful in all your actions, because it will take very little to cause you an annoyance.

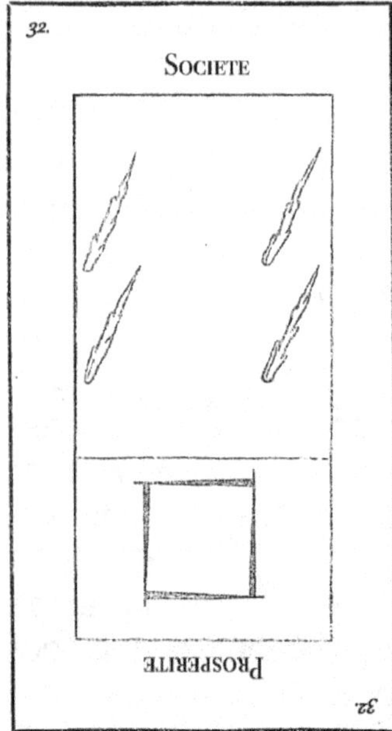

D'ODOUCET

This thirty-second card depicts four sticks or clubs. In the lower part of the card is the number 4 of the Egyptians.

What a sweet picture offered for view! Vegetation 2 is in close union with generation 3. This *prosperous* cooperation can only have the happiest of implications. The product of vegetation will be in due proportion to the consumption made. Nothing superfluous, just the simple necessities which guarantee constant happiness. This is the notion, that must be digested by the 4 of the Clubs, which arranged in a cube, express the rest, the security, which arises from needs met.

MODERN INTERPRETATIONS

This card has by Grimaud been assigned the keywords; CONTRACT AGREEMENT in the upright and PROSPERITY in the reverse.

UPRIGHT: The Four of Clubs implies a period of sentimentality, socialization, community and meeting other people. It may come after a period of hardship. This is a pleasant period, where you may meet someone and contemplate starting a family. In business, you will be viewed positively, projects and contracts will be ample, publicity will be favorable. Finances are protected.

REVERSE: In reversed, this card predicts that there is light at the end of the tunnel. A joyous and happy time. If you are single, this is an auspicious time, you will have opportunities to meet someone and you could end up in a serious commitment. In business, there is recognition for your talents. Generally, a good card, that promises satisfaction in all areas of your life.

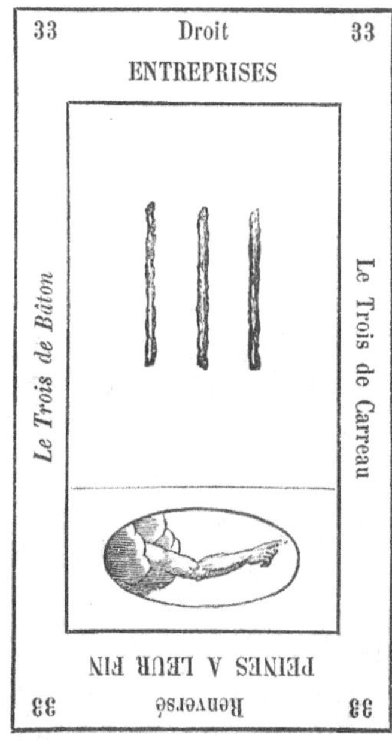

No. 33

Enterprise - Trials at an end[52]
Three of Clubs or Diamonds

If this card follows the querent´s card (No. 1 or 8), a man of extraordinary genius will join your work and make it prosper; happiness will follow him everywhere.

This tarot situated next to a King or a Queen appearing in the Upright, announces literary enterprises, which will bring honor to your family. If this card is found in the Reverse, the querent will be protected by someone influential, who will put an end to the annoyances, he is experiencing.

When this card is drawn by a sailor, it predicts discoveries that will earn him the approval of all mariners.

If this tarot is found in the Reverse, it is a sign of reconciliation. It also warns you that a friend locked up for insanity will soon be brought back to his senses, or that your sorrows will end shortly.

---

[52] Translator: This card in reverse implies pain, endings and interruption, perhaps the figure below is the hand of God handing out penalty for the wicked?

LEMARCHAND

When this tarot[53] follows No. 1, it is an indisputable sign of success and of fame; it announces to the querent, that luck will follow him on many occasions.

Close to a King or a Queen in the Upright, it provides considerable protection to the querent.

After the No. 15, it warns you that many of your friends are conspiring against your purse; and for this reason, you must be on your guard against their plans, if you do not wish to be ruined at any moment.

The card that follows can change the direction of this tarot, when it is in the shape of a card depicting Coins, since this is the announcement of money gains.

---

[53] Translator: The Lemarchand booklet assigns the meaning *Peines Passees* or Passing of Trials on this card in the reverse, rather than *Peines a Leur Fin.*

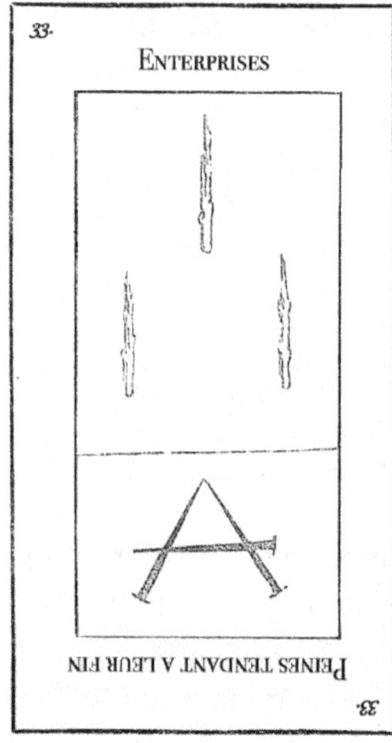

D'ODOUCET

This thirty-third card[54] depicts three sticks or clubs arranged triangularly. In the lower part of the card is the number 3 of the Egyptians.

The abundance of means, undoubtedly excites the desire to undertake. What can be the just motive? The plan to move from a previous situation to a better one, and the double symbol of generation, confirms or rather increases the generating number (3) of Clubs. This is the most favorable omen for the interruption of our sorrows, and the move to happiness superior to that which we enjoyed before; however, seldom is happiness achieved, without some sorrow, nevertheless they will not be sustained, since everything comes together here to facilitate success.

---

[54] Translator: d´Odoucet assigns the word *Interruptions* in reverse for this card.

161

MODERN INTERPRETATIONS

This card has by Grimaud been assigned the keywords; ENTERPRISES in the upright and END OF WORRIES in the reverse.

UPRIGHT: This card implies courage, daring and of new business endeavors. Success is almost guaranteed if you stay committed. Investments are also favored. In relationships, it is card of going for it, your openness and boldness will assist you and if applied with a little sense, will turn in your favor.

REVERSE: The Three of Clubs in reverse is efforts rewarded. Whatever projects you have been working on will be successful and your financial situation improves. A time of less stress, and more emotional satisfaction. You may find yourself with likeminded people. In relationships, this card indicates better times, a period of love and harmony.

No. 34

Sorrow - Surprise[55]
Two of Clubs or Diamonds

This card tells you, that one of your relatives will be forced to go away, he will die on the way; if this trip is made by sea, he will be shipwrecked; however, he will escape death, if this tarot is found with a favorable card.

When a young lady draws this card, it predicts some sorrow regarding the future. It is a sign of jealousy, when it is found after the No. 50.

The 34 after 47 and 49, announces a change or a happy surprise; 34 after 54 and 59, the opposite.

This card in the Reverse announces wonderful news, if found near No. 68 in Reverse; it predicts terror followed by disaster, if accompanied by the No. 14 in the Upright or in the Reverse.

---

[55] Translator: This card in reverse implies hope and surprises, perhaps delivered with a stagecoach like the figure below?

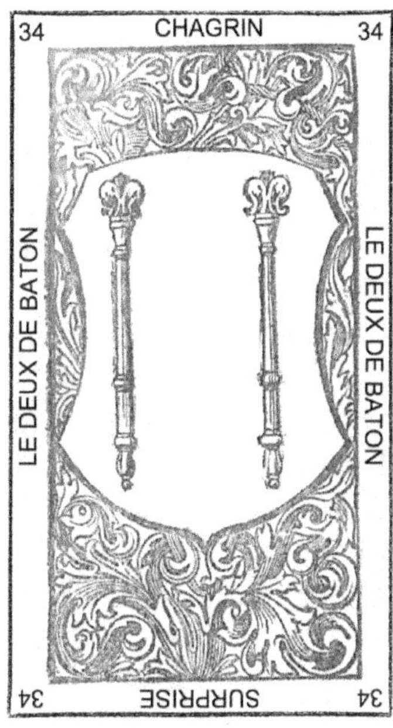

LEMARCHAND

When this tarot appears in the Upright, it is the prediction, that you will experience big annoyances. When it appears in the Reverse, it predicts nice surprises.

After No. 50, it announces jealousy expressed on the part of a husband, if you read for a lady. Or from the wife, if the spread is for the husband.

For a soldier, it tells him that, in order to achieve the rank, he aspires to, he will encounter obstacles; but that there is nothing to be concerned about, when this card is preceded or followed by Nos. 2, 9 or 20.

D'ODOUCET

This thirty-fourth card depicts two sticks or clubs in a St. Andrews Cross. In the lower part of the card is the number 2 of the Egyptians.

We now perceive the entire universe, which seems to submit to the law of generation 3; but as this last symbol 3, is that of animal generation, and man is really an abbreviation of the universe, we begin from this, meaning; man once again resorts to generation, to reproduce himself, (goal is designated by the number 2, the symbol of the first vegetation common to all the rest); if he succeeds, he will experience a pleasant surprise, if not, he recognizes that his vows and his diligent care has been unsuccessful.

MODERN INTERPRETATIONS

This card has by Grimaud been assigned the keywords; SORROW in the upright and SURPRISES in the reverse.

UPRIGHT: The Two of Clubs indicates heartbreak. Small quarrels may lead to misinterpretation, resentment, anger and finally a break-up. A sad time in relationships, made worse by finger pointing. In business, a similar situation, wanting to give up, feeling unappreciated. This card implies the need to take personal responsibility, to assess situations calmly and collectedly and not to let negative emotions overwhelm you.

REVERSE: In the reverse, this card is much more favorable. If you find yourself in a confusing situation, there is help out there, and you will regain hope. A better constructive period is predicted for you, perhaps with a surprise return of a past love or someone you lost contact with. Lots of joy, happiness and surprises is predicted and you will regain your footing. In business, you may be fearful of major changes, however it will turn out ok.

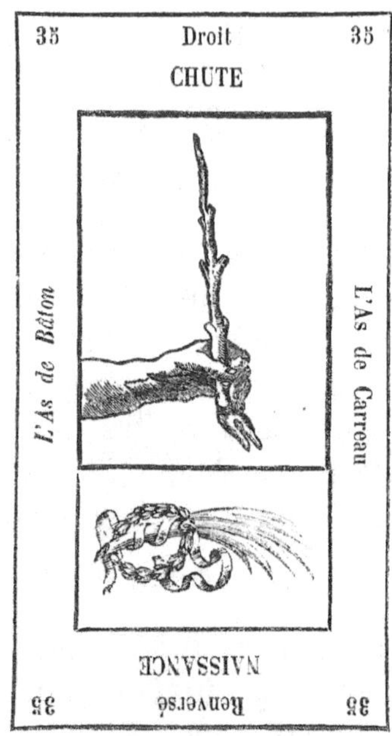

No. 35

Fall - Birth[56]
Ace of Clubs or Diamonds[57]

A complete rout, fire, or serious illness is predicted with this tarot; but you will certainly escape anything that may threaten you.

Next to the No. 19, it should make people fear slavery, after being defeated by enemies to whose power they must submit.

If the cards are read for a young lady, beware if the No. 48 accompanies this card, because love could well make her fall into a trap, dangerous for her chastity and her reputation.

In the Reverse, this card is a sign of birth. If it joins the No. 11, it announces to you and to yours long posterity.

With this posterity, if instead of No. 11 the No. 14 is next to it, several persons missed may resurface.

Near the No. 39, it announces that your descendants will be inclined towards one of the seven deadly sins, in particular gluttony.

---

[56] Translator: The Ace of Clubs on the type II card stock has *Chute* or Fall, in the Upright as per the synonym list, same with Lemarchand. The Version I depicts this however, in the reverse. It seems Orsini flipped around not only this keyword but all the synonyms for this card, when compared to d´Odoucet (Science des Signes, p. 81).

[57] Translator: This card in reverse implies creation, pregnancy and opportunity, perhaps the wreath, in the figure below, illustrates this very fittingly, a symbol of power, victory and legacy?

The Egyptians called this tarot the Rod of Moses, they always regarded it as auspicious, when it appears, reversed.

LEMARCHAND

When this card appears, place it at the head of the row, that forms the spread. This card means birth when reversed.

Near the No. 11, it announces great posterity for the querent.

After the No. 48, it indicates to the person for whom the cards are being laid, that she has much to fear for her reputation, because people who envy her success in the world seek to spread slander about her.

After the No. 39, and in the Reverse, this tarot indicates that epidemic diseases are causing great disruption among savage peoples.

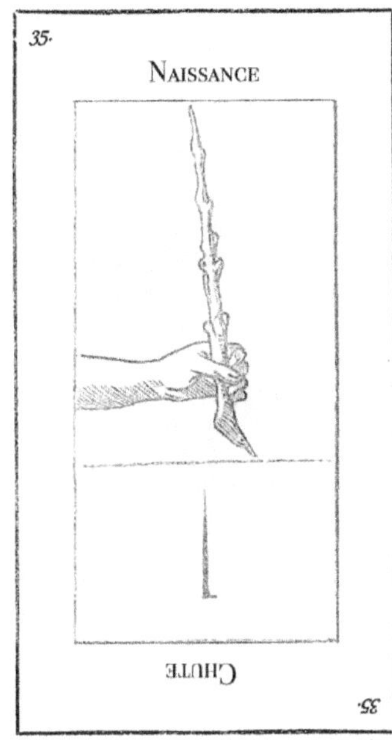

D'ODOUCET

This thirty-fifth card depicts a single rod or club held by a hand. In the lower part of the card is the number 1 of the Egyptians.

The number 5, the symbol of spirit, the universal animator, intimately united with the passive principle of generation 3, which gives rise to relying on the birth of the being, vegetating first, this very reality is subjected to a fall or destruction, always imminent, the apogee of which will be at the highest point. A useful lesson that we must always remember.

MODERN INTERPRETATIONS

This card has by Grimaud been assigned the keywords; BIRTH in the upright and BANKRUPTCY in the reverse.

UPRIGHT: The Ace of Clubs in the upright is very unfortunate. Relationships may be in a poor state, it urges you to study your behavior, a need for mature dialogue. In business things will not work out for you. You may lose your employment, experience a significant loss or delay in finances.

REVERSE: This implies light after difficulty. It may indicate a birth of a baby or just the return something better. This card advices caution still, it is a good time to take advice from others. In business, new opportunities, however you must carefully analyze the offers in order to avoid pitfalls.

No. 36

Blond man – Influential man
King of Cups or Hearts

This card represents the high priest, it indicates a higher will; beware, an influential man wants to hurt you. If the No. 36 is followed or preceded by the No. 18, a hypocrite will pretend to be useful to you, while behind your back he will be your accuser.

When a young lady draws this card, it is a sign of an impending marriage, if it is followed by the No. 48; and of fertility, if it is preceded or followed by the No. 63.

In the Reverse, it predicts to you a change, of considerable losses; but frequently the meaning is modified by the cards that surround it, among which I will name; 7, 32, 41, 47 and 77.

Next to the No. 20, it predicts that before long you will earn a sum of money, which will save you from a very bad situation.

LEMARCHAND

This card announces a higher will, if it appears in the Upright; while, in the Reverse, it is a sign of indecision in the character of the querent.

For a young lady, near card 48 and followed by the 63, this card is the announcement of a forthcoming union with the young man she wishes to marry. It predicts great and beautiful posterity.

In the Reverse and when the no. 7 is found in the row likewise in the Reverse, it announces an unspecified displacement, a change of dwelling, a distant voyage.

After the No. 78, it warns you to be careful of bad advice.

Homme de Place
36.

D'ODOUCET

The thirty-sixth card represents a venerable old man, seated, dressed in a purple robe, wearing a tiara, holding a stem cup in his hand.

After having considered all the cards, in their first aspect, which is common to them, that of physical or purely vegetative existence; it is necessary to examine them, from a moral point of view, meaning those in this group, which are most susceptible to it.

The first entity that presents itself before our eyes is (intellectual) the microcosm or the small world; embodied by the expression of the number 6 of the animating principle, from here it takes on the envelopment of the principle of patience, or generation, 3. Man, we say, is here the evidence, he holds a cup, chalice of choice, and has to hold it to indicate his moral occupation, of the accumulated sciences of the beautiful centuries of Egypt, of the order of the priests. But this same *man* is and must be fair, in order to be able to reveal to us his intellectual capabilities. The genius is symbolized by a light flame, the vulgarity expressed in its color, which is red, and what is, and must be the natural shade of the man, the most approximate in this case is the *blond*. Every educated man, especially from those times, where merit alone was revered, should be distinguished from the common class; indeed, he was priestly, consequently *an influential man*.

MODERN INTERPRETATIONS

This card has by Grimaud been assigned the keywords PROBITY in the upright and DISHONESTY in the reverse.

UPRIGHT: The King of Cups represents the man one can count on. In a relationship he is kind, just, supportive and expresses his feelings. He may have a lot of experience, which he will want to share. For a woman, he would be a good catch. Generally, a good and decent man.

REVERSE: In the reverse, this card takes on another meaning completely. The King of Cups reversed is not to be trusted. He may come off as being considerate and generous but he is unscrupulous, manipulative and acts only from self-interest. He would be a horrible enemy to make, he would not rest until he has destroyed your reputation.

No. 37

Blonde Woman - Wife of an Influential Man
Queen of Cup or Hearts

A lady you love very much is interested in your happiness, she will soon give you news, which will give you the greatest pleasure.

If you are reading for a lady, this card tells her the nicest things; the favorable interpretation of this card is always increased, when it is next to the No. 75.

Near the No. 49, it warns you, that you will be invited to a dinner, where you will be more intemperate than the occasion demands for.

Followed by the No. 63, it tells you that this intemperance will have consequences, it will cause you much inconvenience.

In the Reverse, it predicts for a man, that he will conquer the richest woman he sometimes talks to; and for a woman, that she will be sought after by a very influential person, who will disclose himself to her, and which will end in a marriage.

LEMARCHAND

Card No. 37.[58] A lady of distinction takes great interest in you; you will hear from her shortly; it will be the announcement of a great thing concerning your happiness, undoubtedly a brilliant marriage.

If the person for whom we read is a married woman, this tarot predicts, that she will be much noticed in the first ball she attends.

After the No. 63, it indicates intemperance.

In the Reverse, and when the querent is a young man, this card tells him, that his marriage will take place soon, but that he must be aware of people, who would want him not to succeed.

---

[58] Translator: The Lemarchand booklet assigns the meaning *Femme en Place* or Influential Woman only for this card in the Reverse, not *Femme d´un Homme en Place*, Wife of an Influential Man.

D'ODOUCET

This thirty-seventh card represents a seated woman, crowned with a tiara, dressed in a purple dress, holding a stem cup in her hand.

Life, 7, brought closer to the feminine principle of generation 3, forms a whole, which cannot be better expressed than by a *woman*. It must also express; that no class in society should be deprived of the means to regenerate. This is why her clothing, her attributes, her color, must indicate that she is the worthy companion of the one whose virtues and talents are elevated above the vulgar class of farmers. Indeed, this woman will wear purple, hold a cup, be *blonde* and therefore symbolize the *influential* woman, or be considered as, since she must share the venerations of whom, she is the respectable half of.

MODERN INTERPRETATIONS

This card has by Grimaud been assigned the keywords A WOMAN ABOVE REPROACH in the upright and DISSOLUTE WOMAN in the reverse.

UPRIGHT: The Queen of Cups represents a kind and loving woman. This may be an important woman in your life, such as your mother, girlfriend, etc. She knows how to manage a home, take care of children and she is devoted to her husband, the ideal wife and mother. She may however be too giving and not pay enough attention to herself.

REVERSE: In the reverse this card represents a dishonest woman. She is emotionally unavailable, domineering with a bad temper. She has contempt for people and may wish them ill. The querent may be in a situation where she or he is being used or exploited by someone.

No. 38

Arrival - Deception
Knight of Cups

If this card is accompanied by the No. 71, one of your friends or relatives will come to pay you a visit, which will be very pleasant to you, especially since he is responsible for giving you a sum of money, something you were not expecting. However, if it joins with the No. 30, the visit you will receive, will only have the purpose of granting you a loan.

Next to the No. 50, this card announces an injustice on the part of a magistrate.

Followed by the No. 68, it predicts, you will soon be the owner of a property, that you will buy with the proceeds of a speculation, that could have ruined you.

In the Reverse it implies deceit, you will be deceived in a public meeting, if not far from the No. 14; and if accompanied by the No. 30, you will be prevented from taking part in a pleasurable party.

LEMARCHAND

When this card[59] is next to No. 30, it warns you, that someone you are not expecting will come and give you a loan, which you will not dare to refuse. If it is placed near the No. 71, it is an indication of restitution, it will be one of your relatives, who will visit you and will be responsible for this offer, which you did not expect in any way.

Near the No. 68, it announces, that you will make an advantageous speculation, which will allow you to realize a dream, that you have wanted for a long time.

In the Reverse, it indicates deceit, and urges you to be careful with your purse or your jewelry, when you attend a public meeting.

---

[59] Translator: The Lemarchand booklet assigns the meaning *Duperie* or Deception for this card in the Reverse, rather than *Friponnerie*.

D'ODOUCET

This thirty-eighth card represents a young man on horseback, dressed in purple, and holding in his hand a stem cup.

The 8, the symbol of circulation of generations, is perfect in its place next to the 3, which expresses a particular generation, of a type of animal. Movement. The progressive movement, or the progressions of these generations, which is an actual *arrival*; but in what way? It is the improviser, unexpected, that specifies this principle in general. The individual who increases the family. As in any well-regulated estate, each child arriving must have his or her share of the estate. This frustrates the first heirs, all the more, it is the roguery of fate, although it is not considered as such. Moreover, a good father owes his offspring not less a portion of his property, than an *education* in proportion to its produce. In addition, the figure with which this card is illustrated, has a cup, a symbol of acquired knowledge.

MODERN INTERPRETATIONS

This card[60] has by Grimaud been assigned the keywords ARRIVAL in the upright and CHEATING in the reverse.

UPRIGHT: The Knight of Cups represents visits. A card of meetings, news, letters, gifts perhaps from a young man. It implies sincere emotions, loyalty and harmony. In business, it indicates an opportunity, which may be impossible to ignore.

REVERSE: In reverse, this card represents bad company. A card of slander, criticism and jealousy, someone who will offer you help but not follow through, a friend who seeks to harm you. The Knight of Cups can represent someone disappearing from your life.

---

[60] Translator: d´Odoucet assigns the meaning *Artifice,* or trick in the Reverse, rather than *Friponnerie.*

No. 39

Blond boy - Inclination
Page of Cups or Hearts

A young man will bring you your appointment to a job, which you have been asking for, for a long time and you will make your way. The benefits of a monarch will elevate you to great dignity.

For anyone who draws this card, it predicts that she will marry a fair, learned, witty and wealthy young man; however, if this card is in the Reverse, it tells her, that she will have a thwarted passion; the husband she intends for herself will abandon the plans she relied on.

If it appears in the Reverse (when the spread is made for a man) and when near the No. 27, also in the Reverse, this card announces a thousand obstacles in the inclinations, which have occupied him for a long time.

In general, this card, in the Upright, is a sign of considerations; it predicts approval, success and praise.

LEMARCHAND

When this tarot appears in the Upright, it is of a favorable omen, because it implies consideration, success and praise.

For a young person, it predicts, she will marry a rich and spiritual inclined young blond.

For a man in service, it implies an upcoming promotion, or his appointment to a job, he longs to obtain and which he has sought so far in vain.

After the No. 19, if the cards are being read for a lady, it announces nice gifts to her from an old aunt, of whom she has not heard from in several months.

If we read for a young man, and this card appears in the Reverse, it indicates annoyances that will soon cease.

D'ODOUCET

This thirty-ninth card represents a young man standing, dressed in a purple robe, holding in his hand a stem cup, covered with his cloak.

The 9, or the small earthly being who sheds its germ of life, could not be better placed than next to the patient, who must make evident the product of the secret operations of nature. To express moreover, more appreciably, the species, the type of effusion implied by these two numbers, and the product resulting from it. It offers before our eyes a *boy,* the first physical result, he is blond, to indicate the class from which he was born. He holds the cup as a symbol of his knowledge, he even offers this cup, the sequence of expansive meanings implied in the number 9, to all arrivals. This voluntary offer designates his *inclination* for his fellows, whom he loves, and to whom he wants to embrace with his talents.

MODERN INTERPRETATIONS

This card has by Grimaud been assigned the keywords STUDIOUS BOY in the upright and AFFECTION in the reverse.

UPRIGHT: The Page of Cups represents a hardworking young man. A card of studiousness, diligence, reflection, a person with a fresh perspective. This can represent an admirer, someone who may be very useful to you.

REVERSE: In the reverse, the Page of Cups represents a young devoted man. This may be an unstable person, but still someone who is sincere and loyal to you. He may need advice from you.

No. 40

The City - Wrath[61]
Ten of Cups or Hearts

This tarot is for you a sign of wealth, a future inheritance will help you marry the person you desire, a person your position did not allow you to hope for.

Next to No. 21, it announces a rather lively discussion, which will take place between you and some notable people in the city where you live.

If the spread is laid for a woman, this card warns her, when it shows up accompanied by the No. 29, that gossip has spread in the countryside, where she lives and which will be disturbing to her family.

In the Reverse, this card announces a very nasty quarrel.

When for a man you read, this card predicts, that he will have a duel and that it will end with a good lunch.

To a sailor this card predicts storm, hurricanes, thunderstorms and gales.

---

[61] Translator: The figures below on the Cup cards have been inserted by publisher Blocquel. In reverse this card implies anger, rage and danger. Perhaps that bull in the figure below implies exactly that?

LEMARCHAND

Tarot 40 announces abundance, achievement and success.

If the querent is unattached, this tells him, that he will soon marry a rich heiress, despite the little fortune he personally may have.

After the No. 21, it indicates to the one for whom the cards are laid, great discussions arising between him and some superior person, but that the truth will be on his side and, therefore, reason.

After the No. 29, and when reading for a woman, this is a clue, that some needle pricks were given to her in female council.

For a sailor, this tarot predicts frequent variations in temperature.

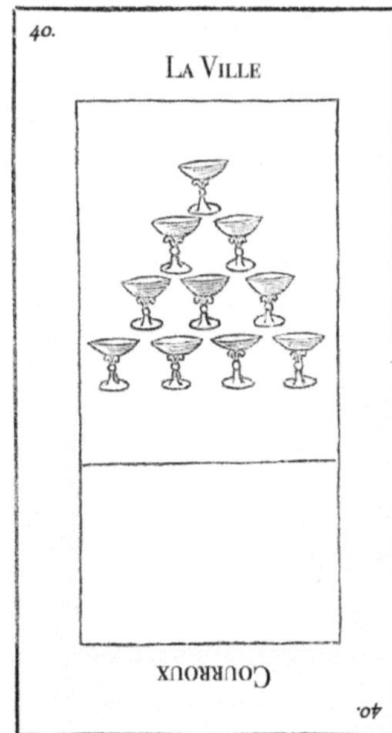

D'ODOUCET

This fortieth card depicts ten stem cups arranged in a pyramid.

We have seen the clubs symbolize rural production; but the place that conceals the sciences, the arts of the highest perfection; the place itself built by a spectrum of these arts, *the city* in the end has to express itself by the Cups. The number 10, which is complete, indicates the central meeting point of insights of all types. The figures on the card recall pleasant things; it is the 0, a symbol of the globe, included in a sphere of 4, a symbol of the universe in general. Nothing represents the universe better than a sumptuous city, except however that all the parts of the universe, are the works of God, and are always, in spite of appearances, in the most perfect harmony, and what is built by man only approaches a certain steadiness. In fact, a big city is chaos, where almost everything is confusing; it is impossible for its innumerable parts to be in complete agreement; the shock of some irritants, incur the wrath of others. This is the fate inherent in complicated establishments. The great number of individual interests generate one way or another an unmistakable *dissatisfaction*.

MODERN INTERPRETATIONS

This card has by Grimaud been assigned the keywords HOME in the upright and ANGER in the reverse.

UPRIGHT: The Ten of Cups is card of emotions. A card of need for family, security and the prioritizing of home life. It is also a card of redecorating or relocating, perhaps to a city. Also, you can expect to see some type of recognition, your job gives you great satisfaction and finances look great.

REVERSE: In the reverse, a card of conflict. A lot of misunderstandings during this time, perhaps a disruption in your family or job. It would not be helpful to react in anger, rather step back and let the storm pass over. There may be risk of financial loss.

No. 41

Victory - Sincerity[62]
Nine of Cups or Hearts

This card has always been auspicious to people of war, it announces great advantage for them over their enemies.

When this tarot is near the No. 71, it reveals, that a one-eyed person, if not physically then morally challenged, will earn you considerable sums.

A soldier who draws this card before leaving for the army is certain, he will return with a high rank.

If this card is in the Reverse, it predicts success in business and loyalty from those you employ.

In the Reverse, and next to the No. 57 also in the Reverse, this card urges you to take advantage of the wise advice given to you by a person, whose sincerity you have more than once recognized.

---

[62] Translator: This card in reverse implies franchise, business and boldness, perhaps that Festina Lente, in the figure below, is a symbol of exactly that, of balance between urgency and diligence?

LEMARCHAND

You have received advice from someone you rightly love; listen again to the voice of friendship in the business you are about to undertake.

If the querent is a soldier, this tarot predicts great success; he will return, in the end of his campaign, full of honors and dignity.

When this tarot is in the Reverse, it indicates, to the querent, great success in commercial speculations.

After the No. 70, it implies a pecuniary annoyance, which will come to disturb you.

Preceded by the No. 50, it recommends, you not to misspeak with people you associate with, because words spoken lightly are always harmful.

D'ODOUCET

This forty-first card depicts nine stem cups arranged in threes.

Here we see man 1, particularly close to the universal 4; their relationship becomes immediate; they derive their full value from one another. The universe includes man; man understands the universe; and the vast knowledge that he gathers here, the soul is able to dispense for the use by his fellows. This is what has to be expressed, and to do this, 9 cups were chosen. The number designates the expansive quality and the cups the type of expansion. The truths learned are a complete *victory* over ignorance. The powerful are *sincere* and generous, weakness alone has recourse to subterfuge.

MODERN INTERPRETATIONS

This card has by Grimaud been assigned the keywords SUCCESS in the upright and BUSINESS SUCCESS in the reverse.

UPRIGHT: The Nine of Cups implies wishes fulfilled. You are reaching your goals, your happiness, or reconciliation. In business, your talents are recognized, you may get a promotion or a bigger pay check. A card of good Luck.

REVERSE: In reversed, it is a card of satisfaction. Exchanges and shared experiences will be joyful. In business, your efforts are appreciated, you will be put in an advisory or motivational role for your other peers. Finances will improve.

No. 42

Blonde girl - Satisfaction[63]
Eight of Cups or Hearts

You have received or will soon be hearing from someone, whom you have a great interest.

If you are reading for a young man, this card tells him, that he will marry a young blonde lady. Near the No. 63, it predicts, that he will have many children.

If for a young lady, and when this card appears with the No. 41, she can expect anything from her lucky star.

Followed by the No. 21, this card warns, that you will have a quarrel with an influential person. Next to the No. 20, it is a sign, you will win a lot of money in a game.

In the Reverse, this card indicates perfect satisfaction, especially when it joins one of the more favorable cards.

---

[63] Translator: This card in reverse implies joy and entertainment. The lyre in the figure below illustrates this very fittingly.

LEMARCHAND

When this tarot is presented in the Reverse, and near favorable cards, it indicates, to the querent, satisfaction in all things.

It also indicates, that the person for whom the spread is being read, soon will receive news from a relative, in whom she is very interested.

For a young man, it is the announcement, that the young lady he will marry will be a beautiful blonde.

If, on the contrary, we read for a young lady, it tells her, that she can expect anything from her star.

Followed by the No. 21, it foreshadows some small quarrels, from which you will emerge victorious.

D'ODOUCET

This forty-second card depicts eight stem cups.

4 and 2 mean, word for word, universal vegetation. The result from it must be a complete whole, articulated by the number 8, a symbol of the succession of generations, illustrated on this card by an equal number of cups. Moreover, indicating here that it is a question of the progressive generation of thoughts, of the insights, which are not less universal than the universe itself, which often is the object of them. It presents to us these cups, the science of symbols, the propagation of which is designated by the attribute *blonde girl*. This propagation has its pleasures, meaning, that which relates to the senses. They are the result of sensuousness; the former gives us a durable *satisfaction*, assuming that it is less lively.

MODERN INTERPRETATIONS

This card has by Grimaud been assigned the keywords SINCERE GIRL in the upright and HAPPINESS in the reverse.

UPRIGHT: This card symbolizes a blonde girl. A gentle, generous, confident, supportive person, often a young woman, student, intern, a niece or granddaughter.

REVERSE: This card in reverse, a card of joy and happiness. A time for love and affection, if you are single, you won't be. In business, projects will succeed and your situation will turn out better than you had expected.

No. 43

Thought — Projects[64]
Seven of Cup or Hearts

This tarot is one of the most difficult to explain, because in the crowd of thoughts, which agitate your mind, it is not possible to guess, which ones occur to you during our reading.

This card signifies idea, purpose, movement. It is only through the cards that surround it, that it is given a meaning. For example, if it was accompanied by Nos. 53 and 54, it would come out as: you have thoughts, that do you no honor and that make you cry. If, on the other hand, it was near Nos. 7 or 22, you would be told, that your thoughts are worthy of praise.

When this card is in the Reverse and accompanied by the No. 47, it is a sign of success in your endeavors. Next to the No. 18, it warns, you will be betrayed, if you do not take due care, and that all your plans will be thwarted.

---

[64] Translator: This card in the Reverse implies purpose and desire. In the figure below perhaps the Cornucopia reflects the desires and the anchor purpose?

LEMARCHAND

The meaning of this card is; designs and projects of all kind; which make an interpretation difficult, because it implies that the querent is subject to great variations in his ideas; also, it only derives its meaning by the tarot cards that surround it. It is in of itself a void card.

When this tarot is accompanied by Nos. 53 and 54, it announces sad, unpleasant, bad thoughts. If, on the contrary, it is close to Nos. 7 and 22, it predicts funny ideas, silly thoughts, cheerfulness in your imaginations.

After the No. 47, it implies success; while together with the No. 18, it indicates unenforceable projects, missed trips.

If we read for a lady, it tells her, that she will be caught by the rain.

D'ODOUCET

This forty-third card depicts seven stem cups.

4 and 3, word for word again, universal generation. To explore this matter, we are obliged to resort to the steps of analogy or to analysis; both require reflection, constituting what we call *thought*; this intellectual function is illustrated by cups in the number of 7. A number which expresses the life of thoughts, whose attributes bring forth *projects*; their benignity depended on the portion of judgment that is left with us, and their nature is almost always relative to the situation, we are experiencing.

MODERN INTERPRETATIONS

This card has by Grimaud been assigned the keywords IDEAS in the upright and PLANS in the reverse.

UPRIGHT: The Seven of Cups indicates your mental state. In relationships, it implies sentimentality, romance and tenderness. It is a good card for singles, who are looking for a partner. This is also an encouragement for you to apply the mind, to visualize your dreams in order to make them a reality. In business, there may be a change, perhaps sparked by a new idea, which will give you some satisfaction. Your finances may need your attention, this will also give you some peace of mind.

REVERSE: In the reverse this car implies contemplations. In relationships you are questioning things, your habits, your behavior, your way of communicating and making positive changes. In business, you may take on new projects, that you did not dare to do before, it could also involve a side hustle, planning big projects, like real estate.

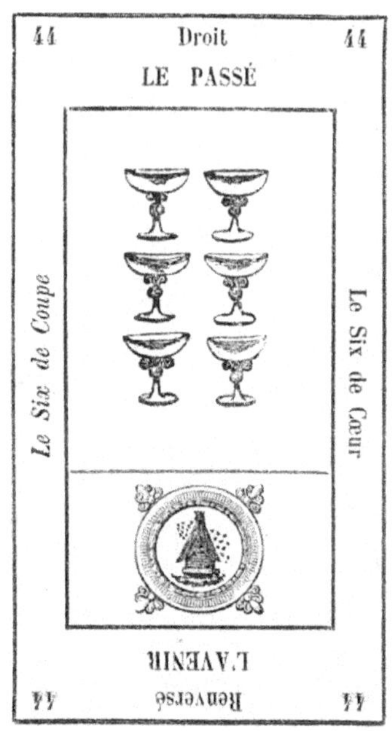

No. 44

The Past - The Future[65]
Six of Cup or of Hearts

When this hieroglyph is presented in the Upright it is a sign of pleasant memories.

Next to the No. 22, it reminds you of a part of the countryside, where you had an adventure, which you should bring to a successful conclusion.

If we see the No. 18, next to this card, we would say; you have committed a nasty deed, for which you must have felt much remorse.

Cards 44-18-51, the last in Reverse, shows an evil woman, who has harmed you in the past.

With the No. 33, this card appearing in Reverse, is a sign of healing, for you, or for a person ill, in whom you are very interested.

This card in the Reverse and arriving accompanied by the No. 17, announces an inheritance, which you have been expecting for a very long time.

---

[65] Translator: This card in Reverse implies the future or things to come. The beehive in the figure below is perhaps a biblical reference to what awaits the virtuous; *the land of milk and honey*?

LEMARCHAND

This tarot announces pleasant memories to you, when it appears in the Upright. In the Reverse and next to the No. 18, it warns you that you will have some regrets.

When this card is accompanied by the No. 33, it indicates the end of a disease, either for the querent, or for a person who, very much so, has his interest.

When the 44, 18 and 51 come in a line to form a spread, they warn you that a dark-haired woman, filled with wickedness, will cause you much inconvenience; however, when one of the three cards is Reversed, it announces the opposite, that is to say, the person in question is saying good things about you, everywhere.

D'ODOUCET

This forty-fourth card depicts six stem cups.

The universe 4 is presented here with two different faces, or rather by a double aspect. One is the *past,* the other is the *future*; but the past and the future are beings of reason, that is to say intellectuals. The cups are therefore used for their design. The number 6 implies the current existence of the universe, represented, in short, by the macrocosm, the spirit of the animating principle. Its existence is guaranteed by its former state, and is the forerunner of its *future* state.

MODERN INTERPRETATIONS

This card has by Grimaud been assigned the keywords THE PAST in the upright and THE FUTURE in the reverse.

UPRIGHT: The Six of Cups is a card of the past. This card represents your experiences, lessons learned, which can be used going forward. It also implies influences from the past affecting your current situation, or things you are urged to hold on to or let go off from the past. It is also a card of improvement.

REVERSE: In the reverse, this card represents the future. Things you are heading towards, projects you may have initiated and the events to come, as indicated by the neighboring cards.

No. 45

Inheritance - Relatives[66]
Five of Cups or Hearts

This tarot is one of the happiest predictions; it predicts inheritance for you, it is also a sign of success in everything you do.

When you read for a young lady, this card tells her, that she will soon marry the husband she wants.

If this card is found before the No. 74, it predicts gifts from someone of high rank.

In the Reverse, this card announces the impending arrival of a relative, whom you have not seen for a long time.

If then near the No. 32, also in Reverse, the arrival of this relative will be a source of prosperity.

But the opposite will happen if in place of the No. 32, the No. 28 in Reverse appears.

---

[66] Translator: This card in reverse implies family and ancestry. The figure below depicts a trident with the intertwining of two fish, perhaps a reminder that blood is thicker than water, of the emotional tie and responsibility, that exists between family members?

LEMARCHAND

The five of cups is always auspicious; it is one of the most favorable cards. It indicates success in the business of the querent.

In the Reverse, this tarot announces the imminent arrival, of a relative of whom you have not heard from for a long time.

If the spread is made for a young lady, No. 45 is the prediction of a longed-for union.

Sometimes also this tarot announces inheritance from foreign countries, as well as from an uncle in America or any other relative, living in distant lands. If this tarot was in the company of No. 32, it would only imply a flattering letter from that relative.

D'ODOUCET

This forty-fifth card depicts five stem cups.

The universal spirit 5 presents us with its general action in the universe. This action constantly pushes for the transmutation of the rest. The mass of matter is determined. No being can be created without others first being destroyed. This profitable destruction is a real inheritance, for the species next, or for the ones current, who benefit from all the spoils. The most common form of inheritance is through *parental* succession; however, the action of inheriting, the degree of kinship even, is illustrated by beings of reason, or intellectuals, which designate the cups, their number is 5, a number which also indicates, with its serpentine shape, the successive progression of individuals.

MODERN INTERPRETATIONS

This card has by Grimaud been assigned the keywords INHERITANCE in the upright and RELATIVE in the reverse.

UPRIGHT: The Five of Cups is a card of family legacy. The experiences with your family, the values, the resources, that have prepared you for what to come. This is a time to tap into that. When you apply your experiences, finances will not be a problem. You may also inherit money, which may be very substantial.

REVERSE: In reverse, this card represents the positive influence of a family member. This may be a parent or sibling. It may indicate the return of someone important to you. Also a card of inheritance and unexpected money.

No. 46

Boredom – New Knowledge[67]
Four of Cups or Hearts

This card is an indication of annoyances, that you will soon experience; people whom you hate will always be near you. If you do make an effort to keep them away, they will put you in touch with schemers.

Next to the No. 28, it predicts that the pleasant party to which you are or will be invited to, will be interrupted by an extraordinary incident.

Next to the No. 60, it indicates that the querent will experience much boredom in a place, where he will be alone.

Followed by the No. 2, in the Reverse, this tarot tells you that you will witness a fire; but if it is preceded by the No. 59 also in the Reverse, it warns you that you will shortly be obliged to mourn a relative, who lives in a very distant country, a relative who is unknown to you, an uncle from America, perhaps!!

---

[67] Translator: This card in reverse implies new instructions and new acquaintances. In the figure below a woman with a lyre and lute, a symbol of peace and harmony, perhaps she is trying out something new?

LEMARCHAND

Here is a tarot[68] which does not predict such wonderful things as the preceding one; it implies annoyances, tribulations, change of weather. You will be caught by a downpour, and you will catch a cold as a result.

Followed by the No. 2 in the Reverse, the card warns you that you will witness a marvelous spectacle, be it a storm, a fire, a waterspout, extraordinary hails, however, it will not cause harm to anyone, because you will only see it in a dream.

After the No. 28, it denotes an invitation to a beautiful house party, in one of the prettiest properties in the region.

---

[68] Translator: The Lemarchand booklet assigns the meaning *Noveaute* or Novelty on this card in the reverse, rather than *Nouvelles Connaissances*.

D'ODOUCET

This forty-sixth card depicts four stem cups.

Who among us has not experienced that the mind, saturated with acquired insights, falls into a kind of boredom, of apathy, which can only be overcome by the idea of acquiring *new knowledge*? Such is the peculiarity of the genie to always seek nourishment from its insatiable greed. Apathy for the rest is expressed by the stable number of Four of Cups; their cubic position indicates a monotonous cessation of action, which this number represents for us. It is first of all on 6, where our globe persistently presents its specific principles and through the steady sphere of the universal 4. Both demonstrate to us in their usual way, no further exercise for the mind; *boredom*, until the activity is reborn, with the hope of making *new discoveries*.

MODERN INTERPRETATIONS

This card has by Grimaud been assigned the keywords BOREDOM in the upright and MISFORTUNE in the reverse.

UPRIGHT: The Four of Cups is stagnancy. A life partner may be disappointing, arguments and upset may have become the daily routine. You could also be investing in people, who do not reciprocate. In business, it is card of difficulty, your finances may become critical.

REVERSE: In reverse it is card of self-reflection. The situation around you may call for a need to change, but you may have a problem seeing it. You may have become a creature of habit. This card implies, that there is a need to expand your horizon, to mix up the daily routine. In business, the old routine does not work anymore and whether you make the change or not, will be the determining factor of your success.

No. 47

Success - Business[69]
Three of Cups or Hearts

If this card is next to the No. 7 in Reverse, you will be successful in a matter, that has preoccupied you for a long time.

When this tarot is near the No. 45 in the Reverse, it announces that one of your relatives, or one of your best friends will obtain great success in a theatre company, the play which he / she will have performed, will be applauded, or will be successful in a major way.

If the querent is a lady, this card tells her that a friend, an actress, will be the reason for the success of a comedy, which would have been booed without her talent, or that she herself will be applauded.

If this card is drawn by a soldier, it predicts benevolence from his superiors, and an unexpected promotion.

With unfavorable cards, this tarot modifies its meaning.

In the Reverse this card means relief, completion, cure, end of business, etc., depending on the querent's situation.

---

[69] Translator: This card in reverse implies responsibility, execution and mastery. The figure below depicts a lion´s head with radiating wings and lightning bolts. The lion is the man in charge, handing out praise or critique, a fitting illustration.

LEMARCHAND

It is particularly to actresses that the interpretation of this tarot [70] applies in a positive way; it announces to the querent that she will have the most brilliant success in a play being rehearsed at the moment; a shower of wreaths and bouquets will come, at the end of the next performance, in order to express to her the impression that her talent will have caused for her admirers.

After the No. 45, it still indicates theatrical success, but very different; it informs you that one of your relatives is preparing a play, that will have huge success, and that this work will put him at the forefront of playwrights.

If the querent were a soldier, it would be the announcement of a victory or success in promotion.

---

[70] Translator: The Lemarchand booklet assigns the meaning *Affaires* or Affairs on this card in the reverse, rather than *Expedition d´Affaires*.

D'ODOUCET

This forty-seventh card depicts three stem cups, arranged triangularly.

Here is something that presents itself to us! 7, life and the universal existence 4, serving us in our penetration. How does the universe 4 survive? By divine goodness, which assigns the generation to it. It is through this, that it renews itself unceasingly. We guessed right, and it is an astounding *success*, because of the wisdom of our genie, which discovers that the generation multiplies the various forms, which appear to us as many different cards, aspects of this same universe. Our intellectual combinations are expressed on this topic by the cups in the number of 3, which implies the result of our research. The *swiftness* with which their principle should naturally present itself to our imagination, is expressed by the last attribute of this card, which receives its confirmation by another meaning of the numbers 7 and 4; designating life and *action*, spread over all parts of the universe, by the generation embodied by the 3 of Cups.

MODERN INTERPRETATIONS

This card has by Grimaud been assigned the keywords RELIEF in the upright and EVERY DAY WORK in the reverse.

UPRIGHT: In the upright, this card denotes success. You are on the right path, making the right decisions in all your endeavors. You may have unnecessary worry, however soon things will be brought back to balance. In business, a time of success ahead, you are recognized for your talents and abilities, and the necessary support is around you. Finances will be good and may last for some time.

REVERSE: In reverse, this card implies conviction. You are taking your relationships seriously, there is a sense of duty and responsibility, you are not easily affected by whims and impulses. A card of happy endings or outcomes too. In business, it implies experience and mastery. Things do not shake you up as easily and you usually know what to do, if things get heated. Finances are managed efficiently.

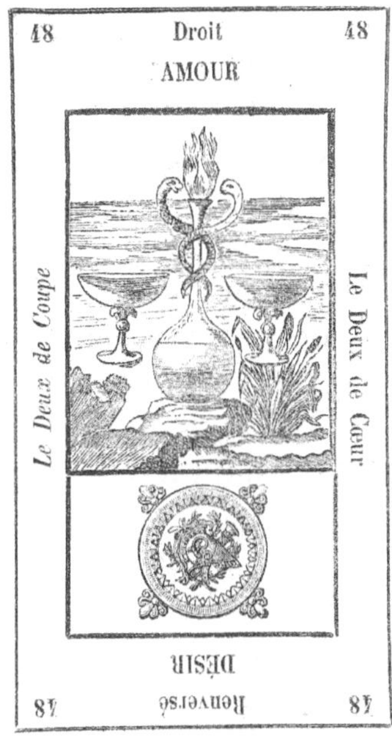

No. 48

Love - Desire[71]
Two of Cups or Hearts

The whole meaning of this tarot is a favorable omen, either in love, or in a commercial enterprise, or in a party of pleasure. If this card appears in the Upright, it predicts fortune for the one who has love of wealth and it announces honors to the ambitious man.

When the querent is a man, this card appearing in the Upright next to the No. 47, announces that he will be happily in love. If, on the other hand, it appears side by side with the No. 54, he will see his offer received badly by the family of the person, whose hand he aspires to have.

If you read for a lady it predicts, that she will be the object of general attention, during a big meeting. She will have an advantageous marriage if the No. 48 is accompanied by the No. 41, however if the first is followed by the No. 61, it will indicate disappointments instead.

In the Reverse and next to the No. 69, this tarot predicts that your desires will be fulfilled. But if this card is followed by the No. 65, also in Reverse, your wishes will be in vain, and you will soon be at odds with a younger person.

Alone, this card signifies passion, will and friendship.

---

[71] Translator: This card in Reverse implies will, appetite and passion. The figure below depicts a trumpet and a Greek helmet, perhaps saying; *here I come, do not stand in my way?*

LEMARCHAND

This tarot predicts fortune to those who love wealth; it announces honors to the one who is fueled by ambition; to the lover, it predicts marriage; to the merchant, good enterprise; to the old man, good health; to the sick, a cure.

When reading for a lady, this card predicts, she will have great success at a ball to which she is invited; it will be more celebratory than any other.

Followed by the No. 61, it is however doubtful; it is an indication of hopes not met and of non-success.

In the Reverse and close to the No. 69, this tarot announces pretty things, of which you will find the explanation to by questioning the spread a second time.

D'ODOUCET

This forty-eighth card depicts two stem cups. This picture is adorned with a vase with a long neck, the elements are contained therein, and fire is emanating from it. Two caduceus[72] serpents crown the vase, which rests on a rock.

Here we obtain the conviction of what we had assumed; the circulations of generations 8, is identified with the universe of 4; but they are not from generation, not without the active and passive principle. Let us examine the two (intellectually since their gender is indeterminable) through two cups whose number 2, specific to man and to the woman, expressing the invariability of vegetation or reproduction. We understand, moreover, that the attractive and respective virtue, which stimulates the mating of the agent and the patient, is, for this last reason, a testimony of *Love*, of which *desire* or magnetic virtue is the precursor, although it is inferior to it (because desire produces nothing in of itself). Let us stress moreover the intelligence, purifying philosophically the two roots and joining them in the right proportion, we thus will become the masters of an elixir, the efficiency of which will not be ambiguous, if one reflects on the results of the combination of the four elements, and the qualities of the three kingdoms, corresponding to the three principles; *Salt, Sulphur and Mercury*.

---

[72] Translator: The *caduceus* or *herald´s staff* was the staff carried by Hermes Trismegistus. The alchemists considered salt, sulphur and mercury to be a representation of divine thought, sacrifice and love.

MODERN INTERPRETATIONS

This card has by Grimaud been assigned the keywords LOVE in the upright and DESIRE in the reverse.

UPRIGHT: The Two of Cups is a card of love. A promising card for relationships, married life will be joyous and very committed with intensity, happiness and passion. A struggling relationship will be reinvigorated. A card of meeting that special someone too. In business, a very creative time, plenty of drive and support. You want to make sure to share your success with others. You also want to reign in any suspicions, as they will not be well-founded.

REVERSE: In reverse, a card of never being satisfied. This may reflect a "the grass is greener somewhere else" attitude, a feeling of inferiority towards your partner or self-doubt, even when nothing is wrong. If not careful, this may lead to actual relationship issues and unhappiness. This is also a card of temptations. Financially you may be tempted to give in to temptations, big purchases that will put your overall situation at risk.

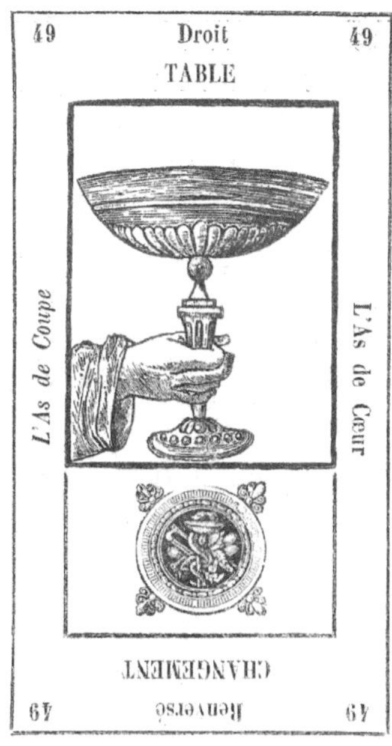

No. 49

Table - Change[73]
Ace of Cups or Hearts

The original meaning of this tarot was law, which was translated to table or table of law, it indicates an inflexible will; next to other cards, it confirms whatever predictions they imply.

Next to the No. 37, it announces, that a blonde woman, who wants to do good by you, will shortly be giving you news, that will reach you in the middle of a celebration.

If you are reading for a young person, and this card is followed by the No. 24, it indicates to him the imminent beginning of his future.

When this card is in the Reverse, it predicts unexpected changes in your position.

If this tarot is found next to the No. 34 in the Reverse, it tells you, that you will see in a dream, what will happen to you.

---

[73] Translator: This card in Reverse implies mutation, metamorphosis and adjustment, the figure below, the Bowl of Hygeia, a symbol of resurrection and healing, perhaps implying a new start with a new improved you?

LEMARCHAND

The meaning of this tarot use to be law; we have translated it to table or table of law. It is the sign of a firm, absolute will; for this reason, it confirms the predictions of any neighboring cards, whatever that prediction may be.

After the No. 37, it brings you long-awaited news from a blond person to whom you have a great friendship.

If you read for young persons, this card warns them that they in future, in order to bring family affairs in order, will take a little trip before getting married.

Next to the No. 34 in the Reverse, this card tells you that you will see in a dream, what will happen to you; but if the dream you have, does not announce pleasant things, there would be reasons to doubt its validity.

D'ODOUCET

This forty-ninth card depicts a stem cup held by one hand.

Here we are at the height of satisfaction. Our intelligence is boundless, as in, without a mold. The image of a single cup expresses, that we are the only being blessed with such an expansion of light. The virtues of the macrocosm are provided to us, as well as the designation of the expansion in the number 9, which itself participates in the universal qualities of 4. Let us celebrate with extraordinary *Joy*, the triumph of our mind .... But alas, we have a dire foreboding, suggesting that it is because of bliss, that the wheel of fortune begins to turn against us .... Let us warn our brothers of this change. It may perhaps become less bitter for them.

MODERN INTERPRETATIONS

This card has by Grimaud been assigned the keywords PARTY in the upright and CHANGE in the reverse.

UPRIGHT: The Ace of Cups implies socializing. Exchanges will be happy, harmonious and joyous. A pleasant time of meeting up, partying. With the support of friends, you may meet a lot of new people, a great new love perhaps. In business, a card of new opportunities, a job, you do not want to miss out on it. Also, a card of caution, not to lose your head or to overspend.

REVERSE: In the reverse, this card implies a reversal. It is card that predicts a change of affection, of second thoughts, a ripple, that may, if not addressed cause a break up in a relationship, a choice, to reinvest or to leave behind. A card of change and inconsistency. In business, dramatic changes, the unforeseen, but with proper diligence these will be overcome, but only if deception does not lead you astray.

No. 50

Magistrate - Wicked Man
King of Swords or Spades

Avoid people of law, lawyers, bailiffs, they always make war on your fortune. Run away from the company of men, you suspect of betrayal.

If this card is found near the No. 22 in the Reverse, an honest magistrate will do you justice.

When the cards are laid for a woman and this tarot is found near the No. 55, she must be careful of a dark-haired man, who makes her eyes soft.

In the Reverse, this tarot urges you, not to start a lawsuit, which will inevitably ruin you.

If this card is preceded by the No. 71 in the Reverse, it predicts that you will be mocked by a dark-haired person.

Next to the No. 61, it announces the death of a person, whom you have lost contact with and who lives in a distant land.

LEMARCHAND

This card urges you to avoid people of the law; run away from the lawsuits and lawyers. When chance brings this tarot near the No. 22 in Reverse, it predicts that an honest magistrate will do you justice.

For a lady, and near the No. 55, it tells her, that she should beware of the fallacious speeches of a dark-haired man with brilliant appearances, but who in the end is of little value.

Next to the No. 61, this is a very unfortunate sign to a person, who has persecuted you for a long time, but to whom you were not entirely without blame.

When this tarot is close to the No. 71, it announces the loss of your purse, which however you will find if the No. 20 is in the row and not in Reverse.

After the No. 78, it indicates that an influential person will be your protector on various occasions.

D'ODOUCET

This fiftieth card represents a man of arms, strong and vigorous, in cuirass, seated, wearing a crown and holding a sword.

After having been expanded by the intellectual sphere, it is time to take up the aspect of the chains of this life. Let's first look at the number that appears. 0, our globe, devoid of the attribute of integration, in fact, it no longer possesses this plenitude, which facilitated an unlimited expansion of its relations, all the more necessary, as this type of consumer has now grown prodigiously. To make matters worse, the universal principle of reproduction no longer directs its movement, only indirectly in favor of our first support. The general vegetation suffers. If new produce is obtained in the future, albeit now becoming rarer, each individual must only have what is necessary, and the sword of justice must make a legal sharing of it. This sword must be entrusted to the one, who will have made a particular study of the respective rights of each applicant. It will therefore be a *man of the robe*, specifically placed between the law and the *wicked man*, who can infringe on it.

MODERN INTERPRETATIONS

This card has by Grimaud been assigned the keywords MAN OF LAW in the upright and WICKED MAN in the reverse.

UPRIGHT: The King of Sword represents the magistrate. It is the man, who advices, decides and passes judgement or a diagnosis. He may be in an actual position of authority or just someone with those character traits. Whether he is good or bad for you, would depend on neighboring cards.

REVERSE: In reverse, this card implies an enemy. An ill-intentioned, spiteful individual, who only cares about himself and abuses his powers. He can be a very dangerous enemy to have. Be careful.

No. 51

Widowhood - Wicked Woman
Queen of Sword or Spades

A widowed woman, with a bad temper, to whom you are a fairly close relative, is about to remarry soon.

If you are reading the cards for a young woman, she should not get married, because she would enter a bad household, unless a favorable card precedes or follows this card.

Next to the No. 1, it indicates that the man will be older than the woman. Next to the No. 8, the opposite.

Next to No. 67, this card announces to a lady, that her husband is not quite as frugal as he could be.

Next to the No. 78, it predicts that you will do something thoughtless; if it is followed by the No. 71, it tells you that you must attend to the conservation of your fortune.

In the Reverse, this card indicates, that a very malicious woman seeks to harm you and that she will succeed, if it is near the No. 47; the opposite will happen if the No. 33 accompanies it.

LEMARCHAND

A shrewd woman, to whom you are a fairly close relative, will soon experience unexpected annoyances.

If one reads for a young woman to be married, it warns her to study well the character of the one she is to marry, because she could well end up in a poor household.

For a married woman, this tarot indicates excessive spending on the part of her husband; near the No. 71, it urges you not to put all your eggs in one basket, and to ensure the conservation of your small fortune.

After the No. 47, this tarot tells you, that a very malicious woman seeks to harm you; but close to the No. 33, the prediction is quite different; it is a person unknown to you, who is looking for an opportunity to do you good.

D'ODOUCET

This fifty-first card represents a woman dressed in velvet red, in cuirass and seated, wearing a crown and holding a sword.

How does man himself feel about the *distance* from the beneficial principle of his existence, which in a way seems to want to escape him? Now, we no longer live as our good patriarchs did. The few days, which are still entrusted to us are in the prey of tribulations. An armed *woman*, therefore *dangerous*, paints this idea; may she make us cautious!

MODERN INTERPRETATIONS

This card[74] has by Grimaud been assigned the keywords WIDOWHOOD in the upright and MALICIOUS WOMAN in the reverse.

UPRIGHT: The Queen of Swords represents an unappealing woman. It may be a widow, single woman or an older woman. She is unpleasant, full of complaint, resentment, sadness, discriminative and hypocritical. Someone to avoid.

REVERSE: In the reverse, this card indicates a wicked woman. In the upright, the Queen is cunning, in the reverse, she is in your face, aggressive, jealous and creates conflict wherever she goes.

---

[74] Translator: d´Odoucet assigns the meaning *Viduite* in the Upright, rather than *Veuvage*, both meaning widowhood.

No. 52

Military - Ignorance
Knight of Sword

A soldier you are interested in will perform some brilliant action and receive a nice reward. If this 52 is joined with the No. 41, his victory will cost him an injury.

If you read for a lady, this tarot tells her unexpected news from a military man, who will give her proof of friendship.

Next to the No. 19, this card changes the prediction.

Next to the No. 38, it predicts, that two old relatives will arrive in your city and one of them, will do you a lot of good.

This card appearing in the Reverse predicts, to a man that he will have an argument with a fool, who will make himself the laughing stock of all, who will listen to him. It predicts to a woman, that she will defeat one of her rivals with a talent, she cultivates with great joy.

LEMARCHAND

You soon learn that a soldier in whom you have some interest, has been talked about, and the rewards he has won on the battlefield are discerning.

After the No. 38, this card lets you know that your city will be visited by famous soldiers.

This tarot, when Reversed, predicts, to the querent, that he will have a discussion with a person full of pretension, and that this person will be made the fool by those, whom he has made judges of the matter.

If we read for a lady, it tells her, that she will shine brightly because of her skills in entertainment, and that her rivals will be eclipsed by her in their very next meeting.

D'ODOUCET

This fifty-second card represents a young man, a Cuirassier on horseback dressed in velvet red and holding a sword in his hand.

We find here what vegetation 2 experiences as a kind of abandonment, from the invigorating principle of 5, the *military* art of attracting again this reproductive spirit, which with great difficulty he will succeed, nevertheless. It is no longer a fortunate time, where the earth produces tasty fruits everywhere. Decadence is coming with great strides even in intellectual matters. The centuries of Barbary follow the heydays of Athens. The predominance of *ignorance* stifles the germ of science, by the carelessness it shows to the arts; the erosion of which increases our misfortunes.

MODERN INTERPRETATIONS

This card has by Grimaud been assigned the keywords SOLDIER in the upright and IGNORANCE in the reverse.

UPRIGHT: The Knight of Swords represents fight. It can be an actual person in the military, but more so, you fighting opposition, obstacles and constraints. You will be able to overcome these with courage and determination.

REVERSE: In reverse this card represents ignorance. Ignorance of people and situations. You must be vigilant, communicate and use your discernment to avoid wasting your time and resources.

No. 53

Spy - Improvidence
Page of Swords or Spades

You are warned, that a very curious man will seek to invite himself into your affairs in order to know your speculations; if this card is preceded by the No. 50 it indicates that it is a magistrate, who seeks to harm you.

With the No. 74, it's an unexpected present; with the No. 19, it is a setback; small distresses will suddenly inconvenience you.

Near the No. 59, this tarot announces loss of money.

When this card follows the No. 13, it predicts a marriage between a relative you love and a young man you hate.

When this tarot is drawn by a military man, it announces a duel where he will be slightly struck.

If it appears in the Reverse you will receive news, that will surprise you singularly; it will be pleasant if this card is near the No. 32, but it will cause you melancholy, if it is accompanied by the No. 34.

When in the Reverse, it presents itself to the No. 1 if the querent is male, or to the No. 8, if the querent is a woman, it predicts that you will be the victim of a carelessness, which will be your fault, but which will not be very serious, a very small bewilderment.

LEMARCHAND

This tarot predicts a good speculation, which could lead to nothing, if you let too many people in on your business. Preceded by the No. 50, it warns you that you must be careful with a magistrate, who does not want you all the good, he seems to wish upon you.

When this tarot follows the No. 13, it announces, that a person who you detest, will marry a young man who you cared enough for and from whom you expected a marriage proposal; but if the No. 20 is very near, it will give you comfort, because it is the promise of something better.

After the No. 32, and in the Reverse, this card tells you, that you will receive news, that will surprise you greatly, also in a very pleasant way.

D'ODOUCET

This fifty-third card represents a young man standing, dressed in velvet red and in cuirass, holding a sword.

We now perceive the generation 3, necessarily languishing, no longer fruitful with the same energy, with the universal spirit of 5 in decline, the people wither or fold, their needs increase due to the obstacles, that are facing them. Everyone *spies*, looks for a way to encroach on his neighbor, one no longer relies on good will. One only offers oneself *unexpectedly*. Let us at least try to settle on a sum, however small it may be.

MODERN INTERPRETATIONS

This card[75] has by Grimaud been assigned the keywords SPY in the upright and IMPROVIDENCE in the reverse.

UPRIGHT: The Page of Swords represent things in secret. This card implies a spy or a secret enemy, someone spreading gossip, rumors and slander. You must remain vigilant, discreet and be very vary, who you trust.

REVERSE: In reverse, this card implies bad surprises. This may be the effects of recklessness or irresponsibility. You will be forced to manage it, with swiftness and determination. It should however go well.

---

[75] Translator: d´Odoucet assigns the meaning *Surveillant* in the upright and in the reverse; *Imprevu* or Unexpected.

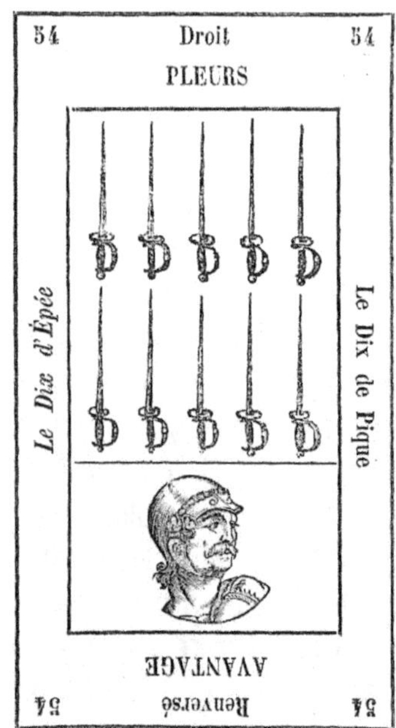

No. 54

Tears - Advantage[76]
Ten of Swords or Spades

When this tarot is next to the No. 17, it is a sign of tribulations in your family; but often when found after the No. 21, it is only a sign of disagreements.

In the Reverse, this card signifies authority, success and advantage.

Near the No. 71, it predicts money-gains in a business deal. To a soldier this card in the Reverse predicts a battle, in which he will be victorious, and which will result in a fortune.

Next to the No. 26, this card shows, that a comparison that favors your rival will cause you sorrow.

If the No. 74 is near this tarot, it implies your sorrows will come from a gift given, without your knowledge, to a person of whom you are jealous of.

---

[76] Translator: The figures below on the sword cards have been inserted by Blocquel. The heads in the lower panels have been traced back to a series of historical instruction cards by Victor-Joseph Étienne de Jouy (1764-1846) and engraver Pierre-François Godard (1768-1838). This much appreciated, important detective work was done by Tarot_John from www.forum.tarothistory.com. This figure represents the unpopular Roman emperor Caligula. Perhaps illustrating this card´s reverse meaning; of might and usurpation?

LEMARCHAND

This tarot indicates, to the querent, that quarrels will disturb the peace of people who are close to him.

In the Reverse, it means advantages, success and some authority.

After the No. 71, it pertains to matters of money, a favorable omen; it predicts a good speculation, profits from commercial affairs.

Close to the No. 26, this card warns you that a person, whose ill-will you do not believe, will harm you, if you have not met his wicked designs.

When the querent is a soldier or a sailor, this card is a sign of advantages in events of war.

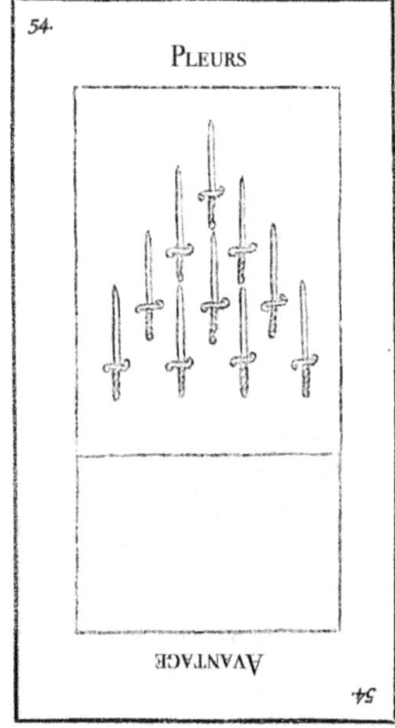

D'ODOUCET

This fifty-fourth card depicts ten swords arranged in a pyramid.

It is in the end the entire universe 4, which sees the main engine of its existence escape in 5; Let's cry! Nature will no longer be an attentive mother to us and polished iron becomes indispensable for us in order to grab for our subsistence and defend our possessions. Let us cry! But the iron becomes cruel in the hand of the oppressor. Let us cry again, but without ignoring the advantage, which remains with us. Let us join forces, let us strike a balance between it, and the usefulness, that we must derive from it. Our designs are manifested in this way, by the symbol of the ten swords, which imply to us, that a tenth will suffice for the defense of the whole.

MODERN INTERPRETATIONS

This card[77] has by Grimaud been assigned the keywords SORROW in the upright and WINNINGS in the reverse.

UPRIGHT: The Ten of Swords predicts sorrows. It implies daily struggle in relationships, complacency, tears, depression and sadness. In business, a stressful period where things do not turn out the way you want, and with bad responses and bad management. Also, a card of endings in all areas of your life. Finances will suffer.

REVERSE: In reverse, a card of advantage. You can expect a meteorite rise, a promotion, which may be greater than you anticipated. A manifestation of things you have wished for and worked for. A card of "all good things come to those who wait." Your finances will reflect your success.

---

[77] Translator: d´Odoucet assigns the meaning *Afflictions* in the upright, rather than *Pleurs*.

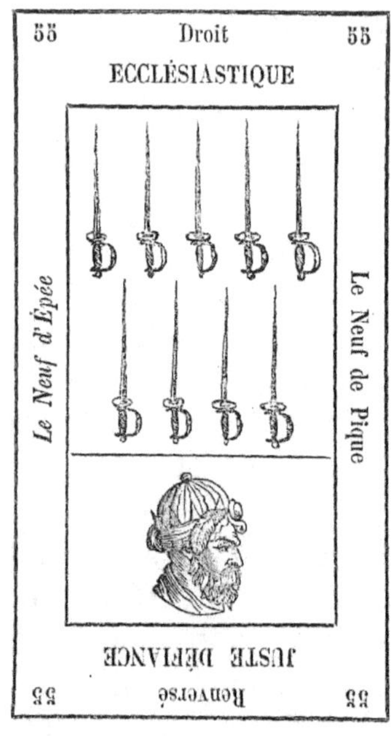

No. 55

Ecclesiastical — Justified distrust[78]
Nine of Sword or Spades

This card presents the nine of sword, it implies, religion and conscience, you will soon attend a religious ceremony. If this card is found next to the No. 13 it predicts that this, will be a wedding ceremony; but if it is near a less favorable card it will be a less pleasant ceremony.

Mistrust is the mother of assurance. In the old days, the Egyptians said; never speak ill of the Gods, or against men. Today it is more than ever necessary to say nothing, there are men meaner, than the demons who accuse you of having spoken badly, so it is wise to be discreet.

In the Reverse, this card tells you; you have walked away from a person, who could have lead you to your ruin.

After the No. 67, it tells you, that the person you should be wary of, is a young brown-haired man.

---

[78] Translator: The figure below represents the Persian King Cambyses, who died of gangrene. Perhaps illustrating one of this card´s reverse meanings; of well-founded fear?

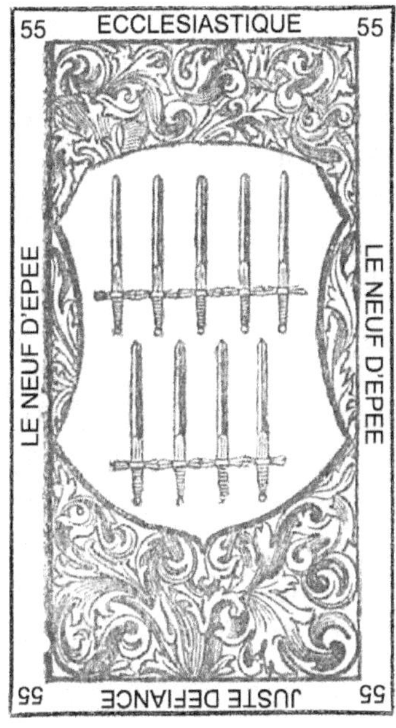

LEMARCHAND

This card[79] relates to great religious ceremonies; it predicts, you will shortly be attending a wedding ceremony; and close to the No. 6, it tells you that it will be a union you never imagined.

If this tarot is in the Reverse, it predicts, on the contrary, a marital breakdown, but between two in favor and from which you were warned all too well.

After the No. 20, this card approves of you not having had too much confidence in an enterprise, which had been proposed to you.

In general, the No. 55 warns the querent to be on his guard.

---

[79] Translator: The Lemarchand booklet assigns the meaning *Ordres* or (Holy) Order on this card in the upright, rather than *Ecclesiastique*.

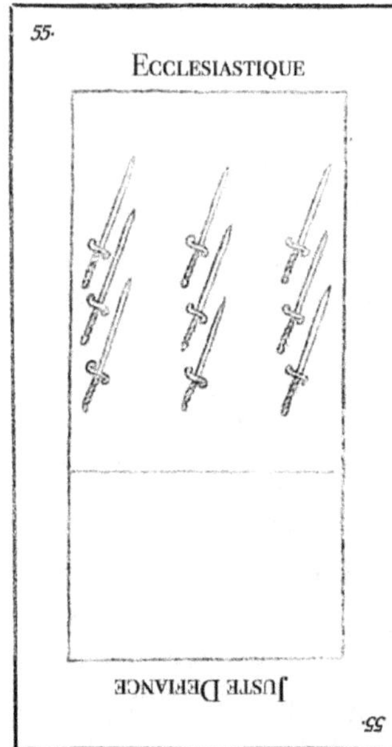

D'ODOUCET

This fifty-fifth card depicts nine swords arranged in threes.

The symbol of the universal spirit 5, here repeated twice, (with due regard to the sensitivity of the preceding cards) indicates to us the current vagueness of its function. The efficiency of it is no longer the same as it was in the past; which should keep us in a *justified distrust* of those among the clients, who provide nothing to the general store, either in labor or in specie. 9 swords designate moreover, that it is by the most arduous work, that we obtain the effusion, that our needs require.

MODERN INTERPRETATIONS

This card[80] has by Grimaud been assigned the keywords CELIBACY in the upright and SUSPICION in the reverse.

UPRIGHT: The Nine of Swords is a card of reflection. It is a time for retreat, solitude, a time to think things through, a decision may be at hand, perhaps involving the future of a relationship. This card is also very spiritual, philosophical, not only from a mental perspective, but can denote actual priests, nuns, religions and so forth. In business, you may seek other pastures, perhaps you feel trapped in your current job.

REVERSE: In the reverse, this is a card of deceit. There may be lies, deceit, drama around a relationship, a partner or a close friend, which causes you distress. In business, you may have people around you, who are trying to harm you, be careful and do not reveal too much. Financially there may be risk of theft.

---

[80] Translator: d'Odoucet assigns the meaning *Celibataire* in the upright.

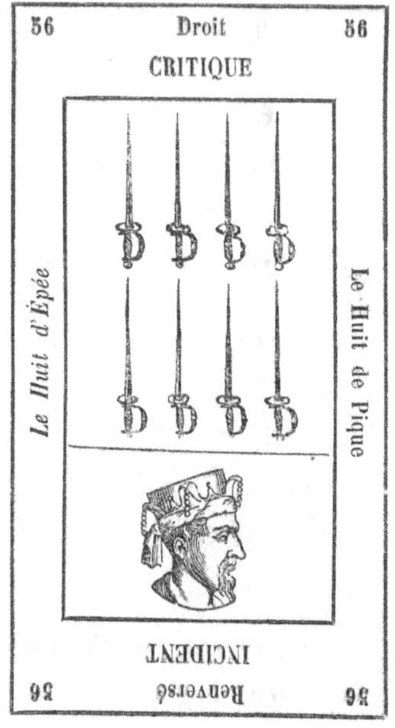

No. 56

Critical — Incident[81]
Eight of Swords or Spades

The eight swords, that are on this card do not bode well for you, if this card is next to the Nos. 13, 20 and 36; and with Nos. 18, 19 or 34, it is a sign of detriment; you will experience a hoax, that you did not expect, and maybe things will go even further.

If this card is drawn by a lady, and next to the No. 46, it alerts her, that gossip has been spread about her, and that she will be in great pain.

Near the No. 44, it predicts dreams that will amaze you.

In the Reverse, if near the No. 78, this tarot announces that a member of your family will go on a pleasure trip. It implies a hasty departure, if seen near the No. 24.

---

[81] Translator: The figure below represents the Chinese legend Fu Xi, who laid down the laws of humanity, instilled moral and social order. Perhaps illustrating this card´s reverse meaning; of fortuitous events and special circumstances?

LEMARCHAND

When this tarot is presented in the Upright and close to the Nos. 13, 20 and 36, it does not predict anything bad.

But with Nos. 18, 19 and 34, it is an unfavorable omen; it predicts you some bewilderment, which will puzzle you all the more, and you will expect more to come.

When the querent is a young lady, this tarot warns her that comments will be made behind her back; and that she will be very upset if same tarot is accompanied by the No. 46.

Near the Nos. 44 and 78, it tells you that you will have surprising dreams; you will attend brilliant parties, balls, shows, but all only in a dream.

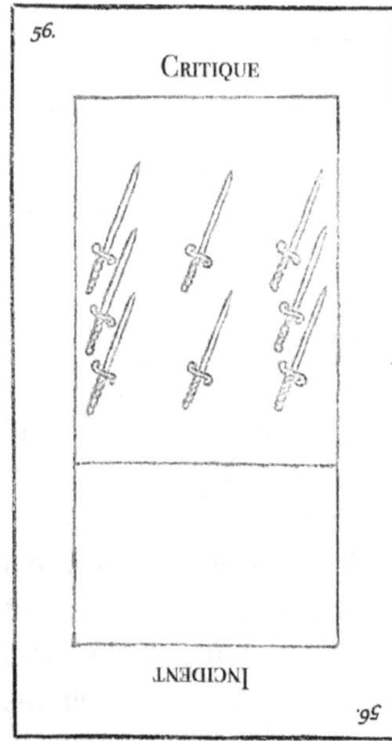

D'ODOUCET

This fifty-sixth card depicts eight swords.

The terrestrial globe presents itself well before our eyes, presented from its specific reproductive principle; but we perceive, at the same time, that the essential agent 5, which, so to speak, irritates the cards, constantly pushes to move away. It is to be expected, that the single principle with which the globe is animated will not be attained, or maintained, renewed by the overarching spirit, which seems to move in an opposite direction. What a *critical* situation! It can result in countless *incidences*. It will nevertheless be possible to ward off a few, by a continual flow of effort, from work that is as painful, as it is dangerous. The 8 of Swords designates our distress in the misfortunes, that characterize them.

MODERN INTERPRETATIONS

This card has by Grimaud been assigned the keywords CRITICISM in the upright and INCIDENTS in the reverse.

UPRIGHT: The Eight of Swords is a card of criticism. You may experience a conflict, where a justified criticism of you is given, which you however do not agree with. This card urges you to put your emotions aside and look at the situation with fresh eyes. In business, you put yourself in a situation, where criticism is raised. Rather than starting an argument, you are advised to take ownership and admit your mistakes.

REVERSE: In the reverse, this card indicates bad circumstances. A card of misunderstanding, tension, confusion, conflict in relationships, perhaps triggered by a serious accident. Often job loss, loss of contracts or loss of clients is connected to this card. Also, finances may be critical, so rein in that spending.

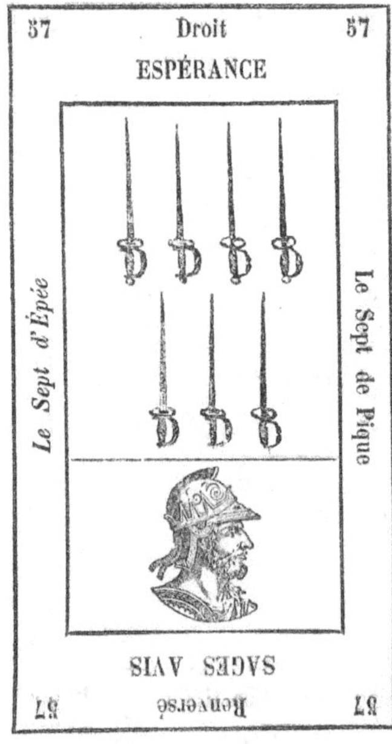

No. 57

Hope – Sound advice[82]
Seven of Swords or Spades

The Egyptians regarded the number seven as one of the most favorable, because the world was created in six days and the seventh was dedicated to rest.

This card tells you that after making a fortune in commerce, you will retire to the countryside.

If you read the cards for a lady, this card tells her that she will soon have a child but then this tarot must be found; next to the No. 63 in Reverse.

With the No. 71, this card foretells of an upcoming inheritance, that will give you much worry before you will enjoy it.

If it appears in the Reverse, it predicts, you will not benefit from the wise advice given to you with regards to a marriage or another important matter.

---

[82] Translator: The figure below represents the wise Roman emperor Probus. Perhaps illustrating this card's reverse meaning; good advice?

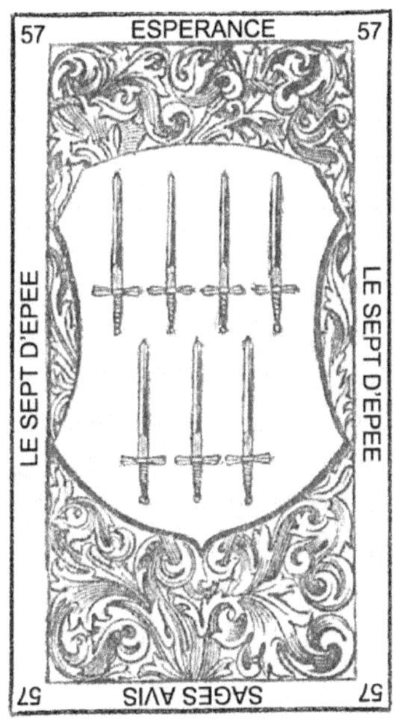

LEMARCHAND

The number seven has always been regarded as very favorable by cartomancers, because the world was created in six days, the seventh was devoted to rest.

If the querent is in business, this tarot tells him, that after making a great fortune, he will retire to a beautiful country estate.

When reading for a married woman, the No. 57 next to No. 63 in the Reverse, is the promise of beautiful posterity.

After the No. 71, it announces an inheritance for which lawsuits will arise between the recipients, but which will end with a good arrangement.

If the querent is about to enter a marriage contract or any other matter of great importance, this tarot warns him to carefully weigh the advice given to him.

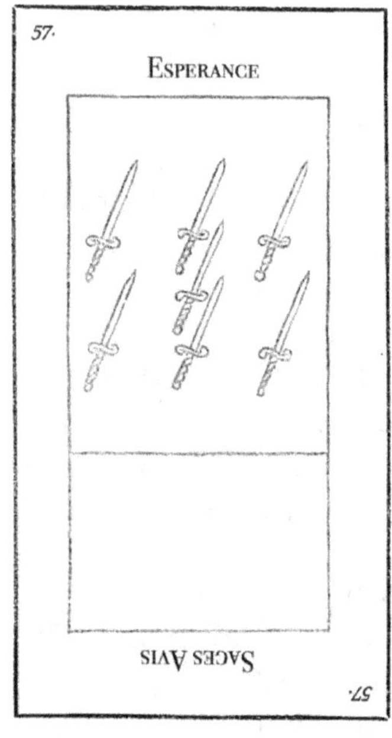

D'ODOUCET

This fifty-seventh card depicts eight swords.

The life willed by 7, takes on the pursuit of the one, who seems not to want his interview. We must hope for everything in these attempts, which *wise precautions* can make effective. As expressed by 7 swords; our conservation is owed only to the union of active efforts, from those who devote themselves more partially to our defense.

MODERN INTERPRETATIONS

This card has by Grimaud been assigned the keywords EXPECTATION in the upright and WISE ADVICE in the reverse.

UPRIGHT: The Seven of Swords is card of dilemma. Although you seek peace, you may find yourself in disputes and arguments, in a head over heart decision. It is a card that urges you to be fair, confident and sincere, which will bring you the solution. In business, things may be very slow, a promotion or career change will have to wait. Financially you may not experience much change.

REVERSE: In the reverse, this card implies advice. You may be waiting for news from a loved one, you are urged to be patient and confident. In business, if you are experiencing problems, you may want to consult a friend or relative. It is useful for you to see things from other people´s perspective, and you may want to consider working in a team

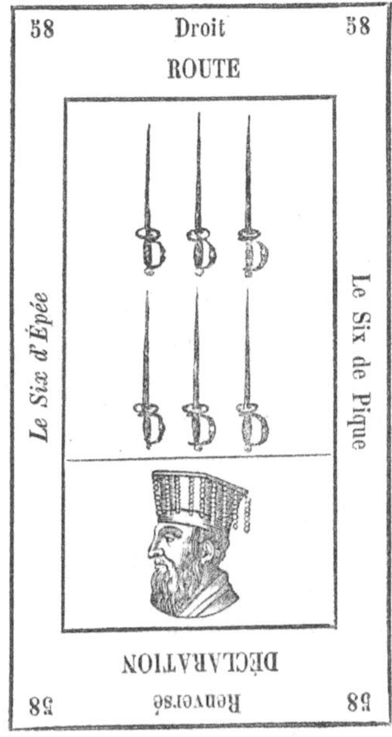

No. 58

Route - Declaration[83]
Six of Sword or Spades

Soon you will be embarking on a journey, where you will experience much fun, however if this card is next to the No. 4, it warns, that you will fear being attacked by a gang of thieves.

Next to the No. 9, this tarot tells you that a trial, that causes you much nuisance, either to you or to one of your relatives, will be judged in a few days.

In the Reverse and near the No. 20, this tarot predicts that an old aunt is busy making her will in your favor; but if instead of No. 20, it is the No. 27 joining the No. 58, expect a delay in the completion of a matter of great importance to you. If you are in a lawsuit, the judgment will not be favorable to you, unless the No. 22 in Reverse precedes or follows this card.

---

[83] Translator: The figure below represents the Chinese philosopher Confucius. Perhaps illustrating this card's reverse meaning; of vision, knowledge and revelations?

LEMARCHAND

This certificate predicts you a fun trip or of great parties of pleasure, such as a wedding, balls and magnificent shows.

Close to the No. 9, this tarot tells you that the trial in question will be judged shortly and to your complete satisfaction.

If this tarot appears in the Reverse with No. 20, it foretells you that a very old aunt is busy making her will and that you will be included there.

After the No. 27, this card indicates delays in an affair that preoccupies you a lot, and of annoyances to which you will be very sensitive, because of the irresolution, that you generally put in all your undertakings; but also, when the No. 22 appears in the row, it predicts satisfaction in what you dreamed of.

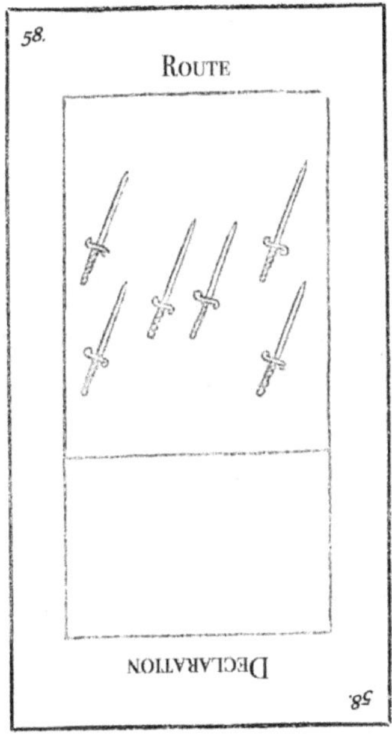

D'ODOUCET

This fifty-eighth card depicts six swords.

The *circulation* of generation 8 constantly pushes to be supported by the agent 5, who modifies it. May these *steps* not be fruitless, and let it all reveal its advantages! Let us expose moreover, with the 6 of Swords, through only the roughest and the most persistent of work, that our globe six, is just a bit beyond our reach.

MODERN INTERPRETATIONS

This card has by Grimaud been assigned the keywords TO TAKE STEPS in the upright and STATEMENTS in the reverse.

UPRIGHT: The Six of Swords represents a change in attitude. You are engaged in constructive dialogue in your relationships and you are fixing things, that need fixing. In your work place, you are taking steps in order to have wanted changes. Generally, a card of progress.

REVERSE: In the reverse, this card indicates expression. In relationships, you are having important conversations, sharing your anxieties, the things that lay heavy on you, which will solve many potential long-term issues. In business, you are able to explain what you are unhappy with, which will be met with understanding and the outcome will prove to be very beneficial to you.

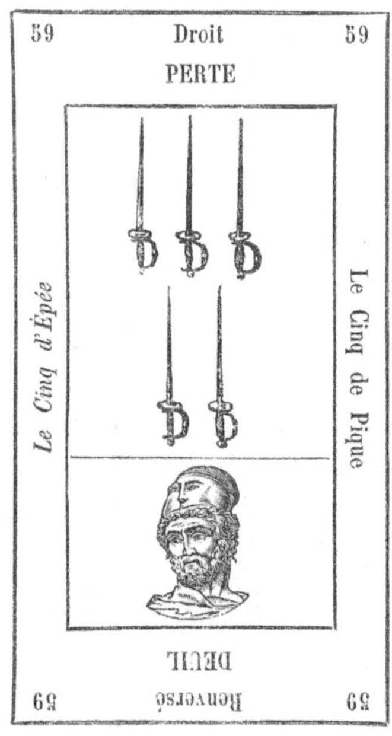

No. 59

Loss - Mourning[84]
Five of Swords or Spades

Mind your purse because soon an attempt will be made on your money.

Next to the No. 66, this card recommends you to use your time for work, because a day will come, when you will regret the time lost.

If we read for a married man, and this card appears accompanied by the No. 24, it urges him to mind those who are eager to call on his wife.

If to a married woman and when this card appears with the No. 33, she must mind a person, who appears to be following her husband´s every move.

If for an unattached person, male or female, and if this card appears with the No. 34 or the No. 76, the querent is in danger of losing the affection of the person he would like to marry.

If this tarot appears in the Reverse, it is a sign of mourning; however, this card is often modified by the cards that surround it.

---

[84] Translator: The figure below represents the Roman emperor Aurelian, who faced devastating internal revolts and barbarian invasions. Perhaps illustrating this card´s reverse meaning; of misfortune and calamity?

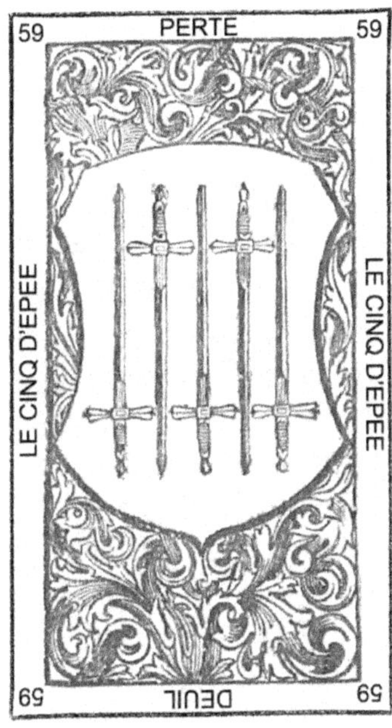

LEMARCHAND

This card warns you that people want more from your purse than from your person; therefore, do not allow yourself to be drawn into speculations, which will cause you irreparable damage.

Next to the No. 66, it warns you to spend your time wisely and to remember, that lost time is never reclaimed.

After tarots 24 or 33, it tells the querent that he must fear domestic annoyances.

When this card appears in the Reverse, it tells you that it will not take long for you to attend some solemn ceremony, where the purpose is anything but pleasant, if not modified by the tarot cards, which follow or precede it.

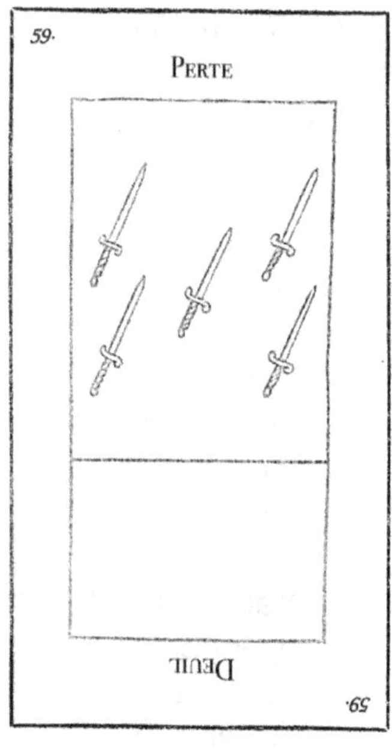

D'ODOUCET

This fifty-ninth card depicts five swords.

However, the effusions or emanations of the globe 9, cannot be decidedly halted; but as it no longer receives as much from the universal principle of 5, there will be a constant *loss*, where we cannot imagine the amount of *suffering*! The 5 of Swords designates therefore henceforth, that it will only be by the continuity of our labor, that we will be able to retain, in part, the reproductive principle of 5, which formerly supplied all of our needs.

MODERN INTERPRETATIONS

This card has by Grimaud been assigned the keywords LOSS in the upright and DEATH in the reverse.

UPRIGHT: The Five of Swords is a very bad card. You may find yourself in a break-up, a divorce or having lost a friend. Sadness, sorrow and mourning, a complete loss of hope may be your current state. In business, you may be facing a loss of employment or bankruptcy. Even in such misery, you are urged to show strength and prudence.

REVERSE: In the reverse this card is even worse. You are experiencing pain, depression and grief, which could be in connection with a death of loved one. In business, despite of much effort and sacrifice, things have gone from bad to worse. A time of saving, what can be saved.

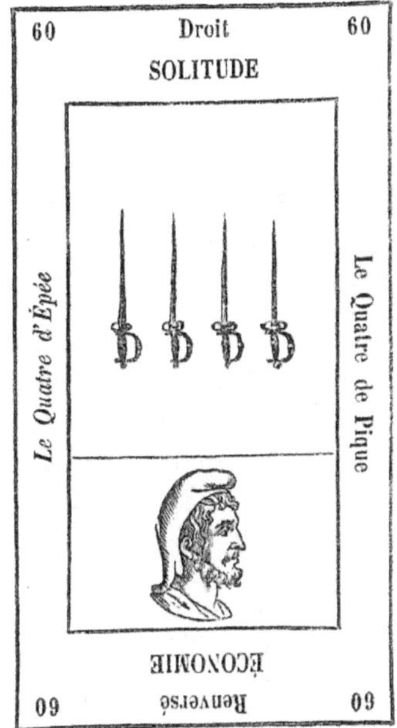

No. 60

Solitude - Economy
Four of Sword or Spades[85]

If you draw this card first, it will predict, that in a little while you will undergo training in order to join a religious community.

Appearing with the No. 56, this card predicts, that your stake will be compromised in a deal. If the querent is a man, be careful when this tarot appears with the No. 14.

When for a woman she should fear abandonment, if this card appears accompanied by the No. 6.

In the Reverse, this card announces a certain success for you, resulting from wise administration of your affairs.

When this tarot appears in the Reverse and near the No. 19, it announces that a failure to save could chip away at your fortune, unless the authoritative advice from a prudent man succeeds in changing your ruinous habits.

Near the No. 21, it warns, that you will be the subject of gossip, and if followed by the No. 17, it announces to you a quarrel, where one of the two antagonists will not be in the right.

---

[85] Translator: The figure below represents the Greek Hero Cadmus, who founded Thebes. Perhaps illustrating this card's reverse meaning; of wise administration, of will and of foresight?

LEMARCHAND

When this tarot is the first drawn, it predicts, that you will soon feel the desire to put yourself in some sort of community.

Close to the No. 56, it is the list of contrarieties; the querent will be subjected to a displacement contrary to his liking; he will be forced to make a trip afar and for which he has complete aversion.

In the Reverse, this card tells you that your business will be successful, if you continue with good order and good administration.

The opposite threatens you, if this tarot is close to No. 19. You will soon be ruined if good advice fails to stop you in your wild spending.

After the No. 21, this card implies discussions or small quarrels followed by reconciliation.

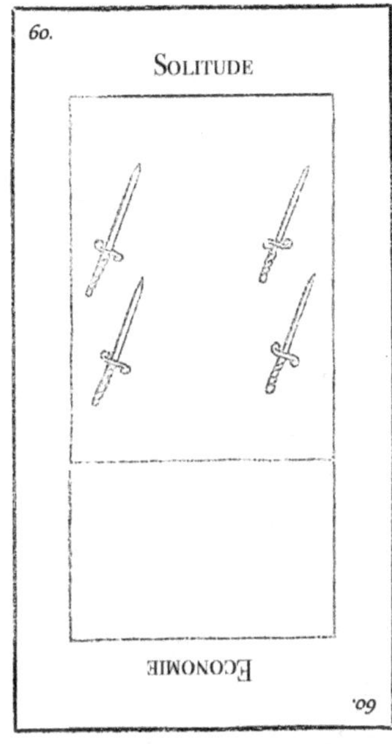

D'ODOUCET

This sixtieth card depicts four swords.

We can see here the globe of the earth 0 is repeated twice in 06. In one of these figures, only in the last, the 6, is presented the spirit animator; a sensitive image of the withering away of the globe, where moors and wastelands express so much *solitude*. The scarcity of production encourages us to *economize*, and the 4 of Swords designates universally, that man is reduced to defense, for his existence and to the means to maintain it.

MODERN INTERPRETATIONS

This card has by Grimaud been assigned the keywords SOLITUDE in the upright and SAVINGS in the reverse.

UPRIGHT: The Four of Swords indicates a time of solitude. A card of withdrawal, limited exchanges, of no communication. You may be in deep reflection, in a state of loneliness, sadness and grieving. In business, you will not have the support, you expected, you will feel isolated and you may be struggling financially with no help in sight. This may be a good time to confide in someone you trust.

REVERSE: In reverse, this card implies discretion. You have learned from the past, you are showing trust, honesty and dialogue, resulting in very harmonious relationships. There may financial burdens, but with the change in your relationships, you should be able to protect your finances.

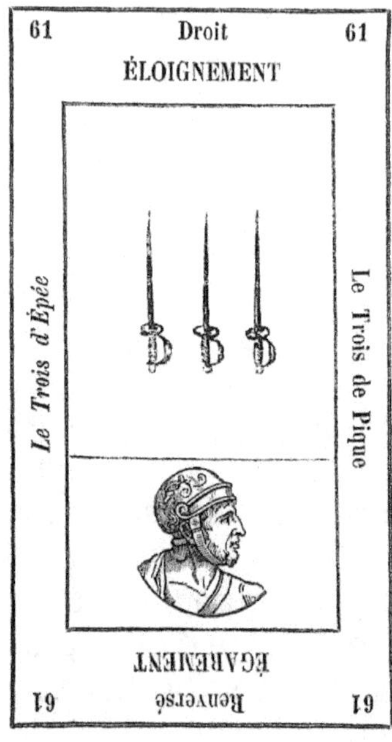

No. 61

Remoteness - Diversion[86]
Three of Sword or Spades

This card, when found near No. 20, is a sign that fortune will always elude you, if you continue to abuse its gifts.

If you read for a young person, this tarot announces to her a scramble of little duration, followed by the No. 13, it predicts, that she will marry a man she has little love for.

Followed by the No. 3 in the Reverse, this card tells you that someone you love will leave; next to the No. 78, it tells you that this person will soon return.

This card appearing in the Reverse, announces, that you regret a reckless mishap, not only for you, but for the person, whom you have compromised by your scantiness.

---

[86] Translator: The figure below represents the Roman emperor Pertinax, a former slave, who was killed by his Praetorian Guards, when he attempted to reform it. Perhaps illustrating the reverse meaning; of losses and of mistakes?

LEMARCHAND

When this tarot appears in the company of the No. 20, it tells you that fortune is capricious, that it quickly tires. It is up to you to know how to keep its favors or to take advantage of its opportunities.

In the Reverse, this card indicates errors of various kind, a perspective on the part of the querent, inconsistent with common sense.

When this tarot is close to the No. 5, it announces a marriage broken or on the verge of breaking up, either in your close family or your own; however, the cards that follow destroy this prediction when a favorable card appears right after, because, it may only be a quarrel that you should expect.

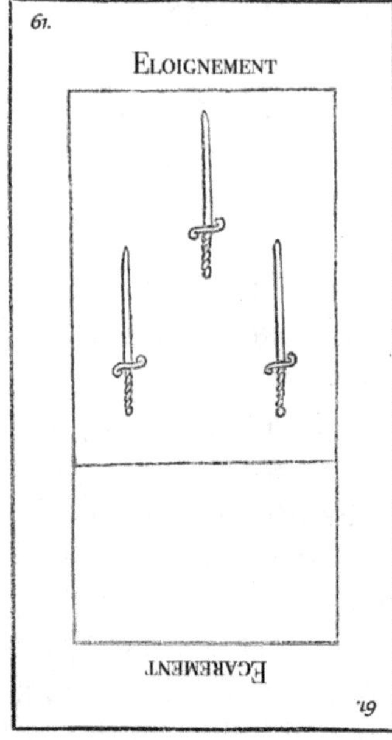

D'ODOUCET

This sixty-first card depicts three swords arranged triangularly.

Man 1 is no longer the prince of the Universe, we see him vegetate at the sphere of the globe illustrated by the 6, which he journeys to, obliged to seek from a *distance* the subsistence, that the soil he did not acquire denies him. Will he *get lost* in his pursuits? Even the generation is hostile (as the three swords express it), it is fire that sustains and protects it. We must now tear apart the bowels of the earth and defend even our children, if we want them to escape slavery.

MODERN INTERPRETATIONS

This card has by Grimaud been assigned the keywords DETACHMENT in the upright and BEWILDERMENT in the reverse.

UPRIGHT: The Three of Swords indicates heartache. You are paying for the mistakes of the past. You may have been careless, disrespectful, prideful or arrogant and now you find yourself in a painful situation. People may have disowned you, pulled away or cut contact. You will need to find a way to get into people's good graces again, however, the prospects do not look good. In business, similarly you can't seem to make things work and you may have painted yourself into a corner with colleagues, resources and finances. A time to take stock and redress.

REVERSE: In reverse, the Three of Swords represents thoughtlessness. A card of consequence, losses. You will have to face the music so to speak, the damage caused by your own irreparable acts, whether a love affair, business mistake or shady dealings, which will require much effort to set straight.

No. 62

Friendship – False[87]
Two of Sword or Spades[88]

This hieroglyph is often a very favorable sign; but the surrounding cards would need to be too.

It predicts very agreeable presents for a lady.

If this card is drawn by a person who solicits, it announces the support of a man of merit.

In the Reverse, this card warns you that you are dealing with deceit; but next to the No. 55, it announces, that the tricks played, which you must mind, will promptly be revealed to you.

When this tarot is drawn by a man of the country, it predicts a mediocre harvest; Otherwise he must draw this card in the Reverse, accompanied by one of the Nos. 19 or 56.

---

[87] False friends, useless relatives. When they are useful they are stingy to the point of not relieving us from our poverty. They are men to be shunned and to be hated, because if you fix your gaze on them, they often pretend to care about you, but behind your back, they oppose anything that could give you relief.

[88] Translator: The figure below represents the Roman emperor Constantine, who summoned the First Council of Nicaea and thus marked the definitive break of Christianity from the Judaic traditions. Perhaps illustrating this card´s reverse meaning; a symbol of betrayal and bad faith?

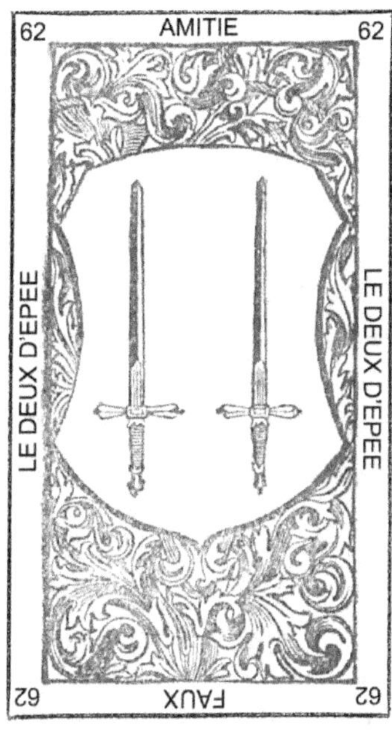

LEMARCHAND

This tarot is very often a favorable omen, but it would be necessary for the cards which surround it to be too.

If the querent is a lady or a young person, this predicts for her gracious gifts; she will receive bouquets with the rarest of flowers.

For a man, it tells him that he will get what he asks for and that he will be supported by some person of influence.

It indicates to the farmer a small harvest, but only when accompanied by unfavorable numbers, such as the 19 or 56; otherwise it would just be an insignificant card.

D'ODOUCET

This sixty-second card depicts two swords crossed.

Vegetation 2, is fortunately constant at the sphere of the presented globe of 6. Still, a few fine days can shine for its sad inhabitants. *Friendship* comes to their aid. Two chiseled swords are the symbol of the union it creates, and of the usefulness of this sweet and inestimable gift from God. The celestial friendship was conceived in the bosom of his mercy! By the same notion, this friendship is the best period of intellectual happiness, which we can have in this world, but the reverse is next; the wheels come off, and once in a bond of sincere and tender friendship, now one finds only personal interest, disguised in a thousand forms, the veil of *falsehood*; may we escape from its traps.

MODERN INTERPRETATIONS

This card has by Grimaud been assigned the keywords TENDERNESS in the upright and DECEIT in the reverse.

UPRIGHT: The Two of Swords is a card of compassion. You can expect understanding, support, kindness, harmony in your relationships. In family, a time of peace. In business, things seem easy and constructive, you will have no problems meeting your obligations. Also, a card of wellness and physical activity.

REVERSE: In reverse, a card of deceit. You may find yourself in an unstable, unfulfilling relationship, feeling neglected, perhaps discovering lies and even adultery. Friends may have let you down, you feel betrayed. In business, someone may take credit for your work, takes the spot light from you. Be careful which people you give your trust to.

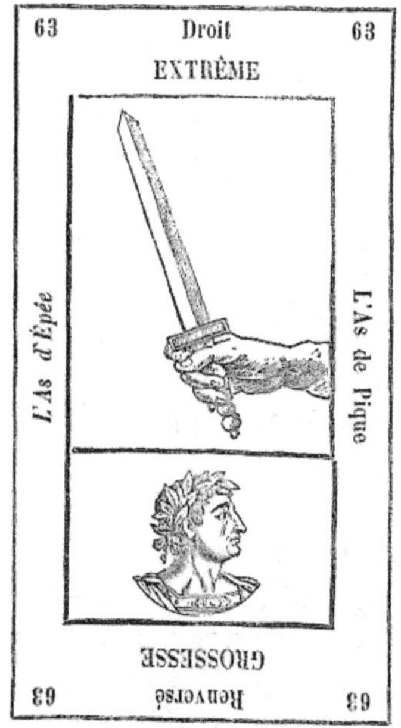

No. 63

Extreme - Pregnancy[89]
Ace of Swords or Spades

You will be surprised by a thunderstorm and lightning will strike near your property or that of a close relative; great misery is predicted for you, do take care to put something aside, or as the saying goes; keep a pear for thirst.

When the querent is in business, this card accompanied by the No. 4, predicts that if he has the misfortune of having creditors, they will be inexorable, and that they will pursue him until they have reduced him to his very end. However, if this tarot is next to the No. 47, a man of power will come to his aid and help him out of trouble.

In the Reverse and if it is for a young person that you read, this card predicts, that a marriage will not take place, because of gossip, which she with proper prudence could have avoided.

But if this card is near the No. 48 and you are reading for a lady, this tarot announces her an upcoming pregnancy.

---

[89] Translator: The figure below represents the Roman emperor Maximinus, the first "barbarian", who rose to become emperor of Rome but which ended up costing him his life. Perhaps a symbol of difficult birth?

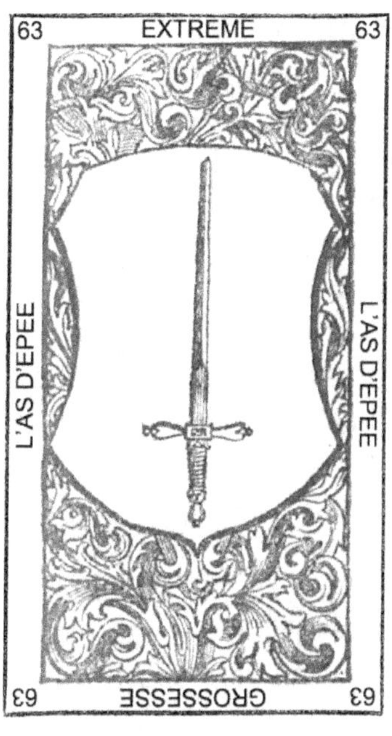

LEMARCHAND

This tarot has sometimes been assigned, from cartomancers, a very unfavorable interpret-tation; they found it to be a sinister omen for persons and for property; sometimes they also saw it as a sign of misery.

The No. 63 is undoubtedly a card of the least happy; close to the No. 4, it announces pecuniary annoyances, and next to No. 47, it indicates that you will be helped by a member of your family.

Sometimes, if this tarot is found in the company of the No. 48, and when you read for a lady, it predicts children for her.

In the Reverse, it indicates, for a young person, some trouble in the plans for a union.

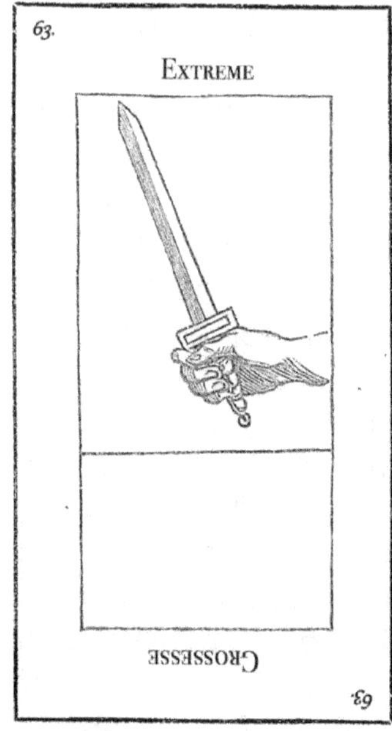

D'ODOUCET

This sixty-third card depicts a blank sword, held by one hand.

Everything has its period, even distress has a term limit; and generation 3, at the sphere of the globe illustrated by 6, is a happy omen. Up to now our misery has been *extreme*, each individual is armed for his own defense and in the defense of his subsistence. However, this can now bring about a new order of more advantageous things; a benign *fructification* is undoubtedly being prepared, bearing in mind, that the heights of misfortune bring back prosperity, as with the universal order, which never disappears, but follows the continual impulses of the wheel.

MODERN INTERPRETATIONS

This card[90] has by Grimaud been assigned the keywords EXCESS in the upright and PREGNANCY in the reverse.

UPRIGHT: The Ace of Swords indicates extremes. In relationships, there may be possessiveness, domination, anger turning to violence and so on. In business, your goals may be unrealistic, what is promised is not kept, a time of conflict and litigation.

REVERSE: In the reverse, a card of rewards. You are reaping the fruits of your efforts, in relationships and at work. This card predicts pregnancy too.

---

[90] Translator: d´Odoucet assigns the meanings *Fructification* or Fruit Produce in the upright and in the reverse; *Extreme*.

No. 64

Brown-haired man - Vicious man
King of Coins or of Clover

If this card is next to Nos. 59 and 62, a black or brown-haired man, that you trust, will deceive you, as well as accuse one of your friends.

If the querent is married, either a man or a woman, he or she should be on their guard, they must fear everything from a person who makes them look good, unless this tarot is preceded or followed by the No. 57 in the Reverse, because, then it will be a person watching out for them.

When this card is drawn by a sailor and when it is next to the No. 24, it predicts, that he soon will be on a long journey.

In the Reverse and accompanied by the No. 58, this card is a bad omen; you will be on a short trip and you will take the wrong path, you will ask a man for directions, he will point out to you the opposite direction, and you will have to take a detour before you can return to your home.

LEMARCHAND

This tarot presents a shady figure or character, who seeks to harm you and your fortune, but his evil designs will quickly be thwarted.

If the querent is a married woman or man, this tarot would be an indication of a household quarrel; but in the company of a favorable card, it predicts that a person, who has sought to be your friend, will succeed with a relentless try in re-establishing the peace in your home.

When this card is drawn by a sailor, it predicts a long journey, where he will experience bad weather, but it will non-the-less be very profitable.

Accompanied by the No. 58, this is a warning, that you on a small trip will experience an unimportant accident.

D'ODOUCET

This sixty-fourth card represents a man of commerce, seated, crowned, dressed in blue, holding in his hand a talisman or a coin.

We finally experience this new aspect, perhaps only as an alleviation. The universe 4 (morally speaking), closes in on the sphere of the globe presented by 6; the production of the aspect furthest opposite will circulate; meaning, from one pole to the other, resulting in a well-being. Soon the country, in the hands of the those most favored by the influences of heaven, will return the lands, to the less privileged, the produce of which, they will have lacked. But what will this movement bring about? Man, alone is capable of this. It is true that he will not do this from a spirit of humanity, of fraternity, his motives are in some respects *vicious*, because of personal interest, his selfishness will make him try to reap a profit, either from his pains, or from his superfluousness[91], both he will supply us. Such is the origin of commerce, which can be pure in form, but the motives remain the same. These are no longer purely moral speculations; the symbolism must square with the object illustrated, the mercantile combinations are thus attributed to *the brown man*, and the coins become his tool.

---

[91] Translator: The *superfluous man* is a 19th century concept (particularly in the 1840s and 1850s). A man of wealth and privilege, who uses his powers for his own comfort and security, and will have very little interest in being charitable or to use it for the greater good.

MODERN INTERPRETATIONS

This card[92] has by Grimaud been assigned the keywords; BUSINESSMAN in the upright and VICIOUS in the reverse.

UPRIGHT: The King of Coins represents a man of influence. He enjoys a high position in society, a man of money. He is competent, successful and has good social skills, is friendly, helpful and pleasant. He is man of science, perhaps a banker, a doctor, or a businessman. He can be counted on, if you need help.

REVERSE: In the reverse, the card represents a corrupt man. He may have the same resources as the King in upright, but he is a bad influence. He is manipulative, perverse, corrupt and will lead you astray, perhaps with a bribe. It is better to stay clear of him.

---

[92] Translator: d´Odoucet assigns the meaning *Vice* in the reverse.

No. 65

Brown-haired Woman – Uncertainty
Queen of Coins or Clover

A relative from the country, rich and generous, will send you presents.

If you are reading for a young man and this card comes first, it is a very favorable oracle, it predicts that he will marry a young brunette, who will bring him much good.

If this card is preceded by the No. 69 in the Reverse, it is a woman mincing, playing you; but if this No. 69 is followed by the No. 45, it announces that you will obtain a donation from one of your distant relatives.

In the Reverse, this card announces an upcoming illness, but it will not last long.

If this tarot is followed or preceded by No. 21, it announces an unpleasant encounter, but with the No. 18, this card is quite the opposite.

LEMARCHAND

The meaning of this card bodes well; it announces lavish gifts to you from an opulent relative, who lives in the countryside.

If the querent is a young man, and this tarot comes first, it tells him that his marriage will take place soon and that the person he will marry will be a very rich young brunette.

After the No. 69, it predicts difficulties; followed by No. 45, a donation from a distant relative.

In the Reverse, this tarot announces a small indisposition, but which will be of short duration.

Accompanied by the No. 21, it implies dueling, this will create much noise, however, it will only cause a fright to the combatants.

D'ODOUCET

This sixty-fifth card represents a seated woman, crowned, dressed in blue, and holding in her hand a talisman or a coin.

Everything is reborn in the attractive sphere of the globe represented by 6, doubly animated by the presence of the universal spirit of 5, the indefinite principle of all reproduction. The balance of trade, the respective exchanges are indicated by a *woman*. She is a brunette because of her field, and carries the caption below; *onto bad*, because indeed on a thousand occasions, the operations in commerce are *risky*; it is at least advantageous to be warned.

MODERN INTERPRETATIONS

This card has by Grimaud been assigned the keywords; RICH WOMAN in the upright and INDECISION in the reverse.

UPRIGHT: The Queen of Coins represents the independent woman. She enjoys good social status, is affluent and manages her own affairs, perhaps a professional. A confident and resourceful person, who may assist you.

REVERSE: In the reverse, this card represents an insecure person. A woman with little confidence in her own abilities, does not know what she wants, makes poor choices and is in the end not a good influence on you.

No. 66

Utility - Inaction
Knight of Coins

This card predicts a few things for you, it announces useful discoveries for your country; friends will ask you for services, that you will refuse without giving cause.

If you are reading for a lady, this card tells her, if followed by the No. 71 and next to No. 74, that her husband will give her some useful gift, which she will be unhappy with at first, but later will grow fond of.

In the Reverse, this card signifies idleness, laziness recklessness.

If you are reading for a soldier, this card appearing in the Reverse, is a sign of peace; near the No. 32 in Reverse, it promises him a rank he will only obtain from favor.

When the querent is an attractive young lady, it urges, when this card is accompanied by the No. 33, to watch herself. This precaution is all the more useful to her future happiness, as without it, the lightness of her character, would make her fall into a trap from which she would never escape.

LEMARCHAND

This card is almost insignificant in any particular reading; it announces discoveries useful to industry; sometimes it predicts, that you will be asked for money, but that you will refuse, despite the trust, the person asking for your benevolence deserves.

In the Reverse, it indicates good opportunities, that you will miss however; it signifies carelessness, idleness and laziness.

When the querent is a soldier, it is the augury of a near peace; near No. 32, it announces, achievements that he will receive as a favor.

For a young person, it is advisable not to behave lightly, because he would experience unexpected annoyances.

D'ODOUCET

This sixty-sixth card presents a young man, on horseback, dressed in blue, holding in his hand a talisman or a coin.

The presented double figure of the globe indicates to us a lavishness in useful *goods*. Up to this moment commerce has only had the object of primary needs. This lavishness leads to *inaction*. O man! Will you always be like the savage who, when he has dinner, throws away what remains by *anticipating* the supplies of the evening! Such is the warning given to us by the caption below on this card.

MODERN INTERPRETATIONS

This card has by Grimaud been assigned the keywords; PROFITS in the upright and INACTIVITY in the reverse.

UPRIGHT: The Knight of Coins represents profits. A card of successful investments, earnings, loans and transactions. Your financial operations will be good. This card can also represent a male friend offering his help.

REVERSE: In the reverse, this car represents carelessness. This is not a time to slack off, to be lazy. You will not be successful, if you do not put in the effort. This card could also indicate an end to a friendship.

No. 67

Brown-Haired Boy - Prodigality
Page of Coins or Clover

This card appearing first, if drawn by a lady, tells her that a strong amiable man will pay her much attention. Next to the No. 34, this card tells her, on the other hand, that she will not be noticed by a gentleman for whom she seems to have more than respect.

If this card appears in connection with a married man, next to the No. 73, it tells him, that there are others as well who find the Madame´s eyes beautiful, but that this is harmless, for she is a tower of virtue.

If, instead of No. 73, the No. 67 is found next to the No. 64 in the Reverse, his wife will have to sustain severe advances, she will have to defend herself against a dark-haired man who has been eyeing her for a long time.

This card in the Reverse, implies luxury, benefit, dissipation and prodigality. To find out what it is, you have to consult the following card.

Near the No. 45, it tells you that you will soon overspend the proceeds of an inheritance, that will come to you from a distant relative, or that after earning a large sum of money, you will not make suitable use of.

When the querent is a gentleman in a high position, and when this card is followed by the No. 59, it is almost certain that he will compromise his assets by some extravagance.

LEMARCHAND

When this card is the first to arrive and we read for a lady, it announces, that a very amiable gentleman will take great care of her; near the No. 34, it means the complete opposite.

In the Reverse, this card signifies dissipation and prodigality; the tarot that follows completes this prediction.

When the No. 45 follows, or precedes this tarot, it indicates that you must take care of your fortune and manage your expenses better; it also says that you will promptly dispel the inheritance you are expecting, or that you will waste money easily earned.

When the querent occupies a high position, it tells him that his extravagance does him more harm than honor.

D'ODOUCET

This sixty-seventh card represents a young man standing, dressed in blue, and holding in his hand a talisman or a coin.

The symbol of life 7 comes in to increase the advantageous existence of the globe presented in 6; that is to say, that everything abounds there with the help of commerce. A *brown-haired boy*, equipped with his mercantile attribute, presents us with the evidence of this; but the all too common fruit of lavishness is misplaced *prodigality*; let us therefore avoid it, if we are worthy of appreciating the lessons inscribed in the profound book of Thot.

MODERN INTERPRETATIONS

This card has by Grimaud been assigned the keywords; STUDIOUS BOY in the upright and PRODIGALITY

UPRIGHT: The Page of Coins represents a student. This is a young man, with a willingness to learn and a willingness to put in the hard work, whether in school or at work. If he is working for you, he will not give you a reason to complain. Generally, a good and serious young man.

REVERSE: In the reverse, this card indicates recklessness. This person may be talented, but does not spend his time sensibly. He overspends, does not put in the effort, fails in what he does. If this is you, you need to change your act, otherwise misfortune is ahead.

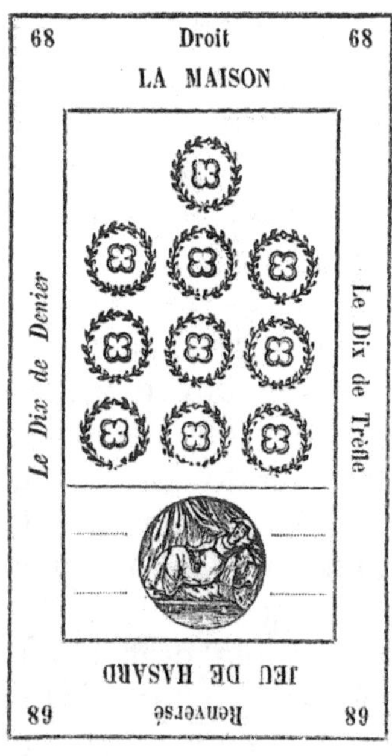

No. 68

The House - Game of chance[93]
Ten of Coins or Clover

This card represents the house, by itself, it has no value; to explain its presence, one must focus on the cards which precede or follow it.

If this card, for example, is accompanied by the No. 31, in the Upright, then it makes it known, the presence of a treasure in the house.

If this card appears in the Reverse followed by the No. 49, it predicts you a win at a game, that will take place at a friend's house on a gastronomic occasion.

When this card is in the Reverse and found next to the No. 21, it announces a great receiving of money.

Next to the No. 47, it warns you that somebody who has owed you for a long time, and who you pursue, will end up paying you, if not voluntarily then by force.

---

[93] Translator: The figures below on the coin cards have been inserted by Blocquel. A card of fortune in the Reverse, no wonder this lady below is relaxing on her couch!

LEMARCHAND

This card has, by itself, only a very weak significance; it means home; it is therefore useful to correctly interpret this card by that which follows or precedes.

When this card is accompanied by the No. 31 in the Upright, it predicts the presence of a treasure in the house.

After the No. 21, it tells you that you will receive money, that you probably did not expect.

Along with the No. 47, it announces to you, that you will shortly receive the sum, that you claim from a person, who was not very eager to pay you back.

Near the No. 49, it announces a celebration in your house, be it a baptism, a wedding or an engagement.

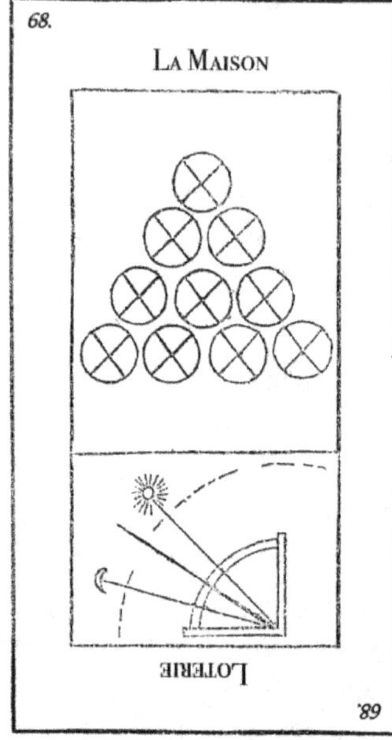

D'ODOUCET

⊗This 68th card depicts ten talismans or coins arranged in a pyramid. In the card below, the fortune game of astrologers, is represented by a circle with the moon in conjunction or new moon.

The circulation of generations 8, brought closer to the globe presented by 6, is a new symbol of the continual circulation of exchanges of all kinds, and of the advantages, which result from them, for the seller and for the buyer. The progression of the species is above all complete, as indicated by the perfection of the number 10, to which it amounts. Their possessions provide what is commonly called a *good house*, however the means that provide it are not very certain. The opposite is next to success, it is a real *lottery*. Happy is the one who bets, who wins and who does not risk anything more! The study of a particular science is essential for the trader; this is partly why this card depicts instruments, specific to common calculation and to astronomy, both absolutely necessary in important and long lasting operations.

MODERN INTERPRETATIONS

This card has by Grimaud been assigned the keywords; HOME in the upright and GAME OF CHANCE in the reverse.

UPRIGHT: The Ten of Coins is a good card. You may find yourself prioritizing home and family. A card of home, joy, and harmonious relationships. In business, a card of steady progress, investing for the long run.

REVERSE: In reverse, this is a very good card. If you are looking for a partner this card predicts a great love. If you are in a relationship, a reigniting. In business, the success of a project, a recognition, a general contentment. If you have made financial investments or gambled, this predict huge gains, which may have a generational impact. Generally, you can expect good fortune with this card in reverse.

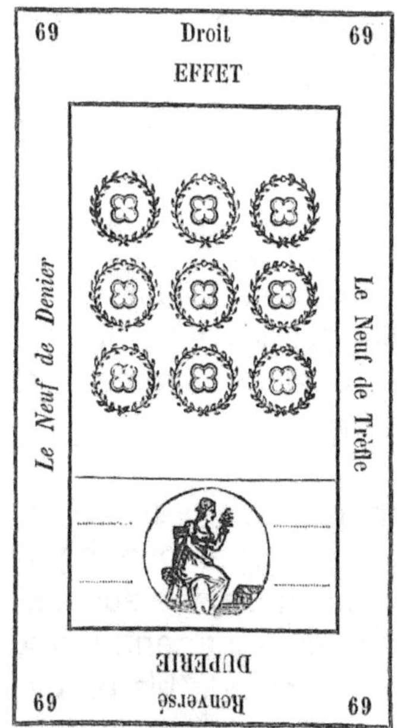

No. 69

Effect - Deception[94]
Nine of Coins or Clover

When this card is found near a significant card, it ensures its prompt effect.

Appearing with the No. 33 and the No. 59, this card announces to you that you are threatened by a most skillful trickery, however this will not impact your fortune, this is just a little trick of some charlatan, which you will shake off at little cost.

In the Reverse, it bears a similar meaning, but if this tarot is found next to more favorable cards, then it is only predicting a bad joke.

With the No. 71, also in the Reverse, it predicts that a person to whom you have loaned a large sum will leave you with great concern about their good intentions.

---

[94] Translator: A card of lure and cunning in reverse, perhaps the figure below encapsulates this in her scrutiny of that flower?

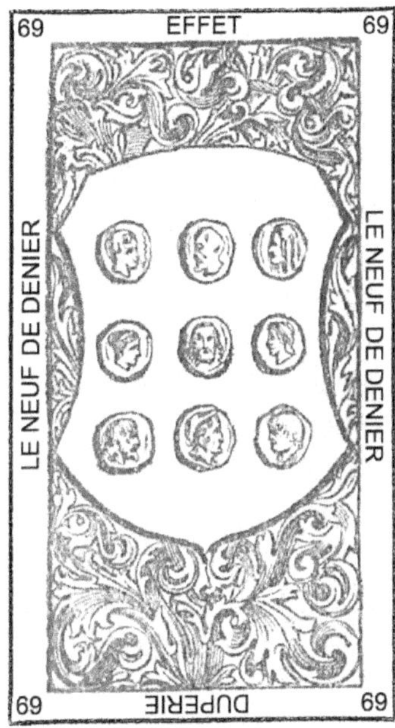

LEMARCHAND

If this tarot is presented in the Upright and close to a card that can be explained without reservation, it would confirm the interpretation.

In the Reverse and near a favorable card, it tells you that you will be fooled by a bad joke.

After the No. 71, it warns you that a person to whom you have lent money is not of good faith, and that you will regret your gullibility; but if the No. 20 accompanies it, there is reason to believe, that you will not lose anything.

It also indicates traps, when the number that precedes it is card 78, making you commit some unreasonable action.

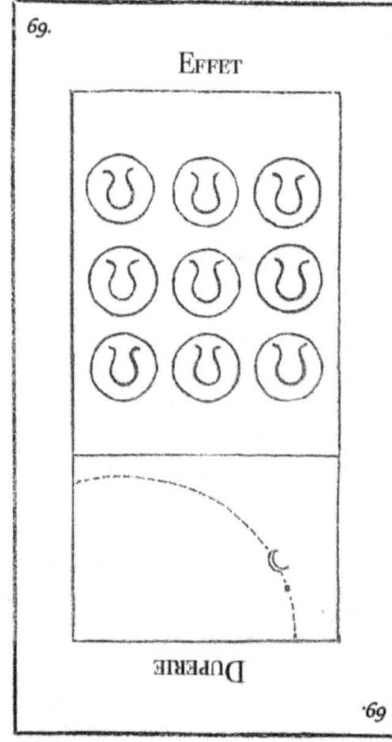

D'ODOUCET

℧This sixty-ninth card depicts 9 talismans or coins arranged in threes. In the card below, the astrologers´ tail of the dragon is presented, or the moon´s descending node.[95]

The globe doubles in its relation to insertion and effusion, indicating to us that from all points of view, the mercantile genie seeks to profit from all production. The number 9 of the coins expresses, that the banker more than anything else, puts to good use its respective value. Nothing is lost, nothing is without effect, all means become good; but often we are outfoxed, too bad for the ones, who let themselves be fooled. Let us notice the bottom of this card, the globe is under the weak light of the new moon; meaning, we are trying to hide the secrets of some lucrative combinations, of that which is done behind the counter.

---

[95] Translator: The South Node.

MODERN INTERPRETATIONS

This card has by Grimaud been assigned the keywords; FULFILLMENT in the upright and DECEPTION in the reverse.

UPRIGHT: The Nine of Coins is a card of rewards. In relationships, a feeling of serenity and happiness, you are heading in the right direction, building for the future. In business, a break-through, your efforts are rewarded. This is also a time where you have that extra energy, so you may start something on the side or pick up a hobby.

REVERSE: In the reverse, this card is unpleasant. There may be people around you, who are taking advantage of you, abusing your trust. You are urged to be careful, not to engage in anything, that does not feel right. A risk of fraud and the loss of money exists.

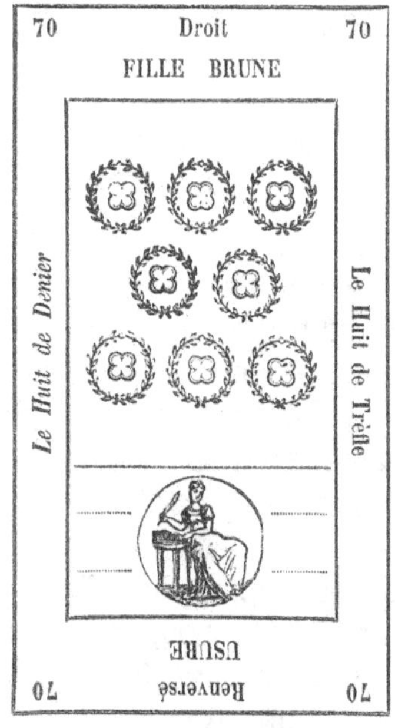

No. 70

Brunette Girl - Usury[96]
Eight of Coins or Clover

This card indicates a brunette girl when in the Upright and she receives her qualifications from the cards that accompany it. In this way, this girl is noble with No. 75; crazy next to the No. 78; bad with the No. 18, etc.

If the reading is for an unattached person, and this card appears followed by the No. 73, it foreshadows success with a dark-haired woman, from whom one wishes to obtain friendship.

If the querent is a man or a married woman, it should be noted that accompanied by the No. 41 in the Reverse, it announces that this querent can have complete confidence in the person that this No. 70 represents. When it is the No. 21 in the Upright, she must expect a quarrel, where she will display more bitterness than sweetness.

When this card appears in the Reverse, it predicts, that one will be an accomplice, guilty of or a victim of usurious action. One will be guilty if the card which precedes is that of the querent, the No. 1 or the No. 8, according to whether the querent is a man or a woman. He will be an accomplice, if it is the No. 7; he will be a victim, if it is one of the Nos. 14, 54 or 59 that accompany it.

---

[96] Translator: A card of usury and avarice in Reverse, perhaps the figure below is trying to come up with the next scheme in her letter?

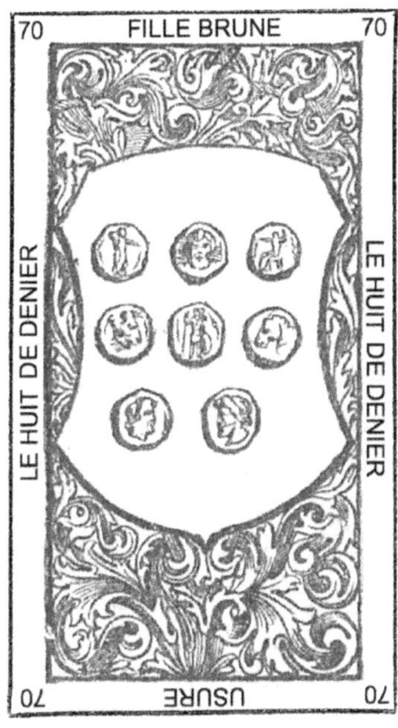

LEMARCHAND

When this card is presented in the Upright, it implies beauty; but it receives its true interpretation from the cards that accompany it.

Close to the No. 18, it warns you that a wicked woman is contemplating harming you; near the No. 75, it is dubious, because the person, who wants to interfere in your affairs has no bad intentions.

If the querent is unattached, and this card is followed by the No. 73, it announces different types of success.

When this card appears in the Reverse, it predicts to the querent that he will be the victim of a misstep in the perception he has in people, believing them to be in good faith, they however are not, they are abusing his trust.

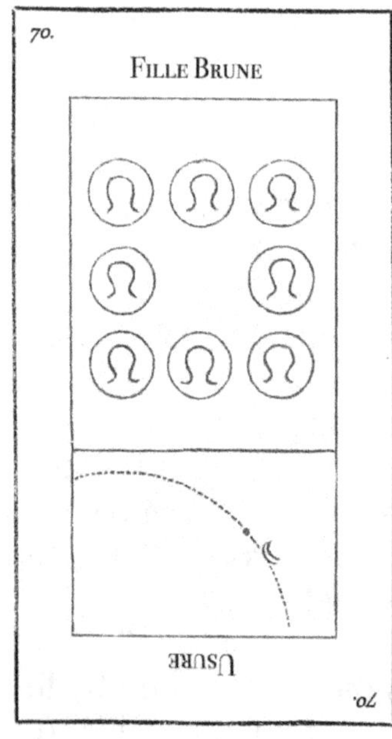

D'ODOUCET

Ω This seventieth card[97] depicts 8 talismans or coins. On the card below, the astrologers´ head of the dragon, is presented, or the moon´s ascending node.[98]

In the end the globe is exhausted by the extent of consumption; which is indicated in the 0 deprived of the symbol of insertion, and which seeks a new life, to become once more prolific. It recovers indeed its fertility (expressed by the attribute of the brunette girl) with the aid of the active industry of the speculator, his appetite of gains, invent new circulations, which bring back *more abundance*, than before. These circulations are indicated by the 8 of Coins. We also see on the bottom of this card, that the world becomes more enlightened and is avoiding the dark maneuvers, which encourage fraud.

---

[97] Translator: d´Odoucet assigns the meaning *Plus* or more in the reverse.

[98] Translator: The North Node.

MODERN INTERPRETATIONS

This card has by Grimaud been assigned the keywords; PLEASANT GIRL in the upright and AVERICE in the reverse.

UPRIGHT: The Eight of Coins represents a female entering your life. A young brunette perhaps, someone who will bring you satisfaction, the missing part, someone who adds the spice in your life. If not a partner, then someone you may offer guidance or support to, a co-worker or a student.

REVERSE: In reverse, it is a card of dissatisfaction. In relationships, you are never satisfied, expecting more from others, than what you bring to the table. This card urges you to make concessions, generosity and to show more consideration. In business, you may be too ambitious, prideful and arrogant, rest assure that such behavior is rarely ever rewarded. This can also represent another person with such qualities.

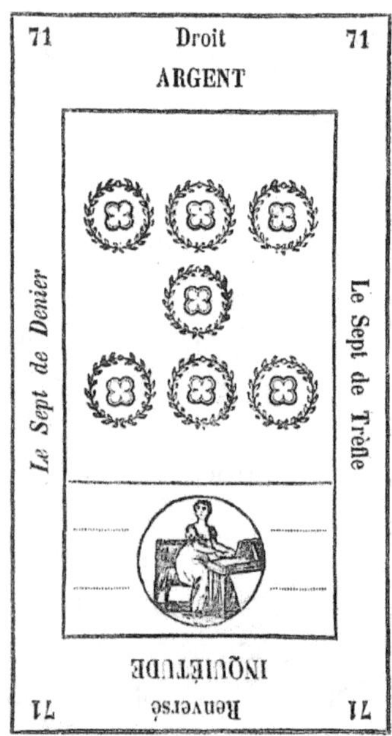

No. 71

Money - Worry[99]
Seven of Coins or Clover

When this card appears first and with the No. 18 or the No. 76, it warns you, that you will be financially victimized by someone who is abusing your trust.

If this card is accompanied by one of the Nos. 20, 31 or 45, then it predicts, that an unexpected sum, gain or inheritance, will come to restore the situation of your affairs, or to add to its satisfactory state.

If the spread is for a young person, first, it tells her that the man, who courts her is not strong financially; second, that she has nothing to fear from her lover's fortune; because even if he does not have it yet, he soon will have a considerable sum, because of the social position he occupies in society.

If this tarot is in the Reverse, it urges you not to worry about the money, that will be asked of you and that you should have faith, especially, if it appears next to the No. 42, also in the Reverse.

When it is next to the No. 45, it tells you the opposite.

In the Reverse, near the No. 78, this card tells you, that you have long been tormented by all kinds of unfounded speculations.

---

[99] Translator: A card of worry and concern in Reverse, perhaps the figure below is trying to distract herself with playing?

When the No. 71 in Reverse is preceded, or followed by cards that do not change its meaning, it announces hassle, instigated by the urge to spend money.

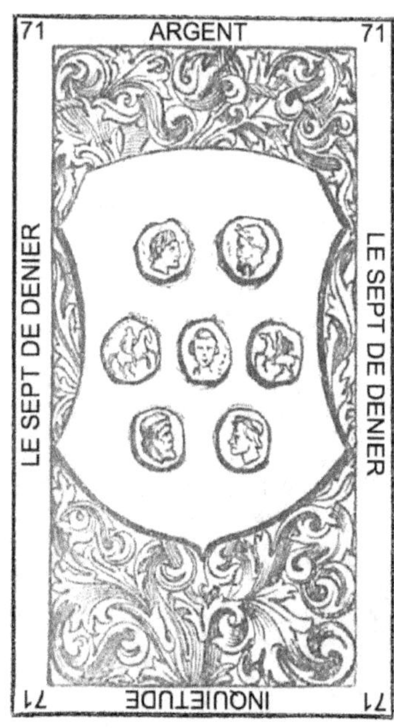

LEMARCHAND

This card warns you to act with caution and only to confide in people who deserve it.

Accompanied by the Nos. 20, 31 or 45, it indicates to you a sum of money, a small inheritance, an unspecified gain, which will go well in re-establishing your financial position.

When reading the cards for a young lady, this tarot tells her that her future has more qualities to offer than riches.

In the Reverse, it tells you; that you will shortly lend out some money, and that you can put your trust in the one who asks you for help.

After the No. 45, it implies the opposite.

Near the No. 78, this card tells you that the worries you are tormented by are unfounded.

When the No. 71, in the Reverse, is found before or followed by the No. 9, it is very auspicious, since it modifies the potentially bad predictions of the neighboring cards.

D'ODOUCET

This seventy-first card depicts seven talismans or coins. In the lower part of the card Saturn is presented in cast ash grey, holding a scythe.

It is not easy to attain fortunes; before getting there, we are often the victim of dark *worries*, stinging concerns; especially since money can only be earned through the slow hand of time; during which time a thousand inconveniences can cause businesses to fail. The two numbers symbolize loneliness. It is man 1, who chases after life 7, whose loss he fears, but this life is not purely animal, it is, according to the spirit of this card, the lavishness expressed by the 7 of Coins.

MODERN INTERPRETATIONS

This card has by Grimaud been assigned the keywords; MONEY in the upright and ANXIETY in the reverse.

UPRIGHT: The Seven of Coins is a card of finances. You may be experiencing financial troubles or you may be very concerned about money. You may even tie money in with self-worth causing ripples in your relationships. In business, it implies someone wishing to make money and opportunities will appear to make money. A card of money coming in, but also a card of caution.

REVERSE: In reverse a card of concern. Things do not seem to work out for you. Your love life may have taken a turn for the worse. Firmness and dialogue may be needed. In business, there may be rumors and a bad climate in general. You are advised to stay focused and not engage in frivolous rumors. Your finances may need a sharper look, you may have a problem with spending.

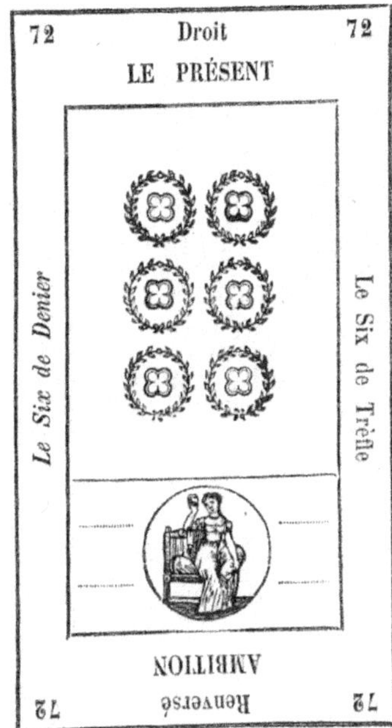

No. 72

The Present - Ambition[100]
Six of Coins or Clover

This card tells you that in the world, in the present, nothing is stable, it announces to you, a fortune, which you will not enjoy, since the thirst for gold absorbs all your thoughts.

If next to the No. 76, it warns you that you are about to find yourself in great embarrassment from which you will escape quickly, however.

A young lady who is the querent and sees the No. 8 preceding this card, and the No. 12 following it and subsequently the No. 20, will find herself in a very advantageous position, because it indicates that the care she has put in her actions has persuaded a man of great fortune to take charge of her situation. This man will work from his own account, if the No. 67 is found in the row of cards; he will work on behalf of others, if the No. 7 is in the row.

In the Reverse, this card announces lack of success in an ambitious project, that preoccupies you to a fault.

Next to the No. 25, it predicts a letter you have been waiting on for a long time, and which will disrupt the beautiful dreams, you hope to see come true.

Next to the number 65, it tells you that your passion is in vain, since the person who is the object of it does not share it, but have patience!

---

[100] Translator: A card of jealousy and illusion in the Reverse, perhaps the figure below finally took off her mask?

LEMARCHAND

This card is the sign of the instability of things around us; it announces a fortune, which the querent will not be able to enjoy because of his ambition.

Close to the No. 76, it predicts inconveniences of all kinds; but this prediction is greatly modified when the No. 33 in the Reverse is found in the same row.

If you are reading the cards for a young person, and the Nos. 20 and 12 precede or follow this card, it tells her, that the protection of a great lady will help her realize a brilliant union.

Close to the No. 25, you will receive a long-awaited letter, which will come to fix the uncertainty you find yourself in.

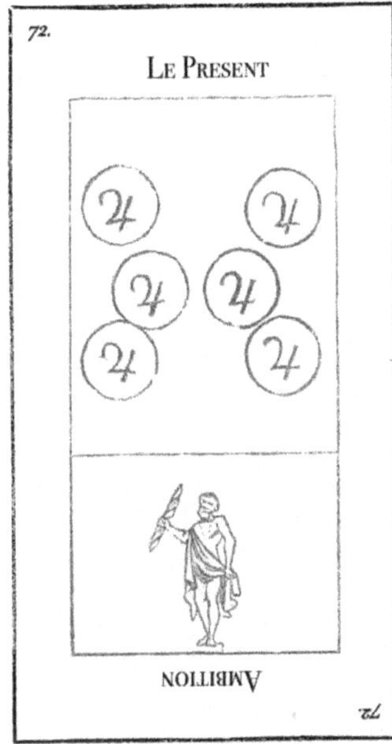

D'ODOUCET

This seventy-second card depicts six talismans or coins. On the card below Jupiter is presented, in the color blue, holding a thunderbolt.

The symbol of vegetation, joined with the symbol of life, indicates the *present time*, which may well be considered as the father of *ambition*; but of what nature is it? The talismanic pieces indicate this to us, their number is *ad hoc*; it is offered to us in 6, the animating spirit, dominating the globe. Power is born from wealth; if man acquires the slightest superiority, he will aspire to the monarchy of the universe.

MODERN INTERPRETATIONS

This card has by Grimaud been assigned the keywords; SURROUNDINGS in the upright and AMBITION in the reverse.

UPRIGHT: The Six of Coins is a card of your situation. This is about the things you are going through right now, whether good or bad, your priorities, where you are heading, as indicated by the neighboring cards. You may be way too preoccupied with the future, concentrate on the now, let what comes come.

REVERSE: In the reverse, a card of ambition. You may try to have it all right away, in a relationship you may consider letting things develop naturally or else you may scare away that suiter. In business, you have set very high goals for yourself, and you may be putting in a lot of work. Again, Rome was not built in a day, take a step back, stay grounded.

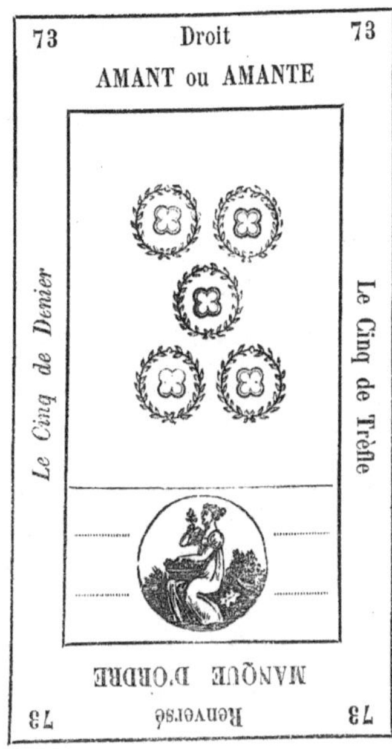

No. 73

Lover - Disorder[101]
Five of Coins or Clover

The inequality between fortunes will cause you to lose a marriage, that you desire, if this card appears with the No. 34.

If you are married, then this card tells you that it will be to someone in your family that this inconvenience will happen; but next to the No. 13, it indicates that this marriage will take place, and if the No. 20 follows, that it will be very fortunate.

In the Reverse, this card announces that the disproportional mess between your savings and your spending will inevitably lead you to great inconvenience. But soon serious protectors will help you improve your compromised finances.

You must fear the coldness and infidelity of the person to whom you have given your heart, unless the No. 62 is nearby, implying having recourse to the friendship of one of your relatives, who will agree to come and help you in this painful situation.

---

[101] Translator: A card of disorder and disharmony in reverse, perhaps the figure below is recognizing her basket of flowers is not as orderly as it should be?

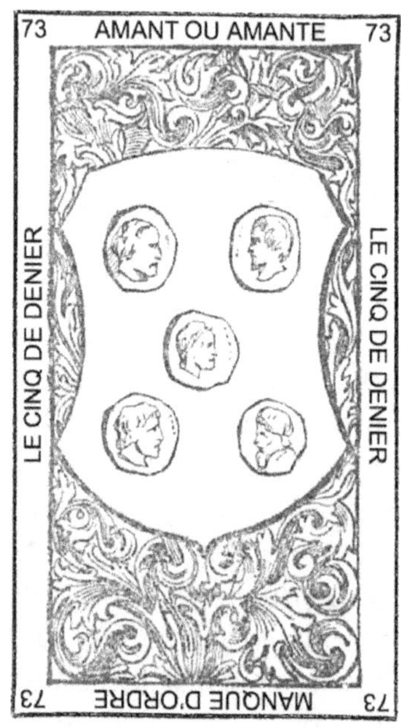

LEMARCHAND

For a man who has marriage on the agenda, this card[102] announces to him the uncertainty on the part of the young lady, because of the disproportional size in fortunes between the two families.

If you are reading for a married person, it is a card for someone in her family; next to the No. 13, it indicates that everything will be fine, and followed by the No. 20, it is the notification of an unexpected success.

After the No. 12, it urges the querent not to let himself be carried away by his passions.

In the Reverse, this card indicates annoying disruptions; preceding or following the No. 62, it makes you hope for precautions which will put you in a position to ward off all the bad situations, which you have to deal with, a result of your excessive spending.

---

[102] Translator: The Lemarchand booklet assigns the meanings *Futur* or Future and *Desordre* or Disorder on this card in the upright and reverse, rather than *Amant ou Amante* and *Manque d´Ordre* or Lack of order.

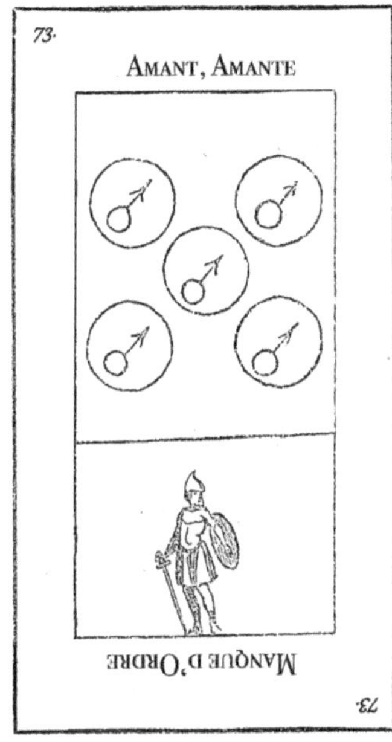

D'ODOUCET

This seventy-third card depicts five talismans or coins. In the card below Mars is presented, in the color red, holding a sword and a shield.

3 and 7; word for word; the *lover* of life 7 is characteristic of generation 3. The number of coins also symbolizes the principle of existence 5. This thus expresses, that money circulates abundantly, favoring *the passions*. This ardor leads however only too often to faulty conduct, *lack of order*, which the wise must nevertheless know how to avoid.

MODERN INTERPRETATIONS

This card has by Grimaud been assigned the keywords; LOVER in the upright and MISCONDUCT in the reverse.

UPRIGHT: The Five of Coins represents a partner. This is the positive influence of partner in a relationship, a husband, a wife or similar. A card of protection, kindness, satisfaction and good advice.

REVERSE: Reversed, this card represents turbulence. You may find yourself in an unsuitable relationship, which affects you and others around you adversely. You may not know what you want, and experience difficulty moving forward. In business, you may not be making sound decisions, making mistakes, a lack of heart or interest. Perhaps you should find a path better suited for you.

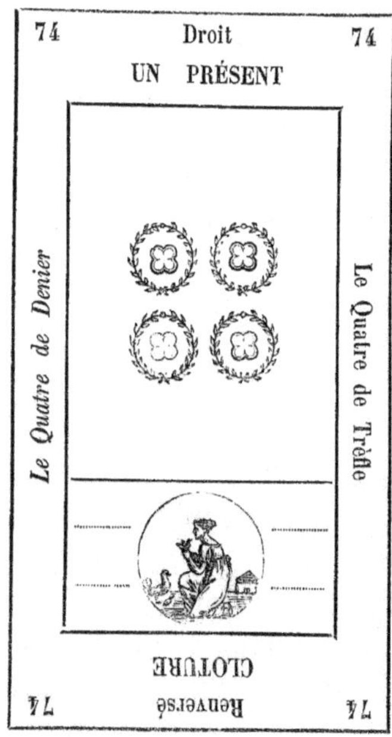

No. 74

A Gift - Enclosure[103]
Four of Coins or Clover

If this card is found with the No. 61, friends or relatives you have in distant countries will send you very nice presents.

If this card is found near the No. 40, it announces for a lady, that a friend, who lives in the nearest town will send you, a gift, which will flatter you. If you are a man and it appears next to the No. 66, it predicts that you will receive news, something very useful has been granted to you.

If you are reading for a bachelor, this card predicts, that a lady will say very kind things to him in an upcoming meeting.

With the No. 36, this card invites you to offer a gift to an influential man, from who you want support.

In the Reverse it means barriers, opposition and obstacles, it should be noted that an affair is not lost, just because of people bickering. An advice to the reader.

---

[103] Translator: A card of enclosure and incarceration in reverse, perhaps the figure below is trying to set that bird free?

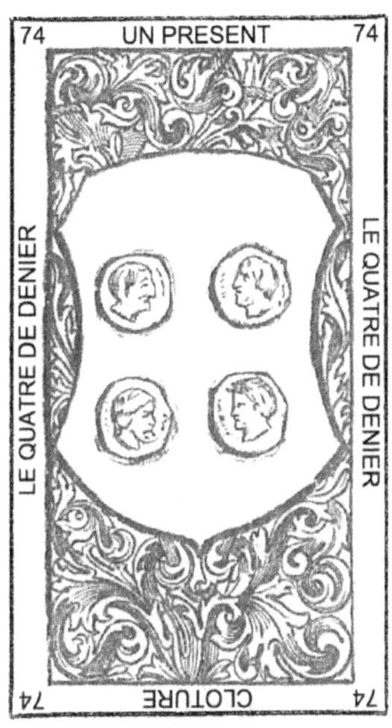

LEMARCHAND

Here is a card[104] of good omen; relatives who live in America will send you lavish presents.

Near the No. 40, when the querent is a woman, this card tells her that she will receive a very gracious gift from a friend.

If you read the cards for an unattached person, this card tells him that the marriage in question will not be successful, he will need to find someone else more suitable with his position.

After the No. 36, you have been warned that you will only get the job you want with gifts, if not at least with something of value to indicate your gratitude.

In the Reverse, this card indicates a certain opposition to your success, but you have to persevere in your affairs. For a soldier, this means enemies defeated.

---

[104] Translator: The Lemarchand booklet assigns the meaning *Don* or Donation for this card in the upright, rather than *Un Present*, a Gift.

D'ODOUCET

This seventy-fourth card depicts four talismans or coins. On the card below is presented Diana, in the color white, holding a torch.

The universe, under the auspices of life, acquires from it the faculty of *dispensing* to us the most precious influences; it incites us to *rest*, which is the fruit of opulence. This is indicated by the perfection of the 4 of Coins, whose cubic structure seems to refuse any movement. This inaction is a real *fence,* in which is circumscribed; to have prudence, to be satisfied with one´s fate.

MODERN INTERPRETATIONS

Grimaud assigns the keywords; PRESENT in the upright and OBSTRUCTION in the reverse.[105]

UPRIGHT: The Four of Coins is a card of opportunity. In business, an improvement in your status, an expansion of customers or finances or other opportunities. Your relationships may be validated by gifts, which will please you. REVERSE: This card in reverse is a card of inconvenience. You may have created a very constraint situation for yourself. You may be experiencing delays, setbacks, where you will need to make some concessions to get out from them. In business, an inopportune time, you may find it very difficult to get a promotion or even change jobs.

---

[105] Translator: d´Odoucet assigns the meaning *Bien Fait* in the upright. Diana is the Roman goddess of hunting. In this card for the meaning in reverse, we can imagine someone returning from a hunt, enjoying the spoils of the hunt or needing to accept it.

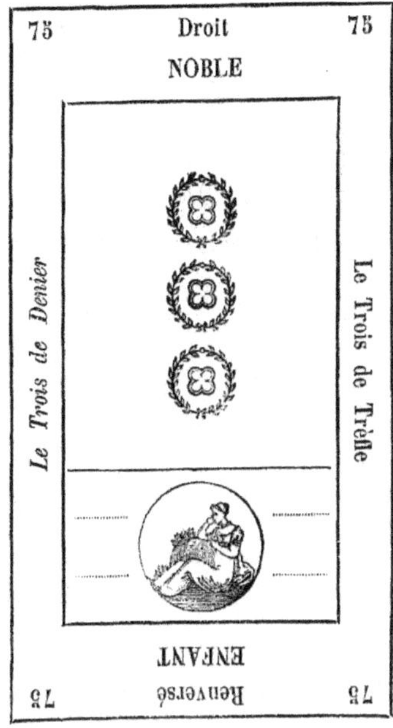

No. 75

Noble - Child[106]
Three of Coins or Clover

When this card appears near the No. 25, it announces to a man that a distinguished stranger is looking after his happiness, especially if it is followed by the No. 68. To a lady, it predicts, if appearing accompanied by the No. 35, that a fall will be the cause of her fortune, which will be secured by a person of nobility. If he is a soldier, and card 75 is followed by the No. 47, then shortly an honorary title is awaiting him.

When this card is in the Reverse and the cards are read for a young lady, you have to pay attention to the neighboring cards; if the No. 63 is there, she will be in grief; if the No. 7, she will be protected.

When the reading is made for a man and if this card is next to the No. 32 in Reverse, it predicts to the querent that his first child born will be very happy, but if the No. 34 accompanies it, it tells him, that his child will one day be a famous man.

---

[106] Translator: A card of weakness and humility in reverse, perhaps this is the reason the figure below needs a rest next to that boulder?

LEMARCHAND

When this card[107] appears in the company of the No. 29; it tells you that a foreign man, with a high social standing, will do a lot for you. It foreshadows money embarrassments, if the No. 35 appears immediately after.

After the No. 47, when the querent is a soldier, this card tells him that he will get some decorations as a result of a brilliant performance.

For a young person, and next to the No. 7, it announces beautiful protections for him.

In the Reverse, this card takes on the meaning only by that which follows it or precedes it; it can therefore be removed from the row, lest it be a card contrary to the meanings of the others.

---

[107] Translator: The Lemarchand booklet assigns the term *Noblesse* or Gentry in the upright instead.

D'ODOUCET

This seventy-fifth card depicts three talismans or coins arranged in a triangle. On the card below Venus is presented in the color green, holding a flaming cauldron.

The universal spirit 5, united with life 7, gives rise to counting on the most flattering of generations, indicated by the 3 of Coins. The one who will appear from this happy combination is a predestined child, to whom true nobility will respond with distributed riches.

MODERN INTERPRETATIONS

Grimaud assigns a different set of keywords; FAME in the upright and MEDIOCRACY in the reverse.[108]

UPRIGHT: The Three of Coins is the card of the noble knight. You may earn the approval of many, by being particularly valiant and courageous. Also, you could meet a prominent or famous person, who could prove helpful to you. In business, your big heart and flexibility could propel you to even greater success and glory.

REVERSE: In the reverse, it is card of immaturity. You may act the child, which will come across as annoying and bothersome to others. In business, you may not take responsibility and engage in childish games, which will not be appreciated. A need to assume a responsible attitude.

---

[108] Translator: d´Odoucet assigns the meaning *Important* in the upright.

No. 76

Inconvenience - Letter[109]
Two of Coins or Clover

For some time, you have experienced inconveniences, whether in your work, or in your business, or in your affairs. The worry for your future is extraordinary, if not for your home, then at least towards those who are close to you. This card commits you to consult the Oracle more often, because your mind is full of worry.

Next to the No. 16, it predicts, that a lawsuit in which you are interested but if not you then a friend, or a relative, will soon be judged in a way that suits your wishes.

If this card is in the Reverse, it tells you that you will be the victim of a superior's ignorance or injustice.

This card in the Reverse is almost always a bad omen, unless it finds itself among more than one favorable card. The annoyances it foretells are always in the shape of correspondences with a magistrate, who finds his pleasures in bickering debates, one could almost say that, the author of this correspondence is or will be a prosecutor or a bailiff.

---

[109] Translator: A card of letters and communication in reverse, perhaps the figure below is trying to send her dog off with a letter, or perhaps teach it a new trick?

LEMARCHAND

The reel meaning of this card is inconvenience, uncertainty. You will only with difficulty complete the business you have undertaken. This card also indicates that those close to you, do not approve of your conduct and tell you to follow the advice of wisdom.

Near the No. 16, it implies success, a trial to your advantage and soon a solution. Card 64 indicates opposition, if it follows the No. 76.

When the Two of Coins appears in the Reverse, it is an omen of something unfavorable; it announces quarrels, disputes; but you must not be discouraged, for it also foretells, it will be almost foreign to you.

D'ODOUCET

This seventy-sixth card depicts two talismans or coins in a flame bath. On the card below Mercury is presented in color red, holding a caduceus and a book.

Here the globe, already sufficiently presented by 6, is still in the sphere of life 7, that is to say, providing an over-abundance of production, indicated by the vegetative number; 2 of the coins. The care of distributing these productions in the most advantageous way is an *inconvenience* for the owner, who is obliged to perform numerous correspondences, the *letters* are for him in this regard a utility appreciated. Let us not forget that these 2 coins in their nature are scouts, the symbol of a double mercury, which corresponds to all the types of existence, to which all the numbers of this card are the hieroglyphs.

MODERN INTERPRETATIONS

This card has by Grimaud been assigned the keywords; DIFFICULTIES in the upright and LETTER in the reverse.

UPRIGHT: The Two of Coins is a card of obstacles. You may be experiencing a lack of support, disagreements and arguments in your relationships, resulting in stress. In business, delays and setbacks. It is a time for patience.

REVERSE: In the reverse, a card indicating news. This can be by any mean; an email, letter, telephone call etc. It may be unexpected and from an unexpected source. The neighboring cards will reveal the contents.

No. 77

Perfect contentment – Money Purse[110]
Ace of Coins or Clover

When in their readings with the Book of Thot, the Egyptians brought forth this card, they regarded it as the greatest sign of happiness; they no longer needed to consult the spread.

Next to cards, which are not favorable, this will change their faulty predictions if not cancel them entirely.

With the No. 13, this card announces a very happy marriage, especially if the person for whom you are reading is a young lady, and card No. 20 is in the vicinity.

In the Reverse, this card predicts that you will play the leading role in finding treasure or finding a well-stuffed purse or something of high value. Despite your search, the owner will remain unknown, if this card is accompanied by one of the Nos. 41, 47 or 71; the opposite will happen if one observes one of the Nos. 4, 19, 26, 34 or 76.

---

[110] Translator: A card of value and wealth in the Reverse, perhaps the figure below is studying her bank statement?

LEMARCHAND

When the old cartomancers brought forth this tarot[111], they regarded it as being completely favorable; they did not inquire into the rest.

Close to cards whose interpretation is most unfortunate, this card destroys their meaning entirely.

After the No. 13, this card announces happiness in marriage. If the No. 20 accompanies it, moreover, a brilliant fortune.

In the Reverse, this card predicts, either for you or for a close relative, the discovery of a good deal, from which you will be, in any case, interested in order to achieve a brilliant fortune, and, thereafter from this fortune you will have superb company, if this card is near the No. 21.

---

[111] Translator: The Lemarchand booklet assigns the term *Bourse* in the reverse, not *Bourse d´Argent* or Money Purse.

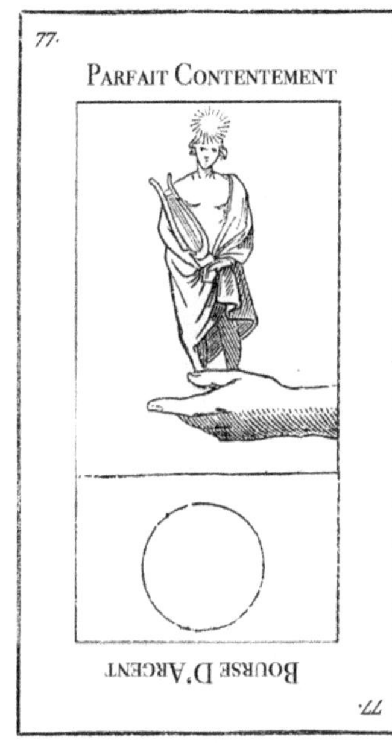

D'ODOUCET

This seventy-seventh card depicts an Apollo or a Sun, yellow in color. On the card below is a single talisman or coin.

The double symbol of life is the symbol of infinite sufficiency. The number 1 of the coin indicates a complete reward of assets, which plunge us into the most *perfect contentment*. But let us bear in mind, that it is from gold, that this beauty is born. Our felicity did not have such a foundation in the early days. Let us elevate our souls above such perishable goods in order to enjoy even greater and more lasting happiness.

MODERN INTERPRETATIONS

This card has by Grimaud been assigned the keywords; PROFOUND HAPPINESS in the upright and MONEY COMING IN in the reverse.

UPRIGHT: The Ace of Coins is a card of joy. This card implies fulfilment, joy, happiness and success in love. A card indicating the offering and the receiving of love. In business, you are appreciated and your work is successful. This also implies a very good time to invest.

REVERSE: In the reverse, this card is still very positive. You may be worried by your finances, but these worries are unfounded. You can expect substantial financial returns. It is a card of good progress, of prosperity and success.

No. 78

Folly - Folly
The Madman or the Alchemist

This card announces the very heights of extravaganza; it makes one fear that one is performing a lot of follies, that one would end up being the victim of, unless some unexpected incident put a stop to it.

Next to the No. 57, this card warns you, that you are about to make it a capital, but that you could avoid it; if accompanied by the No. 41, the opposite would happen; however, it would be too late, if appearing with the No. 27.

Although this card appearing in the Upright or in Reverse, always indicates madness, it is certain that this prediction is considerably modified, when the card appears next to several favorable cards, so that many times, it only indicates happiness obtained by means foreign to science or work.

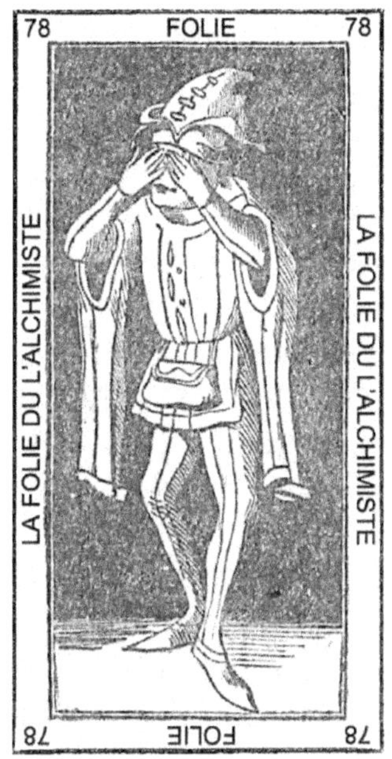

LEMARCHAND

This tarot indicates that the querent is not exempt from extravaganza, and that he could indulge himself in his follies without any restraints, unless another favorable card corrects this unfortunate omen.

Close to the No. 57, it tells you that you are going to make a mistake, that we would label as madness. With the No. 41, you would avoid it; but the opposite would happen, if the No. 27 follows it.

Do not believe that this card, appearing in the Upright or in Reverse, is an absolute sign of madness in the querent; it indicates, together with the No. 20, the vagaries of fortune; it means the querent relies more on luck than on merit.

D'ODOUCET

This card, labeled zero 0, represents a man in madness, who carries his purse, or rather his talismans or coins in a bundle exposed to the sight of all passers-by. From his belt hangs the bell of madness; he is portrayed, pursued by a tiger and trekking along the countryside.

The bell of madness adapts indiscriminately to all the chiming of our chains. The surface of the whole globe is only a theatre of our own extravaganza. Let us back track, in the eyes of the wise man, the symbol of a traveler, on a short journey, whose sorrows, we can alleviate, by behaving in accordance with the healthiest inspiration of the divine ray, which animates us.

MODERN INTERPRETATIONS

This card has by Grimaud been assigned the keywords; MADNESS in the upright and BEWILDERMENT in the reverse.

UPRIGHT: The Fool indicates a period of confusion and disorder, which will be of your own making. You may lack maturity or mental clarity. Is it madness or genius, love or desire? You may have an inability to commit, perhaps running away from serious responsibility. A card of impulse and instinct. On one hand, it is a card of freedom, independence and autonomy, on the other, a card of ignorance and dumb foolery. You may be exploring a childish dream, rebelling against someone, acting out, giving into fleeting passions, go off to change the world, discovering the world anew. Who is to say, what crazy is? Sometimes thinking the impossible makes things happen, sometimes crazy works.

REVERSE: In reverse this card has a similar interpret-tation, albeit only negative. You may be following a mad idea or desire, a distraction, void of reason, common sense and discernment. You may be completely irresponsible with your money, heading straight to bankruptcy. Actual mental disorders can be read into this card as well.

Table of Synonyms

OR THE DIFFERENT MEANINGS

applied in the upright and reverse

ON EACH OF THE CARDS, OR TAROTS OF THE BOOK

OF THOT, in order to facilitate the interpretation of the

spread, formed by, the joining of several, more or less,

impactful cards.

The use of this table is to be understood simply; by studying the words assigned to the relevant card number and applying these to the cards in question. For example, card no. 10 implies, all at once, in the upright; *Temperance, Moderation, Abstinence, Sobriety, Frugality, etc.*, and how these words are applied matters in a reading, it all will depend on the cards that precede or follow the card in question, so it is up to the reader to do so, in accordance with the following table, to choose the appropriate meaning, in order for him to make sense of his spread.

SYNONYMS
No. 1. ETTEILLA.
This means God, All powerful. Eternal. Very high. Unique, **Supreme Being, Central Spirit,** The Male querent, **Chaos,** Thought, **Meditation,** Contemplation, **Reflection, Contention of the spirit.**
Dream, wisdom, ideal, vision, idol, wishful thinking, important male, patience, honesty.[112]

(Reverse) MALE QUERENT.
The Universe, Physical man or the male. The Querent. Philosopher. Philosophical. Philosophically. Philosophize. Wise. Wisdom. Wisely.
Understanding, higher knowledge, skill, thinking ability, life experience, philosophy.

SYNONYMS
No. 2. ENLIGHTENMENT.
Enlightenment, Light, Explanation, Clarity, Unravel. Development, Instruction, Opening, Analysis, Discovery, Interpretation, Revelation, Elucidation, Fire, Sun, Temple of Fire, **Glory, Heaven and Earth, Sulphur, Philosophical.**
Clarification, enlightenment, art, explanation, illumination, illustration, fertility.

(Reversed) FIRE.
Fire, Heat, Glow, Ignition, Flame, Passions, Meteor, Thunderbolt, Lightning, Intervening fire, external and philosophical. Hot, Small clarification, Spark, Ray of light, Glow, Incinerate. Burn off. Ardor. Embracing. Fire of Love.

---

[112] Translator: It is obvious that the synonyms in the original Orsini booklet were copied from d´Odoucet, however many were also left out. I have listed all the synonyms or keywords from the original source, in **bold** text, and where Orsini added keywords, these have been listed as normal. Keywords in *cursive* are modern interpretations.

Light up. Ignite. Lights. Flash. Thunderstorm. Electricity. Fire of Saint Elme. Fire of nature. Magnetism. Outdoor fire, Internal fire, Central light, Salamander, Dissension, Discord in the mind, Cast fire, Pass off one´s anger, Make fire and flame, Bone of contention. Heat, Cooking, Warming up, Inflammation.
Drive, passion, impulsiveness, possessiveness, strive, force, thoughtlessness.

SYNONYMS
OR DIFFERENT MEANINGS OF THE CARD
No. 3. DISCOURSE.
Proposal, Meeting, Conversation, Discourse, Maintain, Speaking, Gossip, Chatting, Slander, Stuck, Deliberation, Purpose. Intention. Resolution. Will. Discussion. Speech, Reasoning. Discuss. Babble. Cackling. Calumny. Defamation. **Moon.**
Disharmony, doubt, hesitation, gossip, discussion, disagreement, harsh words, turmoil, disaffection.

(Reversed) WATER.
Water, Liquid, Cleansing, **Dewy,** Heavy rain, Deluge, **Rain, Sea, River, Flood, Stream, Torrent, Fountain, Current, Lake, Marsh, Swamp, Water table, Pond,** Waterfall. Waves, **Humidity, Steam, Smoke, Mercury, Chaotic and philosophical water, Emanation, Frost, Snow, Exhalation, Evaporation, Instability, Inconsistency, Silence, Murmur, Patient.**
Unsteadiness, imbalance, sadness, doubt, losing it.

SYNONYMS.
OR DIFFERENT MEANINGS OF THE CARD
No. 4. DESOLATION
Clearance, Development, **deprivation, denial, abandonment, analysis, extract, clearance, sorting, separation, depreciation, pillage, theft, losses, deprivation of relief,** Finding out. Deepen. Unravel.

Remove. Deprive. Take off. Ravish. Spoil. Violence. Removal. Abduction. Flight. Skullduggery. Fraud. Swindle. Infidelity.
Disclosure, discovery, revelation, good news, destiny, getting rid of things that do not serve you.

(Reversed) AIR.
Air, Wind, Hurricane. **Storm, Atmosphere,** Native air, Dry, **Climate, Drought. Sky, Star, Subtle, Birds,** Volatility, Turnout, **Volatile, Tone, Manners, Affection, All, Allure, Physiognomy,** Appearance, Likeness, **Resemblance, Wave without consistency, Arrogance, Height, Importance,** Similarity, Beautiful semblance, False pretense, Concealment, Feigned, Pretend, Hypocrisy, Your sound, Acoustic. Air. Sylph. Talk in the air. Light discourse. Vague talk, **Song, Music, Melody.**
Dry spell, increased control, deprivation, delay, bad outcome, effort needed.

SYNONYMS
OR DIFFERENT MEANINGS OF THE CARD
No. 5. VOYAGE.
Travel, Road, Walk, Pilgrimage, **Proceedings, Displacement, Peregrination, Walk, Visit, Race, Incursion, Emigration, Transmigration,** Fugue, Fleeing, **Judge, rout, Rotation, Circulation, Disoriented,** Confuse, **Disconcerted.** Interruption.
On the way, voyage, trip by land, en-route, traveling, opportunities, advantages.

(Reversed) EARTH.
Earth, Matter, Mud, Vase, Silt, Raw material, Forest. Virgin land, **Sulphur and Mercury, Salt of the Wise, Cold, Thick, Gnome, World, Globe, State, Kingdom, Empire, Land, Territory, Possessions, Rural things,** Meadows, Close by, Orchards, Fields, Vineyards, Reptiles, Home, Regions, Country, Places, Site, Local, Landscape, Constancy, Perseverance, Tranquility,

Shores, Shore, Beach, Rivers, Rocks, Reefs, Plains, Mountain, Hill, Valley, Quadrupeds, **Appearance, Permanence, Fixity, Stagnation, Inertia, Animals, Beast, Grave, Tomb, Ash, Powder, Dust, Mature, Salt, Philosophical.**
Simple, village, peasant, rustic, rural, refusal, fear, inability, unsuccessful.

SYNONYMS
OR DIFFERENT MEANINGS OF THE CARD
No. 6. THE NIGHT.
This card signifies in the Upright, *situs*, **night, Obscurity, Darkness, Deprivation of light, Nocturnal, Mystery, Secret, Mask, Hiding, Unknown, Clandestine, Occult,** Eclipse, **Veil, Symbol, Figure, Image, Parable, Allegory, Mystical fire,** Sense of Mystique, Hidden intentions, Mysterious words, Obscure speech, **Occult Science, Deaf, Dark Steps, Clandestine Actions,** In Secret, Clandestinely, Unreason, **Blind, Confuse, Cover, Wrap, Difficulty, Doubt, Error, Ignorance.** Overlook. Oversight. Blanket. Envelope.
Hidden agenda, dark, secrets, things done at night, confidential, mystery, confusion, lack of clarity.

(Reversed) THE DAY.
Day, clarity, Light, Radiance, Splendor, Illumination, Manifestation, Evidence, Truth, Clear, Visible, Luminous, Enlighten, Illuminated, **To give light, To bring to light,** Print, **To publish, To bloom, To break through, To come to light, To clarify, To acquire knowledge,** Public joy, **Expedient, Facilitate, Opening, Window, Empty,** Fireworks, **Zodiac.**
Reality, facts, things done in the open, improvement, essence, authenticity, solutions, good conclusions.

SYNONYMS
OR DIFFERENT MEANINGS OF THE CARD
No. 7. SUPPORT.

Support, Encouragement, Backing, Underpin, Arch-Buttress, Column, Base, Foundation, Basis, Principle, Reason, Cause, Subject, Fixity, Assurance, Persuasion, Conviction, Safety, Security, Confidence, Certainty, Help, Rescue, Assistance, Protection, Relief, Consolation.

Cooperation, protection, support, help, collaboration, good relationships, good legal outcomes.

(Reversed) PROTECTION.

Protection, Influence, Defense, Assistance, Help, Relief, **Benevolence, Beneficence, Charity, Humanity, Kindness, Commiseration, Pity, Compassion, Credit, Authorization.**

Backing, guarding, reconciliation, care, security, offer of help.

SYNONYMS
OR DIFFERENT MEANINGS OF THE CARD
No. 8. ETTEILLA.

This card represents the Female querent, it represents a female or the male querent's person of most interest; Nature, Rest, Tranquility, Private life, Retired life, Lonely life, Hermit life, Religious life, Orphic life, **Retreat, Retired Life, Solitary, The rest of an old man, Temple of Fire, Silence, Taciturnity.**

Endurance, tenacity, perseverance, persistence, serenity, psychic abilities.

(Reversed) THE FEMALE QUERENT.

Imitation, Garden of Eden, Effervescence, Broth, Fermentation, Ferment, Leaven, Acidity.

Recklessness, impaired judgement, led astray, imprudence.

SYNONYMS
OR DIFFERENT MEANINGS OF THE CARD
No. 9. THE JUSTICE
Justice, Equity, Probity, Law, **Righteousness, Rectitude, Reason, Justice,** Courthouse, **Execution, Thot or the book of Thot.**
Law, justice, judication, contracts, forensic, by the book.

(Reversed) THE JURIST.
Legislation, Legislator, Law, Decree, **Code,** Ordonnance, **Statutes, Precepts,** Commandment, Domination, Institution, Constitution, Temperament, Complexion, Natural laws and moral laws, Religious laws, Civil laws, Political laws, **Natural law, Law of Nations**[113]**, Public law, Civil law, Law of war. The Jurist is under the immediate influence of this hieroglyph.**
Rules, restriction, injustice, unfairness, slander.

SYNONYMS
OR DIFFERENT MEANINGS OF THE CARD
No. 10 THE TEMPERANCE.
Temperance, Moderation, Discretion, Continence, Abstinence, Patience, Calm, Sobriety, **Frugality, Chastity, Mitigation, Sparingly, Accommodation, Respect, Consideration, Temperature,** Reconciliation, Conciliation, Tempering by musical sounds, Air temperature, **Climate, Thot, or the book of Thot.**
Frugality, temperance, tenderness, improvement, trust in self, modesty, austerity.

---

[113] Translator: *Droit des Gens* or *Jus Gentium,* a set of minimum rights granted to members of foreign peoples.

(Reversed) THE PRIEST.

Minister, Priest, **Priesthood, Clergy, Church,** Council, Synod, **Religion, Sect, the Priest is under the influence of this virtue.**

Rebuke, guilt, disapproval, self-critical, help needed, things related to religion.

SYNONYMS
OR DIFFERENT MEANINGS OF THE CARD
No. 11 THE STRENGTH.

Advantage by force. Moral strength. Grandeur of Soul. Magnanimity, **Strength, Heroism, Nobleness, Greatness, Courage,** Perseverance. Constancy, **Force, Power, Empire, Ascension, Work of the spirit, Patience, Resignation,** Domination, **Thot, or the Book of Thot.**

Vibrant, force, strength, confidence, dynamics, emphasis, empowerment, vigor, energy.

(Reversed) THE SOVEREIGN.

Sovereign, Kingdom, Empire, **State, Republic, Government, Administration, Reign, Despotism, Sovereignty, Supreme Power, Arbitrary Power,** Authority, Command, **People, Nation,** King, Emperor, General, Commanding officer, Captain, Senior leader, Governor, Dominator, Motor, Regulator, Curator, Protective, **Faith, Imperfection, Discordance.**

Person in authority, intolerant, prideful, abuse, arrogant, subjugation.

SYNONYMS
OR DIFFERENT MEANINGS OF THE CARD
No. 12 THE PRUDENCE.
Prudence, Reserve, Wisdom, Circumspection, Restraint, Discernment, Foresight, Forecast, Premonition, Prediction, Prognosis, Divination, **Prophecy, Thot or the Book of Thot,** Horoscope.
Tact, thoughtful, mindful, prudence, tactical, caution, deliberation.

(Reversed) THE PEOPLE.
Nation, Legislator, Sovereign, **Body politics, Population, Generation.**
Fame, notoriety, encouragement, socializing, dealing with people or the public.

SYNONYMS
OR DIFFERENT MEANINGS OF THE CARD
No. 13. MARRIAGE.
Marriage, Union, Junction, Reunion, Hymn, Vow, Oath, Intimacy, Liaison, **Assembly,** Junction, Conjunction, Copulation, Coupling, **Bond, Alliance, Chain, Slavery, Bother, Captivity, Bondage.**
Commitment, contract, agreements, bond, marriage.

(Reversed) UNION.
Society, Acquaintance, Cohabitation, Adultery, Incest, **Alliance, Fusion, Mixture,** Amalgamation, **Peace, Concord, Agreement, Harmony, Good intelligence,** To set right, Reconciliation.
Link, coherence, connection, animosity, infidelity.

SYNONYMS
OR DIFFERENT MEANINGS OF THE CARD
No. 14. FORCE MAJEURE.

Force majeure, Human strength, **great Movement, Vehemence, Extraordinary Effort, Force, Extraordinary Power,** Physical force, Violent impulse, **Powers, Virtues, Impulse, Outbursts of genius, Ravage, Violence,** Constraint, **Work, Physical,** Firmness. Strength of mind. Manual or physical work.
Charisma, success, instinct, passions, aggression, control, compulsion.

(Reversed) MINOR FORCE.
Lightness, Weakness, Smallness, Tenderness. Weakening, **Failure,** Fainting. Abatement. Overwhelmed. Languor. Sagging. Drag. Insulted. Sacrilege.
Defenseless, obstacle, infidelity, dominated, vulnerable, be under the thumb or a pawn of somebody.

SYNONYMS
OR DIFFERENT MEANINGS OF THE CARD
No. 15. SICKNESS.

Illness of body, soul or spirit, Poor state of health or business, **Illness, Infirmity, Disturbance, Ache,** Poison. Epidemic, Plague, Gangrene, **Anguish, Hurt, Displeasure, Shame, Pain, Misfortune, Disaster.**
Depression, sadness, grief, pain, suffering, heartache, worry, distress, health issues.

(Reversed) SICKNESS.
Illness of mind, Headache, Indisposition, Heartache. Languishing disease, **Unhappy situation, Disgrace, Inconvenience, Worry,** Melancholy, **Affliction,** Remedy. Charlatan, **Doctor,** Empirical, **Mage.**
Depression, disorder, discomfort, nervousness, mental issues.

SYNONYMS
OR DIFFERENT MEANINGS OF THE CARD
No. 16. THE JUDGMENT.

Judgment True, Good, Healthy, Fair, False, **Discernment, Intelligence, Conception, Reason,** Understanding, **Common sense,** Right attitude, mind, **Reasoning, Comparison,** Deliberation, **Sight, Suspicion, Thought, Opinion, Feeling, Dissolution,** Last judgement.
Urge, counsel, clarity, opinion, clue, warning, reconciling.

(Reversed) THE JUDGMENT.
Arrest, Decree, Deliberation, Decision, Arbitration, Pacification, Bad judgment, **Weak spirit, Cowardliness,** Dementia, Injustice, **Simplicity,** Foolishness.
Arbitration, unfairness, regret, relief, defeat, judgment.

SYNONYMS
OR DIFFERENT MEANINGS OF THE CARD
No. 17. MORTALITY.

Dead, Mortality, Annihilation, Destruction, End, Death, Last sigh, Extinction, Extermination, Attack, Murder, Assassination, Homicide, Suicide, Regicide, Massacre, Carnage, Butchery, Slaughter, Killing, Poison, Poisoning, **Alteration, Rot, Corruption, Putrefaction.**
Ending, rupture, renewal, dead, played out, passing.

(Reversed) NOTHINGNESS.
Inertia, Sleep, Paralysis, **Lethargy,** Fainting. Negation. Nil. Not at all. Paralyze. Fall asleep, **Petrification, Annihilation, Sleepwalking.**
Death, loss of hope, Impotence, powerlessness, despair.

SYNONYMS
OR DIFFERENT MEANINGS OF THE CARD
No. 18. TRAITOR.
Hypocritical. Fanatic. Impostor, **Betrayal, Disguise, Concealment, Hypocrisy, Traitor, Deceiver, Corruptor, Seducer**, Fanaticism, **Disguise, Cunning,** Deceit, **Imposture.**
Disloyalty, foul play, suspicious, betrayal, infidelity.

(Reversed) HYPOCRITE.
Hermit, **Solitaire, Anchorite, Hide, Conceal, Disguise, Politics, End,** Cunning.
Lie, ailment, deception, self-deception, fabrication, distress, hurt, unsuccessful.

SYNONYMS
OR DIFFERENT MEANINGS OF THE CARD
No. 19. MISERY.
Misery, Distress, Indigence, Poverty, Shortage, Need, Necessity, Calamity, Adversity, Woe, Unfortunate, Grief, **Penalty, Torment, Pain, Affliction, Disagreement Punishment,** Correction, **Retribution,** God´s Punishment. **Setback, Disgrace, Severity, Rigidity, Rigor.**
Affliction, misfortune, upheaval, misery, hardship, shocks, loss of money.

(Reversed) PRISON.
Imprisonment, Detention, Arrest, Captivity, Slavery, **Oppression, Tyranny,** Despotism, Yoke, Dungeon, House of God, Servitude, **Chains, Subjection, Subjugation.**
Detention, difficulty, trapped, prison, dominated.

SYNONYMS
OR DIFFERENT MEANINGS OF THE CARD
No. 20. FORTUNE.

Happiness, Felicity, Improvement, Bonus, Blessing, **Prosperity, Goods, Wealth, Benefits, Graces, Favors, Destiny, Fate, Adventures, Good fortune.**
Prosperity, fortune, clear up, ability, profits, rewards, luck, enjoyment, good health.

(Reversed) INCREASE.

Increase, Enlargement, Abundance, Increase, Growth, Vegetation, Production.
Build up, increase, irregular, promotion, strengthening.

SYNONYMS
OR DIFFERENT MEANINGS OF THE CARD
No. 21. DISSENSION.

War, Dissention, Dispute, Noise, Unrest, Riots, Agitation, Insurrection. Revolt. Sedition. Faction. Conjuration. Rebellion. Defection, **Battles, Fight, Combat, Vainness, Pride, Vanity, False-glory, Pomp, Ostentation, Audacity, Recklessness, Violence, Disorder, Anger, Injury,** Outrage, **Presumption, Revenge.**
Courage, Course of action, path, daring, pride, process, trials.

(Reversed) ARROGANCE.

Noise, Uproar, Dispute, **Quarrel, Differences, Contestation, Litigation, Bother,** Argumentation, **Debates.**
Achievement, confrontation, conflict, change in direction.

SYNONYMS
OR DIFFERENT MEANINGS OF THE CARD
No. 22. COUNTRY MAN.

Country man, Good and stern man, Well-intentioned man, Honest man, Conscience, Probity, Villager, Rustic, Peasant, **Agriculture, Laborer, Farmer.**
Leader, reliability, loyalty, singular minded, good advice.

(Reversed) GOOD AND STERN MAN.
Good and stern man, Indulgence, Severity, Complacency, **Tolerance, Condescension.**
Waiver, indulgent, remission, tolerant, fair.

SYNONYMS
OR DIFFERENT MEANINGS OF THE CARD
No. 23. COUNTRY WOMAN.

Country woman, Household economy, Honest woman, **Honesty, Civility,** Courtesy, **Sweetness, Virtue, Honorable, Chastity.**
Quality, understanding, discreet, devotion, sincerity, singular minded.

(Reversed) GOOD WOMAN.
Good woman, Kindness, Excellence, Obliging, Unofficial, Helpful, Benefit, Service, Obligation.
Attention, care, commitment, charitable.

SYNONYMS
OR DIFFERENT MEANINGS OF THE CARD
No. 24. DEPARTURE.

Leaving. **Departure, Displacement, Removal, Absence, Abandonment, Change, Flight, Desertion, Transmigration, Immigration, Transposition, Translation, Transplantation, Transmutation, Evasion.**
Change, adaptation, moving on, arriving, information.

(Reversed) DISUNION.
Disunity, Quarrel, Rupture, Dissension, Division, Part, Separation, Partition, Faction, Party, Quarrel, Untangle, Cut, Fracture, Discontinuation, Interruption.
Separation, quarrel, departure, conflict.

SYNONYMS
OR DIFFERENT MEANINGS OF THE CARD
No. 25 GOOD STRANGER.
Stranger, Unknown, Extraordinary, Strange, Unusual, Inquisitive, Unbelievable, Surprising, Admirable, Wonder, Prodigy, Miracle, Episode, Digression, Anonymous.
Creativity, search, encounters, surprise.

(Reversed) NEWS.
Announcement, Instruction, Advice, Warning, Admonition, Anecdotes, Chronicle, History, Tales, Fables, Notions, Teaching.
Announcement, interference, message, news.

SYNONYMS
OR DIFFERENT MEANINGS OF THE CARD
No. 26. TREASON.
Treason, Perfidy, Deceit, Deception, Cunning, Surprise, Disguise, Concealment, Hypocrisy, Prevarication, Duplicity, Disloyalty, Darkness, Villainousness, **Falsehood, Conjuration, Conspiracy, Imposture.**
Malice, deceit, deception, lies, jealousy,

(Reversed) OBSTACLE.
Obstacle, Hurry, Bar, Inconvenience, Opposition, **Obstruction, Annoyances, Difficulty, Pain, Work,** Inconvenience, Objection, **Abjection, Chicane, Reclamation, Pitfall, Hedge, Entrenchment, Redoubt, Fortification.**
Obstacle, threshold, blockages, impediment.

SYNONYMS
OR DIFFERENT MEANINGS OF THE CARD
No. 27. DELAY.

Delay, Delays, Removal, Postponement, Dismissal, Suspension, Elongation, Slowly, Slowness, **Slowdown.**
Delay, ailment, misunderstanding, setbacks, hindrance, complications.

(Reversed) ADVERSITY.
Crossing, Obstacle, Impediment, Contrariety, Disadvantage, Adversity, Pain, Misfortune, Misfortunes, Calamity.
Misery, isolation, adversary, misfortune, sorrow.

SYNONYMS
OR DIFFERENT MEANINGS OF THE CARD
No. 28. COUNTRYSIDE.

Countryside, Field, Plain, Agriculture, Cultivation, Labor, Immovable property, Farm, Hall, Garden, Orchard, Meadow, Wood, Grove, Shade, Pleasure, Entertainment, Amusement, Pastime, Recreations, Joy, Peace, Calm, Tranquility, Innocence, Country life, Forest, Valley, Editing, War campaign. Sheepfold.
Harmony, trips, own pace, self-employment, countryside.

(Reversed) INTERNAL DISPUTES.
Internal dispute, Examination, Reasoning, Our intelligence, Regrets, Remorse, Repentance, Internal agitation, Irresolution, Uncertainty, Indecision, Inconceivable, Incomprehensible, Doubt, Scruple, Timorous Consciousness.
Uncertainty, suffering, doubt, remorse, upset.

SYNONYMS
OR DIFFERENT MEANINGS OF THE CARD
No. 29. TALK.

Talking, Speech, Interview, Conference, Seminar, Conversation, Dissertation, Deliberation, Discussion, Speech, Pronunciation, Grammar. Dictionary, **Languages, Idioms,** Jargon, **Clumsy speech, Negotiation, Mischief, Exchange, Measure, Commerce, Traffic, Correspondence, Speak, Say, Deliver, Confer, Gossip, Bring, Divide, Chat, Chatter.**
Change, conviction, flaking, persuasion, discussions, resolve.

(Reversed) INDECISION.
Indecision, Irresolution, Uncertainty, Perplexity, Inconstancy, Lightness, Variation, Variety, Diversity, Hesitate, Hesitation, Stagger, Flicker, Versatility.
Hesitation, uncertainty, doubt, indecision.

SYNONYMS
OR DIFFERENT MEANINGS OF THE CARD
No. 30. DOMESTIC.

Maid, Waiter, Page, Valet, Servant, Mercenary, Inferior, Slave, Courier, Commissioner, Messenger, Announcement, Commission, Housework, Servitude. **House Interior, Message, Family, All of the servants and of the house.**
Familiar, comfort, cozy, gifts.

(Reversed) WAIT.
Expectation, Trust, Hope, Foundation, to Trust, to count on, to Promise, Confidence, Foresight, Fear, Apprehension.
Delay, impatient, needing to wait, need for effort.

SYNONYMS
OR DIFFERENT MEANINGS OF THE CARD
No. 31. GOLD.

Gold, Wealth, Opulence, Magnificence, Splendor, Radiance, Luxury, Abundance, Goods, Sun, Physical, Philosophical and moral.
Windfall, abundance, support, happiness, pay off.

(Reversed) TRIAL.

Lawsuits, Litigation, Differences, Trouble, Contestations, Disputes, Authority, Instruction, Pursuit, Annoyances, Discussions, Chicanery, Bother, Contradiction, Inconsequence.
Dismissal, testing, lawsuit, break-up, trial.

SYNONYMS
OR DIFFERENT MEANINGS OF THE CARD
No. 32. ASSOCIATION.

Society, Association, Assembly, Liaison, Federation, Confederation. Church, **Alliance, Assemblage, Reunion, Circle, Community, Gathering, Multitude, Mob, Crowd, Troops, Band, Company, Cohort, Army, Convocation, Accompaniment, Mixed, Mix, Alloy, Amalgam, Contract, Convention, Covenant, Treaty.**
Contract, agreement, approval, business outcome.

(Reversed) PROSPERITY.

Prosperity, Growth, Increase, Advancement, Success, Achievement, Happiness, Bloom, Felicity, Beauty, Embellishment.
Sentimentality, well-being, flourishing, socializing, recognition.

SYNONYMS
OR DIFFERENT MEANINGS OF THE CARD
No. 33. ENTERPRISE.

Company, Undertake, Begin, Usurp, Seize, Audacity, Temerity, Boldness, Imprudence, Enterprising, Daring, Foolhardy, Bold, Enterprise, Inconvenience, Confused, Lost, Effort, Trials, Attempt.
Work, trade, endeavors, enterprise, boldness.

(Reversed) TRIALS AT AN END.
Interruption by Misfortune, Torment, Pain, Work, End, Cessation, Discontinuation, Release, Rest, Suspension, Intermission, Intermittence.
Endings, rewards, satisfaction, better times.

SYNONYMS
OR DIFFERENT MEANINGS OF THE CARD
No. 34. SORROW.

Grief, Sadness, Melancholy, Affliction, Unhappiness, Pain, Desolation, Mortification, Mood, Annoyance, Vapors, Dark ideas, Bitterness, Anger, Spite.
Concern, heartache, pain, sorrow, unappreciated, regret.

(Reversed) SURPRISE.
Deceit, Deception, Cheating, Misunderstanding, **Surprise, Enchantment, Shock, Trouble, Unexpected event, Unexpected fact, Fear, Emotion, Fright, Awe, Terror, Consternation, Astonishment, Admiration, Rapture, Alarms, Wonder, Phenomena, Miracle.**
Amazement, surprise, hope, regain your footing.

SYNONYMS
OR DIFFERENT MEANINGS OF THE CARD
No. 35. FALL.

Fall, Cascade, Decadence, Decline, Withering, Depletion, Dissipation, Insolvency, Bankruptcy, Ruin, Destruction, Demolition, Damage, Ravage, Fault, Error, Misunderstanding, Dejection, Overwhelm, Discouragement, Perdition, Abyss, Chasm, Precipice, Perish, Drop, Decay, Demean, Profundity.[114]
Failure, insolvency, job loss, infertility.

(Reversed). BIRTH.

Birth, Commencement, Nativity, Origin, Creation, Source, Beginning, Principle, Primacy, First, Extraction, Race, Family, Condition, House, Lineage, Posterity, Occasion, Cause, Reason, First, First fruit.
Origin, better times, new opportunities, pregnancy.

SYNONYMS
OR DIFFERENT MEANINGS OF THE CARD
No. 36. BLOND MAN.

Blond man, Honest man, Probity, Equity, Arts, Science.
Reliability, fidelity, supportive, fairness, good manager.

(Reversed) INFLUENTIAL MAN.

Influential Man, Distinguished man, Man of high rank, **Honest man**[115], **Dishonest man, Extortion,** Rascality, Looting, **Concussion, Injustice,** Waste, Dilapidation, **Brigand, Thief, Rogue, Vice, Corruption, Scandal.**

---

[114] Translator: The keywords by d´Odoucet for card 35 have been flipped (Upright and Reverse) in order to reflect Orsini´s booklet. Please note, the modern interpretations do seem to go in the direction of Orsini´s flip, regardless of the Etteilla cards used...

[115] Translator: *Honnete homme* is listed by d´Odoucet both in Upright and in the Reverse.

Untrustworthiness, manipulative, back-stabbing, corrupt, unscrupulous.

SYNONYMS
OR DIFFERENT MEANINGS OF THE CARD
No. 37. BLONDE WOMAN.
Blond woman, Honest woman, Virtue, Wisdom, Integrity.
Unique, loving, special, exemplary, too giving.

(Reversed) WIFE OF AN INFLUENTIAL MAN.
Woman of a distinguished rank, Dishonest woman, Vice, Dishonesty, Depravity, Maladjusted, Corruption, Scandal.
Scorn, dishonest, emotionally unavailable, domineering.

SYNONYMS
OR DIFFERENT MEANINGS OF THE CARD
No. 38. ARRIVAL.
Arrival, Coming, Approach, Manner, Reception, Access, Reconciliation, Conformity, Event, Reunion, **Approximation, Accessory, Affluence, Comparison.**
Letters, opportunity, gifts, visits.

(Reversed) DECEPTION.
Deception, Villainy, Deceit, Cunning, Artifice, Finesse, Address, Flexibility, Cheating, Trickery, **Subtlety, Irregularity, Darkness.**
Bad company, jealousy, infidelity, criticism, deceit.

SYNONYMS
OR DIFFERENT MEANINGS OF THE CARD
No. 39. BLOND BOY.
Blond boy, Studious, Study, Application, Work, Reflection, Observation, Consideration, Meditations, Contemplation, Occupation, Trade, Profession, Employment.
Diligent, studiousness, hardworking, a flirt.

(Reversed) INCLINATION.
Fondness, Incline, Propensity, Inclination, Attraction, Taste, Sympathy, Passion, Affection, Attachment, Friendship, Heart, Envy, Desire, Attractiveness, Commitment, Seduction, Invitation, Pleasure, Flattery, Cajolery, Sycophancy, Adulation, Eulogy, Praise, Courtier. Seducer, Alluring, The song of the Syrenes, **Inclinations which create ruin, that which blows up in the end.**
Sympathy, friendship, devoted, unstable admirer.

SYNONYMS
OR DIFFERENT MEANINGS OF THE CARD
No. 40. THE CITY.
Town, City, Motherland, Country, Township, Village, Place, Site, Location, **Residency, Dwelling, Residence, Citizen, Bourgeois, Inhabitant of the city.**
Within, relocation, moving to the city, security, home life.

(Reversed) WRATH.
Wrath, Indignation, Agitation, Irritation, Emotion, Anger, Violence, Fury, Frenzy, Rage, Hatred, Aversion, Animadversion, **Animosity, Resentment, Revenge, Danger, Risk, Peril, Injury, Contempt, Outrage,** Blasphemy, **Thunderstorm, Storm, Uproar, Cruelty, Inhumanity, Atrocity, Enormity.**
Conflict, disruption, anger, misunderstanding.

SYNONYMS
OR DIFFERENT MEANINGS OF THE CARD
No. 41. VICTORY.
Victory, Success, Achievement, Advantage, Gain, Pump, Triumph, Trophy, Majesty, **Pre-eminence, Superiority, Show, Appliances, Paraphernalia.**
Wish fulfilment, Success, appreciation, reconciliation.

(Reversed) SINCERITY.

Sincerity, Truth, Reality, Loyalty, Good faith, Franchise, Ingenuity, Candor, Openness, Simplicity, Naivety, **Freedom, License, Privacy, Familiarity, Boldness, Ease, Deregulation.**

Business, trade, craft, motivational, joy.

SYNONYMS
OR DIFFERENT MEANINGS OF THE CARD
No. 42. BLONDE GIRL.

Blond girl, Honest girl, Modest girl, Honor, Decency, Modesty, Restraint, Shyness, Fear, Apprehension, Sweetness, Pleasure.

Gentle, generous, honest, loyal, pure.

(Reversed) SATISFACTION.

Pleasure, **Satisfaction, Happiness, Contentment, Gaiety, Joy, Elation, Rejoicing, Entertainment, Feast,** Sabbath, **Excuse, Reparation, Exoneration, Public joy, Show, Appliances, Preparing, Preparative, Disposition.**

Happiness, health, affection, welfare, satisfaction.

SYNONYMS
OR DIFFERENT MEANINGS OF THE CARD
No. 43. THOUGHT.

Thought, Soul, Mind, Intelligence, Idea, Memory, Imagination, Understanding, Conception, Meditation, Contemplation, Reflection, Deliberation, Sight, Opinion, Feeling.

Sentimentality, romance, visualization, insight, awareness.

(Reversed) PROJECTS.

Project, Design, Intention, Desire, Will, Resolution, Determination, Premeditation.

Contemplation, assignment, enterprise, making changes, task.

SYNONYMS
OR DIFFERENT MEANINGS OF THE CARD
No. 44. THE PAST.
The Past, Preterit, Fading, Withering, Dried out, **Earlier, Formerly, Previously, A While back, In the old days, Old age, Decrepitude, Antiquity.**
Lesson, past influence, background, past.

(reversed) THE FUTURE.
Things to come, Future, After, Then, Posteriorly, Later, Regeneration, Resurrection, Reproduction, Renewal, Reiteration.
Heading towards, perspective, prospects, events to come.

SYNONYMS
OR DIFFERENT MEANINGS OF THE CARD
No. 45. INHERITANCE.
Heritage, Succession, Legacy, Gift, Donation, Dowry, Legal Gift, Inheritance, Transmission, Will, Tradition, Revolution, Cabal.
Values, inheritance, legacy, estate.

(Reversed) RELATIVES.
Consanguinity, Blood, Family, Having, Ancestors, Father, Mother, Brother, Sister, Uncle, Aunt, Cousin, Adam and Eve, **Filiation, Extraction, Race, Line, Alliance, Affinity, Acquaintance, Relationship, Bonds.**
Positive influence, family affairs, parents.

SYNONYMS
OR DIFFERENT MEANINGS OF THE CARD
No. 46. BOREDOM.
Boredom, Displeasure, Discontent, Disgust, Aversion, Intimacy, Hatred, Horror, Worry, Pain of spirit, Some grief, Affliction, Painful, Annoying, Unpleasant, Sorrowful, Afflicting.
Struggle, stagnancy, arguments, unpleasantness.

(Reversed) NEW KNOWLEDGE.
New instructions, New information, **New insights,** New details, New clarifications, **Clue, Indication, Conjecture, Omen, Presage, Hunch, Prognosis, Prediction,** Oracle, Prophecy, Divination**, New.**
Need to change, old routine, self-reflection, new acquaintances.

SYNONYMS
OR DIFFERENT MEANINGS OF THE CARD
No. 47. SUCCESS.
Success, Science, Happy exit, Happy outcome, Victory, Healing, Cure, Relief, Accomplishment, Perfection.
Output, success, relief, recognition.

(Reversed) BUSINESS.
Expedition, Dispatch, Execution, Completion, End, Conclusion, Termination, Accomplishment.
Conviction, duty, responsibility, occupation, mastery.

SYNONYMS
OR DIFFERENT MEANINGS OF THE CARD
No. 48. LOVE.
Love, Passion, Inclination, Sympathy, Attraction, Proclivity, Friendship, Benevolence, Affection, Attachment, Relish, Bond, Courteousness, Attraction, Affinity.
Passion, affection, reinvigoration, support, love.

(Reversed) DESIRE.
Desire, Likes, Wishes, Will, Envy, Lust, Greed, Lustful, Jealousy, Passion, Illusion, Appetite.
Self-doubt, temptation, risk, desire, urge.

SYNONYMS
OR DIFFERENT MEANINGS OF THE CARD
No. 49. TABLE.
Table, Meal, Feast, Gala, Feast, Nourishment, Food, Nutrition, Guests, Services, Invitation, Prayer, Petition, Summons, Host, Hotel, Hostel, Cabaret, Log, Tavern, **Abundance, Fertility, Production, Solidity, Stability, Fixity, Constancy, Perseverance, Continuation, Duration, Suite, Attendance, Persistence, Firmness, Spirit, Table, Painting, Image, Hieroglyph, Description, Tablets, Portfolio, Office, Secretary, Table of nature, Brass table, Marble table, Law, Catalogue, Table of contents, Harmonious table, Garden table, Holy table.**
Socializing, reception, dinner appointment, entertain, overspending.

(Reversed) CHANGE.
Mutation, Permutation, Transmutation, Alteration, Vicissitude, Variety, Variation, Volatility, Lightness, Exchange, Barter, Purchase, Sale, Market, Treaty, Convention, Metamorphosis, Diversity, Versatility, Reversal, Upheaval, Revolution, Reversion, Version, Translation, Interpretation.
Turn, inconsistency, change, adjustment, modification, correction.

SYNONYMS
OR DIFFERENT MEANINGS OF THE CARD
No. 50 MAGISTRATE.
Magistrate, Man of the Law, Judge, Counsellor, Assessor, Senator, Businessman, Practitioner, Lawyer, Prosecutor, Doctor, Medical Practitioner, Jurist, Jurisprudence, Litigant, Legal advisor.
Diagnosis, judgement, robe, mantel.

(Reversed) WICKED MAN.
Evil intention, Wickedness, Perversity, Perfidious, Crime, Cruelty, Inhumanity, Atrocity.
Ill-intentioned, angry, evil, spiteful.

SYNONYMS
OR DIFFERENT MEANINGS OF THE CARD
No. 51. WIDOWHOOD.
Widow, Widowhood, Deprivation, Absence, Famine, Sterility, Indigence, Poverty, Empty, Vacant, Unoccupied, Unworked, Idle, Free.
Loner, survivor, sad, hypocritical, unpleasant, left behind.

(Reversed) WICKED WOMAN.
Wicked woman, Malignancy, Malice, Deceit, Craftiness, Artifice, Mischief, Bigotry, Prudery, Hypocrisy.
Cunning, aggressive, evil, difficult woman.

SYNONYMS
OR DIFFERENT MEANINGS OF THE CARD
No. 52. MILITARY.
Soldier, Man of the Sword, Man of Arms, Fencing master, Swordsman, Chasseur, Officer, **Soldier from any body and of any weapon, Fighter, Enemy, Disputes, War, Combat, Battle, Duel, Attack, Defense, Opposition, Resistance, Destruction, Ruin, Overthrow, Enmity, Hatred, Anger, Resentment, Courage, Valor, Bravery, Satellite, Hand for hire.**
Soldier, courage, competitor, fighter.

(Reversed) IGNORANCE.
Impudence, Ineptitude, Foolishness, Drivel, Stupidity, Carelessness, Impertinence, Extravagance, Ridiculous, Nonsense, Swindle, Trickery, Rascality, Fabrication.
Stupidity, ignorance, waste of time.

SYNONYMS
OR DIFFERENT MEANINGS OF THE CARD
No. 53. SPY.

Spy, Curious, Observer, Scrutineer, Amateur, Spy, Questioner, Examination, Note, Remark, Observation, Annotation, Speculation, Reckoning, Calculation, Guesswork, Scholar, Artist.
Disguised, enemy, secret, spy, gossip.

(Reversed) IMPROVIDENCE.

Improvidence, Sudden, Suddenly, Out of the blue, Astonishing, Surprising, Unexpectedly, Fortuitously, Hopelessly, All of a sudden, Improvise, Act or speak without preparation, Compose and recite on the spot.
Indifference, recklessness, negligence, the unforeseen.

SYNONYMS
OR DIFFERENT MEANINGS OF THE CARD
No. 54. TEARS.

Crying, Tears, Sob, Wailing, Sigh, Complaints, Lamentations, Grief, Affliction, Sorrow, Sadness, Pain, Complaining, Tales, Desolation.
Grumble, complacency, depression, lament, tears, bad outcome.

(Reversed) ADVANTAGE.

Advantage, Gain, Profit, Lucre, **Success, Grace, Favor, Benefit, Ascending, Power, Rule, Authority, Might, Usurpation.**
Income, advantage, promotion, profit, results.

SYNONYMS
OR DIFFERENT MEANINGS OF THE CARD
No. 55. ECCLESIASTICAL.

Bachelor, Celibate, Virginity, Puberty, Apostle, Ecclesiastic, Pope, Cardinal, Archbishop, **Bishop, Abbot, Priest, Monk, Hermit, Religious, Non, Temple, Church, Monastery, Convent, Hermitage, Sanctuary,**

Worship, Religion, Piety, Devotion, Rite, Ceremony, Ritual, Recluse, Anchorite, Vestal virgin.
Solitude, reflection, spiritual, philosophical, religious things.

(Reversed) JUSTIFIED DISTRUST.
Justified distrust, Suspicions well-founded, Legitimate fear, Mistrust, Doubt, Conjecture, Scruples, Fearful Conscience, Pure, Shyness, Modesty, Disgrace, Shame.
Assumption, deceit, drama, hunch, distrust, theft.

SYNONYMS
OR DIFFERENT MEANINGS OF THE CARD
No. 56. CRITICAL.
Criticism, Bad position, Critical decision, Critical moment, Decisive moment, Unhappy situation, Delicate circumstance, Crisis, Examination, Discussion, Research, Blame, Censorship, Gloss, Epilogue, Control, Disapproval, Condemnation, Annulment, Judgment, Contempt.
Criticism, discussion, readjustment.

(Reversed) INCIDENT.
Incident, Difficulty, Objection, **Special circumstance, Conjuncture, Event, Accessory, Inconvenience, Obstacle, Lag, Delay, Abjection, Dissent, Contradiction, Opposition, Resistance, Quibble, Stray, Unexpected, Fortuitous event, Adventure, Occurrence, Destiny, Fatality, Accidents, Misfortune, Disgrace, Unfortunate, Symptom.**
Obstacle, dispute, incident, tension, confusion.

SYNONYMS
OR DIFFERENT MEANINGS OF THE CARD
No. 57. HOPE.

Hope, Expectation, Hopefulness, Desire, **Claim, Founded, Trust, Make up, Purpose, Volition, Will, Wish, Way, Envy, Taste, Fantasy.**
Dilemma, illusions, stagnancy, outlook.

(Reversed) SOUND ADVICE.

Sound advice, Good advice, Salutary warnings, Instruction, Lesson, Observation, Reflection, Remark, Advice, Thought, Rebuke, Reproach, News, Announcement, Poster, Consultation, Admonition.
Recommendation, advice, hint, team work.

SYNONYMS
OR DIFFERENT MEANINGS OF THE CARD
No. 58. ROUTE.

Road, Lane, Path, Course, Passage, Trail, Way, Walk, Leave, Motion, Thoughtfulness, Conduct, Middle, Manner, Fashion, Expedient, Journey, Career, Promenade, Example, Trace, Vestige, Dispatch, Commissioner.
Fixing things, constructive dialogue, mission, messaging.

(Reversed) DECLARATION.

Declaration, Declarative Act, Development, Explanation, Interpretation, Charter, Constitution, Diploma, Manifest Law, Ordinance, Publication, Proclamation, Ostensive, Poster, Publicity, Authenticity, Notoriety, Denunciation, Enumeration, Recitation, Denotation, Designation, **Knowledge, Discovery, Disclosure, Vision, Revelation, Appearance, Showing, Confession, Protest, Approval, Authorization.**
Pronunciation, expression, explanation, disclosure, conversation, assertion.

SYNONYMS
OR DIFFERENT MEANINGS OF THE CARD
No. 59. LOSS.

Loss, Alteration, Wretch, Degradation, Waste, Withering, Destruction, Deterioration, Detriment, Decrease, Damage, Failures, Prejudice, Tare, Tort, Damage, Business decay, Spoilage, Disadvantage, Devastation, Dilapidation, Dissipation, Unfortunate, Misfortunes, Reversal, Reversal of fortune, Ruin, Defeat, Confusion, Debauchery, Shame, Defamation, Dishonor, Infamy, Ignominy, Affliction, Ugly, Deformity, Humiliation, Robbery, Theft, Abduction, Plagiarism, Kidnapping, Hateful, Horrible, Steal, **Disgrace, Corruption, Deregulation, Seduction, Unattachment.**
Sorrow, Sadness, break-up, affliction, loss, bankruptcy.

(Reversed) MOURNING.

Mourning, Dejection, Affection, Regret, Desolation, Affliction, Sadness, **Sorrow,** Calamity, Misfortune, **Pain, Pains of spirit, Funeral cortege, Funeral dress, Mournful, Funeral,** Ceremonial Burial, **Burial.**
Sorrows, pain, grief, mourning.

SYNONYMS
OR DIFFERENT MEANINGS OF THE CARD
No. 60. SOLITUDE.

Solitude, Desert, Retreat, Hermitage, Exile, Banishment, Proscription, Uninhabited, Isolation, Abandon, Abandonment, Tomb, Grave, Coffin.
Excluded, withdrawal, isolation, reflection.

(Reversed) ECONOMY.

Economy, Good conduct, Wise administration, Foresight, Discretion, Household, Savings, Avarice, Economize, Order, Arrangement, Report, Convenience, Concert, Accord, Concordance, Harmony, Music, Disposition, Testament, Reserve,

Restriction, Exception, Circumspection, Circumscription, Restraint, Wisdom, Symphony, Sparingly, Precaution.
Discretion, trust, financial burdens, past.

SYNONYMS
OR DIFFERENT MEANINGS OF THE CARD
No. 61. REMOTENESS.
Remoteness, Departure, Absence, Deviation, Dispersion, Distant, Delay, Disdain, Repugnance, Aversion, Hatred, Disgust, Horror, Incompatibility, Contrariety, Opposition, Unsociability, Misanthropy, Incivility, Separation, Division, Rupture, Antipathy, Section, Cut off.
Dismay, heartache, painful, estrangement.

(Reversed) DIVERSION.
Diversion, Dementia, Raving, Alienation of spirit, Distraction, Crazy conduct, Error, Misunderstanding, Loss, Detour, Deviation, Dispersion.
Distraction, thoughtlessness, losses, mistakes.

SYNONYMS
OR DIFFERENT MEANINGS OF THE CARD
No. 62. FRIENDSHIP
Friendship, Attachment, Affection, Tenderness, Benevolence, Relationship, Relation, Identity, Intimacy, Suitability, Correspondence, Interest, Conformity, Sympathy, Affinity, Attraction.
Intimacy, support, kindness, friends, peace.

(Reversed) FALSE.
False, Falsehood, Lie, Imposture, Duplicity, Bad faith, Deception, Concealment, Deceit, Trickery, Superficial, Appearances, Surface.
Neglected, stolen credit, enemy, betrayal, adultery.

SYNONYMS
OR DIFFERENT MEANINGS OF THE CARD
No. 63. EXTREME.

Extreme, Large, Excessive, Outrage, Furious, Carried away, Extremely, Passionate, Excessively, Vehemence, Animosity, Transport, Emotion, Anger, Fury, Rage, Extremity, Bounds, Confined, End, Limits, Last, Last breath, To the last, Scramble.
Rage, anger, possessiveness, domination, litigation.

(Reversed) PREGNANCY.

Pregnancy, Germ, Semen, Sperm, Womb, Pregnant, Delivery, Conception, Fruiting, Birth, Childbirth, Fertilization, Production, Composition, Growth, Enlargement, Increase, Multiplication.
Birth, reaping the fruit, pregnancy.

SYNONYMS
OR DIFFERENT MEANINGS OF THE CARD
No. 64. BROWN-HAIRED MAN.

Brown(haired) man, Trader, Merchant, Banker, Stockbroker, Calculative, Speculator, Physicist, Geometry, Mathematics, Science, Master, Professor.
Businessman, money, educated, successful.

(Reversed) VICIOUS MAN.

Vice, Defect, Weakness, Imperfection, Defective Conformation, Formless Nature, Deregulation, Ugly, Deformity, Corruption, Stench.
Negative thinking, manipulative, dishonest, perverse.

SYNONYMS
OR DIFFERENT MEANINGS OF THE CARD
No. 65. BROWN-HAIRED WOMAN.
Brown-haired woman, Opulence, Wealth, Pomp, Luxury, Sumptuousness, Assurance, Safety, Confidence, Certainty, Affirmation, Security, Boldness, Freedom, Franchise.
Successful, resourceful, affluence, generous.

(Reversed) UNCERTAINTY.
Bad, Doubtful, Uncertain, Doubt, Indecision, Uncertainty, Fright, Dread, Fear, Timidity, Apprehension, Vacillation, Hesitation, Indeterminate, Irresolute, Perplexed, who is suspended.
Insecurity, hesitation, doubt, poor choices.

SYNONYMS
OR DIFFERENT MEANINGS OF THE CARD
No. 66. UTILITY.
Useful, Advantage, Gain, Profit, Benefit, Profitable, Favorable, Advantageous, Important, Necessary, Compelling, Unofficial.
Profits, transactions, earnings, pay-out.

(Reversed) INACTION.
Peace, Tranquility, Rest, Sleep, Apathy, Inertia[116], Stagnation, Inactivity, Disappointment, Leisure, Passages, Recreation, Carelessness, Nonchalance, Indolence, Laziness, Idleness, Numbness, Discouragement, Destruction.
Laziness, carelessness, idleness.

---

[116] Translator: d´Odoucet lists the word *Mertie* instead of *Inertie*.

SYNONYMS
OR DIFFERENT MEANINGS OF THE CARD
No. 67. BROWN-HAIRED BOY.

Brown(haired) boy, Study, Instruction, Application, Meditation, Reflection, Work, Occupation, Learning, Schoolboy, Disciple, Pupil, Apprentice, Amateur, Student, Speculator, Negotiator.
Inexperience, student, apprenticeship, willingness.

(Reversed) PRODIGALITY.

Profusion, Superfluous, Largeness, Indulgence, Sumptuousness, Magnificence, Lavishness, Multiplicity, Liberality, Benefit, Generosity, Charity, Hosting, Multitude, Degradation, Dilapidation, Pillage, Dissipation.
Excess, reckless, mischief, intemperance, over-spender.

SYNONYMS
OR DIFFERENT MEANINGS OF THE CARD
No. 68. THE HOUSE.

House, Household, Economy, Savings, Residence, Domicile, Dwelling, Manor, Home, Housing, Hotel, Palace. Store. Shop. Lodge. Barracks, **Building, Vessel, Place, Archive, Chateau, Cottage,** Hut. Tent. Pavilion. Hotel. Hostel. Cabaret. Log. Tavern. Religious house. Monastery. Convent. Hermitage. Burial. Tomb. Grave. Stable, **Family, Extraction, Race,** Line, **Posterity, Den, Cave, Lair.** Retreat.
Dwelling, resort, home, the long run.

(Reversed) GAME OF CHANCE.

Lot, Fortune, Game, Fortuitous event, Chance, Ignorance, Fate, Doom, Destiny, Fatality, Happy or unlucky occasions. Stop. Decree. Decision. Dowry. Legitimate. Go. Share. Donation. Gratification. Pension. Opportunity.
Good luck, investment, speculation, gambling, fortune.

SYNONYMS
OR DIFFERENT MEANINGS OF THE CARD
No. 69. EFFECT.

Effect, Sequence, Result, Consequence, Evidence, Conviction, Conclusion, Event, Execution, Achievement, Accomplishment, Perfection, Goods, Furniture, Buildings.
Serenity, break-through, consequence, rewards.

(Reversed) DECEPTION.

Deception, Surprise, Error, Lure, **Hour, Trickery, Fraud, Deceit, Cunning, Cheating, Swindling, Embezzlement, Roguery, Infidelity.**
Lie, ruse, deception, abuse.

SYNONYMS
OR DIFFERENT MEANINGS OF THE CARD
No. 70. BRUNETTE GIRL.

Brown-haired girl, Honest girl, Welcome, Obliging, Thoughtfulness, Politeness, Honesty, Civility, Complacency, Condescension, Hospitality, Manners, Character, Natural.
Young lady, co-worker, assisting, candor, guidance.

(Reversed) USURY.

Advantage, Increase, Majority, More, Much, Copiously, Abundantly, Wear, Exorbitant, Exaction, With wear and tear, Usurious, **Avarice, More than, Over, Again, Importance, Elevation, Height, Pride, Vainness, Vanity.**
Greed, pride, indulgence, arrogance, dissatisfaction.

SYNONYMS
OR DIFFERENT MEANINGS OF THE CARD
No. 71. MONEY.

Money, Wealth, Sum, Currency, Silverware, Purity, Parity, Candor, Innocence, Ingenuity, Moon, Purging, Purification.
Settlement, finances, making money, win, self-worth.

(Reversed) WORRY.

Worry, Torment of mind, Impatience, Affliction, Sorrow, Anxiety, Loneliness, Care, Attention, Diligence, Application, Apprehension, Fear, Defiance, Distrust, Suspicion.
Concern, anxiety, bad climate, turmoil.

SYNONYMS
OR DIFFERENT MEANINGS OF THE S CARD
No. 72. THE PRESENT.

Currently, Presently, the moment, Incontinent, Suddenly, Now, At this time, Today, Assistant, Witness, Right away, On the hour, At First, **Contemporary, Attentive, Careful, Vigilant.**
Presently, the present, preoccupation, priorities.

(Reversed) AMBITION.

Desire, Wish, Ardor, Eagerness, Passion, Research, Greed, To come, Jealousy, Illusion.
Purpose, striving, ambition, diligence, grounding.

SYNONYMS
OR DIFFERENT MEANINGS OF THE CARD
No. 73. LOVER.

Lover, in Love, Chivalrous, Gallant, Husband, Wife, Consort, Spouse, Friend, Amateur, Mistress, Loving, Cherishing, Adoring, Matching, Accord, Convenience, Connection, **Compatibility, Kindness.**
Affection, protection, lover, kindness.

(Reversed) DISORDER.

Disorderly, Counter-order, Misconduct, Disorder, Trouble, Confusion, Chaos, Damage, Ravage, Ruin, Dissipation, Consumption, Deregulation, Libertinism, Discord, Disharmony, Discrepancy.
Bad behavior, turbulence, imprudence, difficulty, mistakes, change of direction.

SYNONYMS
OR DIFFERENT MEANINGS OF THE CARD
No. 74. A GIFT.

A Present, Gift, Generosity, Benefit, Liberality, Holiday gifts, Grace, Offering, Donation, Gratification, Service, White color, Lunar medicine, White stone. Precious stone.
Enjoyment, expansion, opportunity, satisfaction, gifts.

(Reversed) ENCLOSURE.

Enclosure, Circuit, Circumvallation, Circumscription, Circumference, Circle, Circulation, Intercept, Obstruction, Congestion, Grabbing, Cloister, Monastery, Convent, Incarceration. Imprisonment. Arrest, **Stop, Fixed, Determine, Definitive, End, Boundaries,** Barricades, **Limits, Terms, End, Barrier, Partition, Wall, Hedge, Walls, Obstacles, Bars, Impeachment, Suspension, Delay, Opposition.**
Obstacle, impediment, inconvenience, hindrance, inopportune time.

SYNONYMS
OR DIFFERENT MEANINGS OF THE CARD
No. 75. NOBLE.

Noble, Consequence, Famous, Important, Great, Major, Extended, Vast, Sublime, Renowned, Famous, Mighty, Elevated, Illustrious, High standard, **Illustration, Consideration, Soul Greatness, Noble processes, Generous** actions, **Magnificently, Splendidly.**

Rank, elevated, valiant, courageous, influence, glory.

(Reversed) CHILD.

Puerility, Child, Childhood, Frivolity, Weakening, Lowering, Decrease, Politeness, Smallness, **Lowness, Mediocracy, Minuteness, Bagatelle, Frivolity, Baseness, Yellow, Cowardice, Reject, Petite, Puerile, Puny, Bas, Rampant, Lowly, Abject, Humble, Abjection, Humility, Humiliation.**

Average, immaturity, child, petty.

SYNONYMS
OR DIFFERENT MEANINGS OF THE CARD
No. 76. INCONVENIENCE.

Inconvenience, Obstacle, Congestion, Obstruction, Hitch, Glitch, Trouble, Hassle, Emotion, Scramble, Scrambling, Difficulty, Impediment, Kink, Obscurity, Agitation, Worry, Perplexity, Solicitude.

Obstacles, stress, difficulty, set-backs, delays.

(Reversed) LETTER.

Ticket, Written, Writing, Sacred scripture. Secular writing, **Text, Literature, Doctrine, Erudition, Work, Book, Production, Composition, Dispatch, Epistle, Message, Character, Literal** meaning, **Alphabet, Elements, Principles, Letters of exchange.**

Message, email, letter, telephone call.

SYNONYMS
OR DIFFERENT MEANINGS OF THE CARD
No. 77. PERFECT CONTENTMENT.

Perfect contentment, Felicity, Happiness, Rapture, Enchantment, Ecstasy, Wonder, Complete satisfaction, Complete joy, Unspeakable pleasure, Color red, Perfect medicine, Sun medicine, Pure, Prayer answered, **Accomplished.**
Happiness, fulfilment, joy, prosperity.

(Reversed) MONEY PURSE.
Sum, Capital, Principal, Treasure, Wealth, Opulence, Rare, Expensive, Precious, Invaluable.
Gain, prize, profit, success.

SYNONYMS
OR DIFFERENT MEANINGS OF THE CARD
No. 78. FOLLY.

Madness, Insanity, Extravagance, Unreason, Delusion, Drunkenness, Delirium, Hot fever, **Frenzy, Rage, Fury, Transport, Enthusiasm, Blindness, Ignorance, Mad, Senseless,** Unreasonable, **Irresponsible, Innocent, Simple, Foolish.**
Dumbfounded, impulse, instinct, dismay, foolish, amazement, childish dream, fleeting passion, crazy.

(Reversed) FOLLY.
Imbecility, Ineptitude, Carelessness, Foolishness, Carelessness, Negligence, Absence, Distraction, Apathy, Fainting, Annihilation, Sleep, Nothingness, Nullity, Emptiness, Nothing, Futile.
Mad idea, void of reason, distraction, mental disorders.

LIST
OF THE ONE HUNDRED MAIN QUESTIONS

making reasonable use

OF THE BOOK OF THOT

1. Who am I among men[117]?
2. Will my affairs clear up?
3. Will I be able to prevent slander?
4. Will I be stripped of my hopes?
5. Will my trip be happy?
6. Will my experiences help me?
7. Will I be supported?
8. Who am I among the women?
9. Is my main virtue to be fair?
10. Is my main virtue to be temperate?
11. Is my main virtue to be strong?
12. Is my main virtue to be careful?
13. What will be the outcome of a marriage?
14. Will I have *force majeure* in what concerns me?
15. What will be my health or the outcome of an illness?
16. My judgment on others and others on me?
17. Tell me about death?
18. Will I be warned of any betrayal?
19. Will I endure prison or an extreme misery?
20. Will I become really rich?
21. Will I have quarrels?
22. What kind of men will I have more interest in?
23. What kind of women will I have more interest in?
24. What should I focus on?
25. Will the foreigners be favorable to me?

---

[117] This question has several meanings and, like all the others, leads to unique answers, to the point of wonder.

26. Am I being betrayed and should I challenge myself?
27. Are the delays at their end?
28. Will I go to the countryside?
29. Should I go talk to my protector?
30. Tell me about the order of my housekeeper?
31. Am I going to get some gold?
32. Is my company honest?
33. Should I start?
34. I am in pain, what should I do?
35. Will I have children?
36. Name me my true friend?
37. Name me my enemy?
38. Will he arrive without delay?
39. Who will be in my life, a young man or a widower?
40. The city, the provinces, or going abroad, what is more favorable to me?
41. Will I achieve a victory?
42. Who will be in my life, a young woman or a widow?
43. What should I concentrate my thoughts on?
44. Does the past decide my future?
45. Can I expect an inheritance?
46. Does my boredom arise from the moral or the physical?
47. Can I hope to be successful?
48. Is my love well founded?
49. Will abundance come into my home?
50. Will my judges be convinced in depth and with the justification of my cause?
51. Will I be a widower or a widow?
52. What profession, Science, Art, Commerce, Outfit, Sword, fits my person?
53. Are they watching my conduct, my actions?
54. Are my tears foolish or legitimate?

55. Should I think on celibacy? What suits me; the result?
56. Should I prepare for some disease or is there something wrong, I don't know?
57. Do I have to give up on to my aspirations?
58. Will I get what I was promised?
59. Will I find what I lost?
60. Which way to begin in the world?
61. Will I get out of my worry soon?
62. Is the friendship that I am shown real?
63. What will be the result of my strong passions?
64. Do I have to rely on a man?
65. Should I rely on a woman?
66. Is it true, that they want to be useful to me?
67. Should I listen to a person?
68. Will I support my household?
69. Will I have effects, or will I lose effects?
70. What will become of the words?
71. Will he get any money?
72. How do I spend the present?
73. Should I be attached to a person?
74. Will I receive a present?
75. Will we act nobly?
76. Will I get out of my predicament?
77. Will I have perfect contentment?
78. What will be my greatest madness?
79. Do I have recourse to a good man, sincere?
80. Do I have to take care of a person?
81. Do I break up with who I think on?
82. Is the news I have heard true or false?
83. How to overcome the obstacles that stand in the way of my success?
84. Is my enemy powerful?
85. Does the flexibility of my character depend on the moral or the physical?
86. Will someone's indecision go on for a long time?

87. Will I bloom?
88. Will I have a trial? or what will be the outcome of a trial?
89. What end will the case that concerns me have?
90. Are my sorrows at an end?
91. What will be my first surprise?
92. Shouldn't I be wary of the last victory I achieved?
93. Should I break up with someone, who doesn't give me hope?
94. I would like to break up with a woman but I fear her retaliation. Am I wrong?
95. Am I deceived, as I fear?
96. Will death break my bondage?
97. Do you think I'll lose my jewelry?
98. Are they speaking the truth to me?
99. Will I have fun at a party, I plan to go to?
100. Will I do well to stick to the project before me?

GAME RULES

OF VARIOUS GAMES WITH TAROT[118]

MUCH FUN

TAROT GAME ACCORDING TO THE EARLY

AND MOST KNOWN EGYPTIAN

The book of Thot took the name of *Tarot, or the Royal Game of Human Life.*

Not only is the Tarot capable of advising and instructing the solitary, as he entertains as many people as he can assemble, relieving him of his worries by the superiority of the wise advice it offers him; since he is persuaded by the intelligence of the wise men who have composed it.

I. Once the players have chosen their Mage among themselves, they also choose from the non-playing persons, a man and a woman, whom they name *Osiris* and *Isis*.

2. When sitting down at the table to play, the Mage has the dominant place, we agree on the price of the main fine which is assumed here to be 1 sol (Parisis), and to collect the fines, we place a basket in the middle of the table.

3. Once all the players have taken their seat, the Mage takes the book of Thot, shuffles its pages taking care to put them both in upright and reverse without looking at them, has them cut to his left, and distributes the cards on his right, with such division as he likes, but up to the number seven, to all the players, including himself.

---

[118] Translator: This chapter on game rules in the Orsini booklet matches a text from *Cours Theorique et Pratique,1790 by Etteilla (p.145-148).*

4. Each player should notice what the top card is (when the Mage deals) i.e. opposite to his front; it is in this way in the progressive order of the appearance of the cards, that the players must read the cards which are drawn, and which they read to whom they please of all the people, who are in the room.

5. When one of the players expresses an oracle, he takes on the role of *interpreter*, and if the person to whom he gives the oracle, does not give him a present, he is obliged to pay half of the fine.

6. When a person has had three true oracles either past or present or in any order wished, and he refuses to reward the reader; the players hold a committee and judge by majority vote, whether the refusal from the person is founded or not. In the latter case the Mage pronounces the word *Pamenes*, which warns the whole room, that there is in the assembly a person, who does not take part in the Royal Game of Human life, and then, Osiris and Isis are obliged to pay for him, because they are compelled by their title, which they have accepted, to always spread peace and abundance to the heroes, being the players.

7. When one of the spectators asks for a player's hand, the Mage fixes the price, which is divided into three; the first third to the fines fund; the second to the Mage, and the third to the player; the player can refuse this sacrifice by paying with his hand the first two thirds of the price fixed above.

8. If one of the spectators has acquired the hand of a player; he runs all the chances of that player, the fines and the presents.

9. When a player cannot return an oracle, he puts his seven cards down and pays a quarter of the fine.

10. If, when able to read an oracle, the player does not know to whom to address it, he lays his cards facing up onto the table, giving the speech of what he sees and pays nothing. If, on the contrary, he reads incorrectly, which the

other players must judge, the Mage sentences him to half a fine.

11. When the interpreter has returned an oracle, high or low, and has received a present, he can have his seven cards switched out by the Mage, who offers back the cut, and finally, if one player's cards produce three presents from the same or from several people, for whom the three oracles are given, all players except the Mage give the interpreter the value of three times the fine. That is the Civic Crown.

12. It is the Mage who orders and directs everything at will; he pronounces the fine, according to the nature of the fault, such as; to show his cards to other players, hide them from spectators, be discreet in the reading out loud of oracles, make oracles that are not proven, etc.

13. The spectators can enter the game until the moment when the Mage indicates the end of the game by saying; in a quarter of an hour, or half an hour and so on.

14. If the Mage forgets to announce the end of the game, the spectators would be entitled to take their share of the charged fines with the other players, which is then divided equally.

15. At this Royal Game of Human life, people who do not know divine political and philosophical science have the least fun and lose the most. You can only spark your interest by practicing it.

THE PLEASANT GAME OF TAROT

Why this card deck of Tarot was not brought forth earlier in our France, is as I believe, because the French only ask for a summary of all things, and what has made them less popular, is the fact, that very few people have had the knowledge of the rules, which must be observed in order to play them. It is the most entertaining game, that can be found and of which I can say, with truth, where there is no deceit, no trickery.

The Swiss and the Germans do not usually play other games, and even in France, as in Lyon, Marseilles and other places, where we know of this type, it is very much in use.

It should be noted that the ordinary deck of cards, that is played in France is made up of 52 cards and that of Tarot 78.

The 52-card deck has four suits each consisting of 13 cards, or 13 in all four suits; the deck of 56 has an additional knight in each suit, making up 14 in the four suits; the Tarot in addition to the 14-card suits has 22 extras named the majors.

By removing the 22 majors and the four knights, there will remain 52 cards, with which we can play all the games that are played in France, such as *Piquet*, *Triomphe*, *Brelan*, etc.

Rules of the pleasant game of Tarot

1. When we play the 78 cards of tarot, we can be two, three, or four players; each one is dealt twelve cards, we then turn over one card, which we place under the deck pile and which is made known to all and thus forms the bottom. The first to play may replace from one up to five of his cards; the second one to four, the third one to three. The cards, replacing those discarded are taken successively from the pile by the players, starting with the first player. The cards turned in cannot be used again; they remain under the deck.

2. The 22 majors out-trump all the others, which we will call minors and which are the 14 cards of each suit, in their numerical order. So, for example, if the play is in swords or spades, the value of the majors will be counted as follows, and in descending order:

1. Chaos which is the superior trump, among those named the Majors.

2. Light etc., until the 22nd trump which is Folly or the No. 78, the lesser of the Majors. Then come all the Minors. Know this: 23 the King of Swords or Spades, 24 the Queen, 25 the Knight, 26 the Page, 27 the Ten, 28 the Nine, 29 the Eight, 30 the Seven, 31 the Six, 32 the Five, 33 the Four, 34 the Three, 35 the Two, 36 finally the Ace of the same suit, which in this game is considered the least valuable card. We will proceed in the same way when the suit belongs to the cards of Clubs or Diamonds, to those of Cups or Heart, and to those of Coins or Clover.

3. When the turn involves one of the all-important Majors, we understand that only these of this order can compose the trumps, and that the 56 other cards have no other value, then what is special to them, meaning, the King of the suit played takes the Queen and she then takes the Knight, and so on, as long as one of the Majors does not appear to take them away.

4. In this game we consider all the majors as a fifth suit, and we can play with them as with the cards of the other suits, thirds, fourths, fifths, etc., as in *Piquet*. The numerical order of these is used to compose the odds. For example, the Nos. 7, 8 and 9 will form a third; the 12, 13, 14 and 15, a fourth; those 17, 18, 19, 20 and 21, a fifth, etc., the Folly does not fit into any combination.

5. All the Majors also compete for points with the other suits, and with equal points, however they win over them. All courts are worth ten points and the other cards, even the Ace, are worth the points they score.

6. We also count as in *Piquet* the three and the fourteen of Kings, Queens, Knights, Pages, Ten and Aces. The latter, contrary to what is practiced in *Piquet*, are erased or cancelled, by the three or fourteen of ten, and the superiors.

7. The one who makes the greatest number of tricks has ten points.

8. As to the number of points, which form the game, it is up to the players to fix that before start, usually we play with a hundred points.

9. The players' bets are fixed by them and deposited in a basket. All of the bets go to the one, who first reaches the agreed upon number.

10. For anything that is not stated above, we follow the rules of the game of *Piquet*.

One of the big differences that we should notice from *Piquet*, is that we do not recognize all cards[119], but in this one, we recognize two kinds; some called Majors and some Minors.

---

[119] Translator: Piquet is played with cards 7 through to Kings with Ace as the highest.

ANOTHER GAME THAT THE SWISS ORDINARILY PLAY

With these same 78 cards, the Swiss play with three people, and deal all the cards into a reserve of three, which the dealer cuts, after turning over the last card, which indicates the trump or the all-out. The rules of this game differ from those of the previous, only with regard to the number of players and that of cards, that are dealt to them and in that it does not give rise to extras.

All of the 22 Majors cards are as follows:

1 Le Chaos.	12 La Prudence.
2 La Lumiere.	13 Le Grand Pretre.
3 Les Plantes.	14 Le Diable.
4 Le Ciel.	15 Le Magicien ou Bateleur
5 L´homme.	16 Le Jugement dernier.
6 Les Astres.	17 La Mort.
7 Les Oiseaux.	18 Le Capucin.
8 Le Repos.	19 Le Temple foudroye.
9 La Justice.	20 La Roue de Fortune.
10 La Temperance.	21 Le Despote Africain.
11 La Force.	78 La Folie.

As for the different ways of playing tarots, that goes beyond our subject, we have recalled here some of these rules, the reader will find still others in the Academy of Games by Bonneveine, in 12 volumes, which has just been published.

Let us conclude by noting that Tarots for cartomancy differ from Tarots in playing cards; those generally used are:

LE GRAND JEU DE L'ORACLE DES DAMES.
78 tarot cards printed in chromolithography an imitation of the xv century miniatures, enclosed in an illustrated box and accompanied by an explanatory book.

GRAND JEU DES 78 TAROTS ÉGYPTIENS.
or book of Thot, in service of the Grand Etteilla. 78 colored cards.

As for tarots in playing cards, these are: Swiss, Italians, Spaniards, etc., these are not ordinarily used for spreads.

THE INTUITIVE APPROACH

The reader may be a little overwhelmed so far, by the information given in this book from the old sources, however let us bear in mind that a lot of experience has gone into using these cards since 1789 and that some information provided here may be less relevant, in particular from a practical and intuitive reading approach. There is always a difference between theory and practice.

In the following pages the modern spreads are described and this is perhaps the most important practical take-away from this book. The reader will see that certain methods are not used today by modern Etteilla readers; i.e. the various card games described in the earlier chapters, the meanings attributed to the "sets" such as the appearance of 2 jacks and 3 kings etc. in a spread, the "pairing" between cards, left and right of the spread, and basically all the old spread techniques.

As with any tarot reading approach, your own intuition is what matters the most. The spread itself can give a frame to the reading, such as a basic time line; past, present and future, the modern spreads better than the old, but it will be the card itself, its upright or reverse meaning and it´s "interaction" or inertia with neighboring cards, that will give the reader the most important information.

Intuition is more a "feels right" approach rather than a logical or mechanical; "this is what the keyword on the card says or this is what Etteilla´s technique was", so the reader must follow his or her own intuition rather than any rule.

ADDITIONAL CARD SPREADS

The Cross Spread[120]

Shuffle the cards and cut with your left hand. Articulate your question, and put the cards as indicated in the figure below. The first card on the left represents the querent's state of mind or the determining event, that in this moment comes into his spread. The second card, opposite the first and on the right, will be the element which will hamper the question or reinforce it, depending on whether it is in the Upright or in the Reverse. The third card, on the top and in between the other two, will inform him about possible events, meetings, forces needed in order to achieve his goals. The fourth card, opposite the third, below, will reveal the answer.

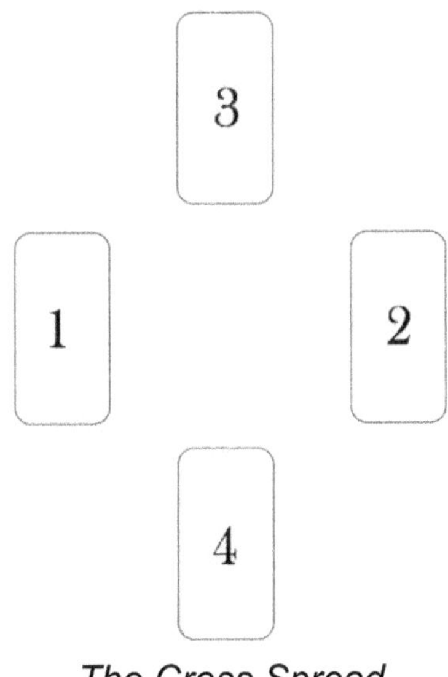

The Cross Spread

---

[120] Translator: This spread is a recap from Claude Darche.

Example.
The cards 2, 52, 72R and 41 have been drawn.

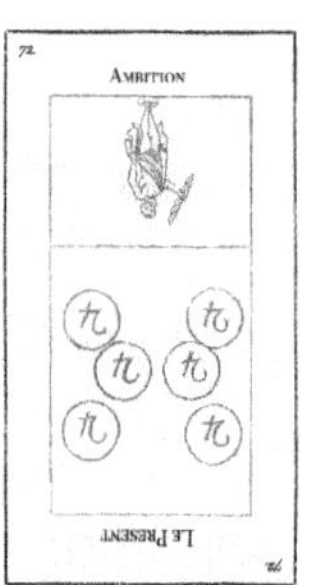

The cards are laid out as in the figure. The interpretation may come out something like this: Cards show someone looking for clarity, to receive feedback or to speak his mind, perhaps in connection with a job, his demeanor and candor will assist him, and this will turn out to his advantage.

The 5 card spread[121]

Mix the cards on a flat surface, pick them up and shuffle. Once the cards are shuffled, cut the deck with your left hand, while asking your question. Pay attention to the wording of your question. It should be concise and clear, so as to avoid any confusion. Now count the cards to five, and take out that fifth card and put it down, face up, in front of you. Repeat this operation 4 times, so you in the end obtain five cards, which you will have arranged in a spread, as in the figure below.

1. Cards 1 and 2 represent the past influence to the question asked.
2. Card 3 is the present. It is the objective reflection of the querent´s state of mind, what his situation is.
3. Card 4 and 5 represent the future. It is the answer to the question, with the elements currently available.

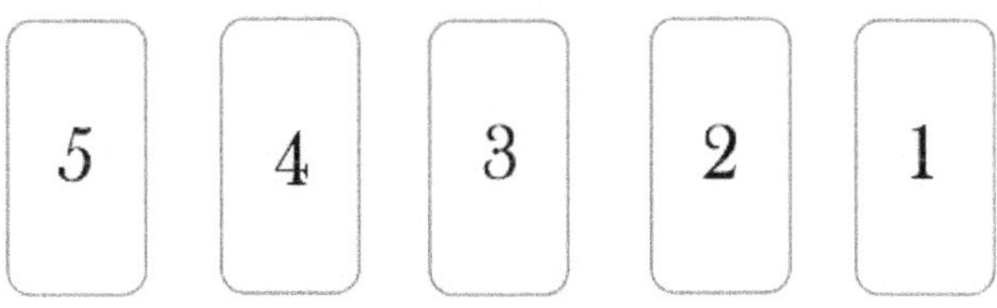

The 5 Card Spread

---

[121] Translator: This spread is a recap from E. San Emeterio.

Example.
The cards 51R, 18, 44, 60 and 66R have been drawn.

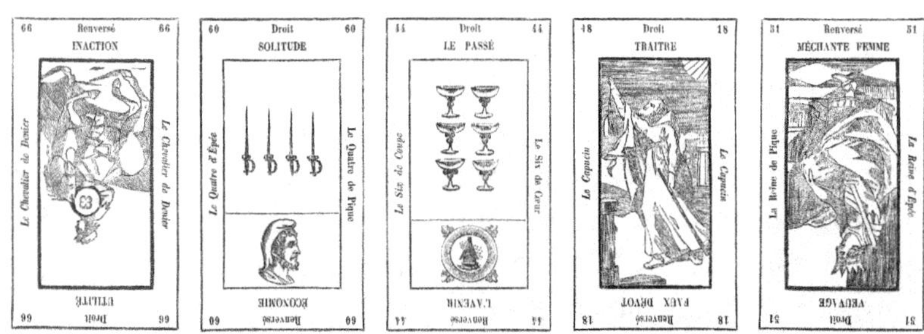

The cards are laid out and read from right to left. The interpretation may come out something like this: Cards show a nasty woman, who has hurt you in the past, from which you are still recovering, keeping you in hermit mode and preventing you from moving on.

Example.
The cards 78, 66R, 57, 54 and 49R have been drawn.

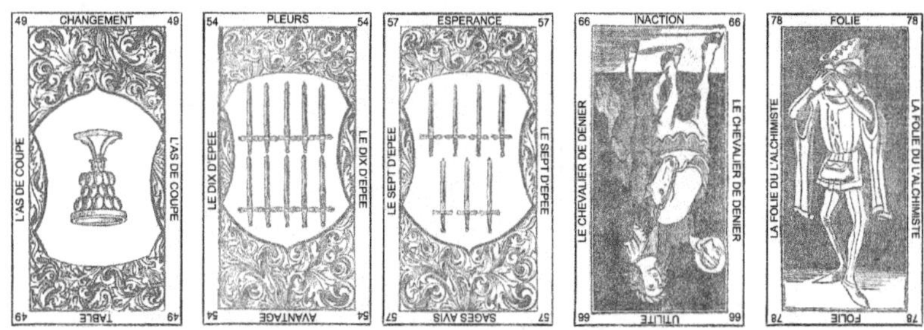

This interpretation may come out something like this: Cards show in the past a foolish person, or perhaps a thoughtless person, who did not act in time or did not act at all, who now although hopeful but perhaps not realistic, is going to suffer the consequences and will have to adjust to the changes as best she/he can.

The Draw of the 3 Worlds[122]

Mix the cards on a flat surface in front of you, then pick them up and shuffle them. Once the cards are shuffled, you put the deck in front of you and cut it with your left hand. You then draw three times five cards, which you will spread out as in the figure. The top row is 1, second 2, bottom 3. Card 1 in each row will always represent the querent, his personality, his current state of mind etc. You will then read the cards as follows: 2, 3, 4 and 5.

1. The First Row: Concerns the querent´s emotional life or his past.
2. The Second Row: Concerns the querent´s professional life or his present.
3. The Third Row: Concerns the querent´s future or his future material situation.

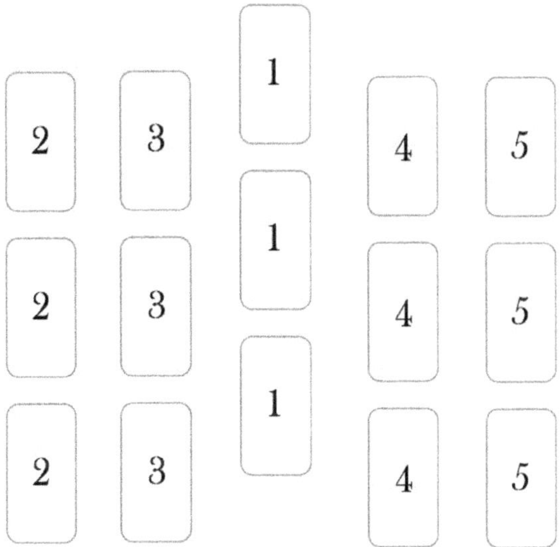

The Draw of the 3 Worlds

---

[122] Translator: This spread is a recap from E. San Emeterio and Claude Darche.

Example.
For the past, from left to right, the cards 34, 9, 13, 21 and 36R have been drawn. For the present, the cards 4, 61R, 59, 65 and 5R have been drawn. For the future, the cards 39, 10, 11, 1 and 44R have been drawn.

The marriage card is in the center, representing the past. Card 9 Justice with card 21, a card of dispute and 34 a card of sorrows, indicates a divorce. Moreover card 36, the King of Cups in reverse, traditionally a card representing the father, perhaps here, him racing off as the Charioteer. It is obvious that, the querent is still affected by a divorce in the past.

Card 59 in the present, a card of grief, so certainly some issues here needing to be addressed. A card of denial in 4, a card of diversion in 61R, a card of money making in 65 and 5 a card of stagnation in reverse. We can see that the querent is still grieving and has issues moving on from this, he or she is diverting his or her attention towards other things, such as work, making money. We can assume that this is affecting his or her relationships to people around him or her too.

The future does however look much brighter. Strength is drawn as the first card. With card 39, he or she is bit by bit putting in the effort, healing that hurt, balancing out those emotions with the Temperance card, gaining that insight, with card no. 1 and putting the past behind, looking to the future, with card no. 44 in the reverse.

The Inverted Pyramid Spread

This spread is used, when the querent wishes to ask a question concerning a relationship between 2 people. The relationship can be of any type; a couple, to a family member, a friend, a business partner etc. The cards are shuffled as in the previous spreads. All 78 cards are shuffled for this spread. Proceed as follows:

1. Draw six cards and lay them out as in the figure below. The first row concerns the present. The first card represents you, the querent, while the second represents the person you are inquiring into (Note; not specifically cards no. 1 and 8!). The other four cards are placed between these two cards. These cards represent the state of mind of the two people. The cards are read two by two for each.
2. The second row represents the next three months, indicating the events, the state of mind, feelings, victories and defeats. Card 7 is the querent, card 9 is the other person. Card 8 is the synthesis between the two.
3. The third row represents the general situation, emotionally, between the two people, six months from now. The left side describes the querent, the right, the other person.
4. The last card in the fourth row indicates the trajectory, the outcome after one year.

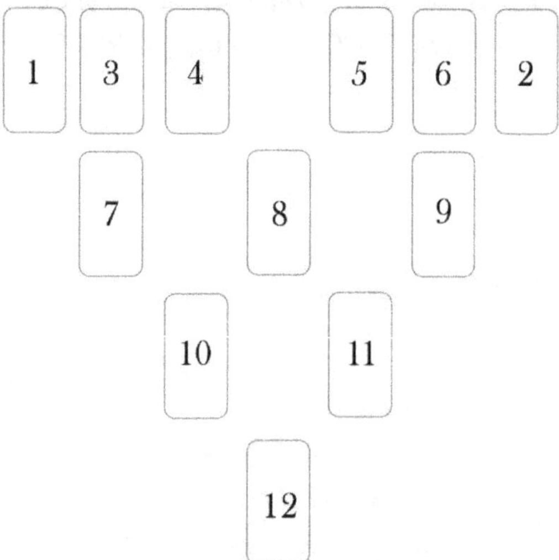

The Inverted Pyramid Spread

Example.
The following cards have been drawn for a female querent with regards to her spouse. In the first row from left to right; 49, 60, 44R, 67, 31, 53. The second row; 51R, 56, 77R. Third row; 30R, 46R. Outcome; 19R.

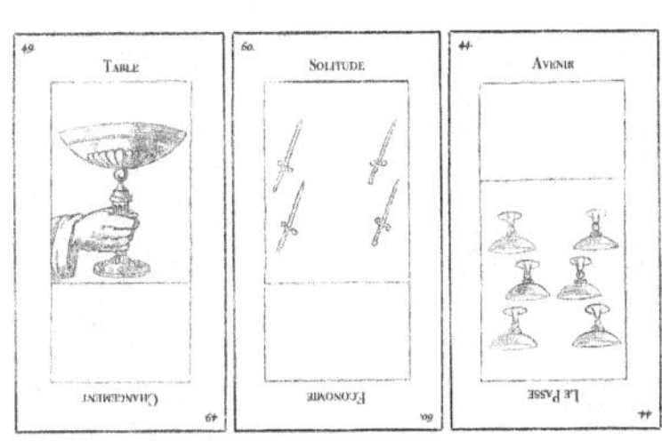 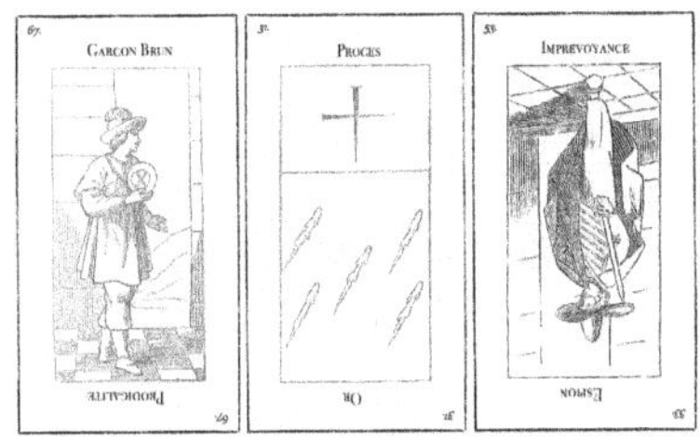

 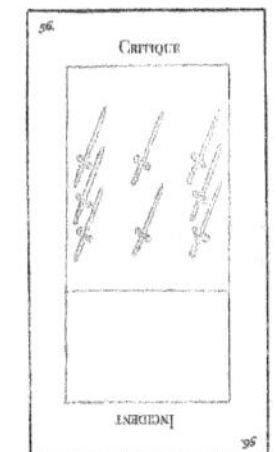 

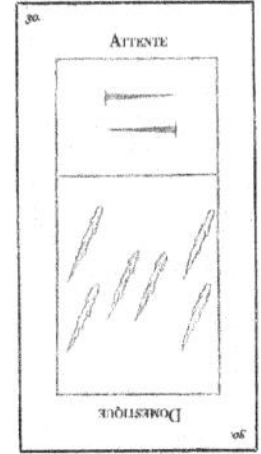 

This interpretation may come out something like this: The female querent is represented by the Ace of Cups, emotionally available, perhaps in a new relationship, putting in the effort, looking to push the relationship in the right direction, but feels neglected, the communication between them is not good, she might be questioning the future of the relationship. The spouse is represented by the Page of Swords, indifferent, preoccupied, caught off guard, perhaps in some sort of dispute or legal issue, probably in connection with a work situation, where he is inexperienced and which takes up his time.

The second row implies a worsening of the situation between the two. She will not end up happy, she will become resentful towards him, and will become difficult to deal with. He may still be preoccupied with work, but can still be fully invested in the relationship. The synthesis between them however will become difficult and will deteriorate.

The third row implies she holding off, not investing any longer, waiting for him to make the change. He will be on the defensive, but may try different approaches, which however, will not be successful.

The outcome is more hardship, difficulties, this will most probably end up in a break up, if things do not change. It may also indicate an actual prison situation with the Tower, an ending by force, so to speak, which could tie back to that legal issue from before.

OLD CARD SPREADS

The 7 Card Spread[123]

The direct question generally takes place, where the querent has not received in a previous reading the particular solution of what affects him. In such cases, the querent expresses and exposes in a clear and precise manner the subject that affects him, the reader then, after having shuffled the cards of the book in both upright and reverse, gives it to the querent to open. Once the cut is made, and the whole book returned; he takes the first seven cards, then orders them from right to left, successively and in the natural order of their coming. He first reads the appearing cards (A, B, C, D), then reads the cards two by two (1+7, 2+6, 3+5, see table below), and if the solution is found, answers the question; however, if the solution is doubtful or obscure, it would be necessary to draw follow up cards in the same quantity, order them as with the first and read the appearing cards first. Otherwise, we must lay out the spread again, we draw in a row, the same number of cards and we read as described.

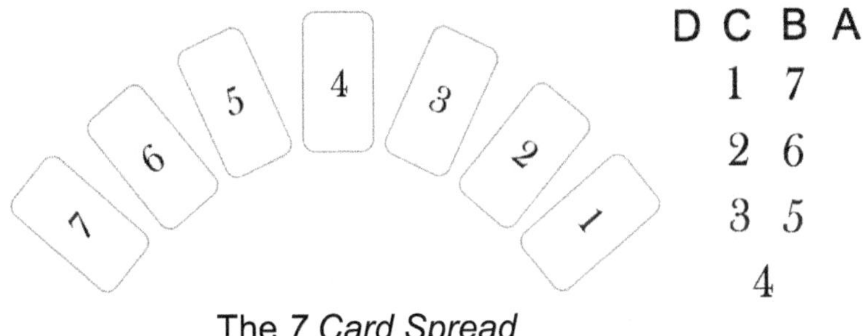

The *7 Card Spread*

---

[123] Translator: This text on the *Quatrieme coup* is a translated excerpt from *Science des Signes, 1806*, by M. M. d´Odoucet p. 76-78.

If on the third try the question cannot be resolved, it is left unresolved for the moment; but we invite the querent to make the heavens favorable, and we urge him to present his question another day.

Now consider, for example, the following question to be answered: Who is my most formidable enemy, both morally and physically? and then we are presented with the following cards, ordered from right to left; 47: 31: 69: 33: 32. 57. 41: Note that the cards which are accompanied with two points, have come in the reverse, the others in the upright, *situs*. They say; you foolishly give all your confidence to a company, which could put an end to the discomfort you feel; however, someone plays with your candor, it is in the envious shrewdness of the necessary quibbles of business affairs. Thus, injustice keeps you waiting. Deceit predominates in this company, and your bad luck remains.

Summary: With due care to the sensitivity of this question; you have to fear, morally, too much frankness; and physically, fraudulent losses.[124]

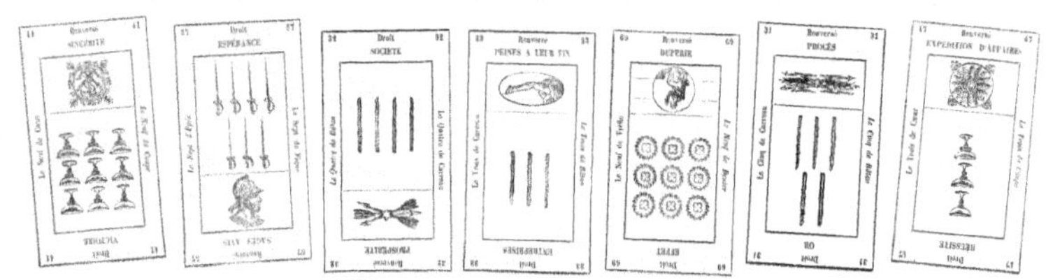

The example spread

---

[124] Translator: The breakdown of this spread; the spread is read right to left; the first 4 cards; *Business (affaires), Trial, Deception, Penalty in the end (misfortune)*. The pairing: *Business on Sincerity, Trial on Hope, Deception on Association, Penalty in the end*. The sets: 2 Threes in Reverse *Savings*, 2 Nines in Reverse *small profit*. Card 69R next to 31 implies *pitfall, enemy* and 69 arriving with 33 *a most skilful trickery*.

The Wheel of Fortune Spread[125]

After having shuffled the cards of the book in reverse and upright, we remove card 1 or 8, depending on the sex of the querent. After the cut, we form two columns each comprising 11 cards, which are topped by a bar with 11 cards; thus, making up 33 cards.

In the interior is laid out a wheel comprising of three times 11 cards, in order to correspond to the 33 previous cards; making a sum set of 66 cards to be interpreted. The 11 remaining cards are put aside and left without further explanation; however, the card which had to be withheld from the deck, 1 or 8, depending on the sex of the querent, is now placed in the center of this wheel.

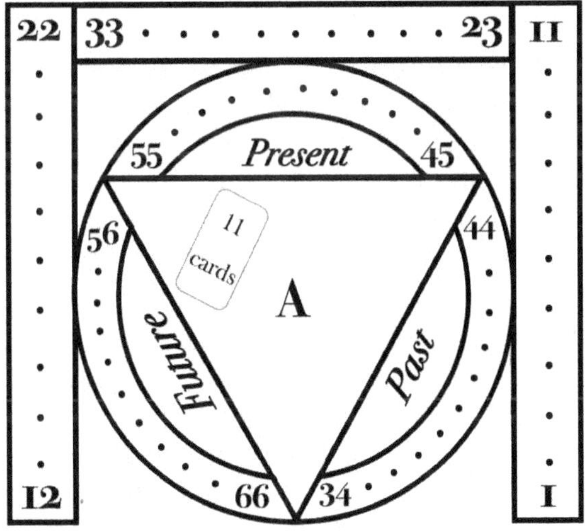

Wheel of Fortune Spread[126]

---

[125] Translator: This text is a translated excerpt *from Science des Signes, 1806, by M. M. d´Odoucet p. 60-64.*

[126] Translator: A rendition of the *Troisome Coup* from *Cours Theorique et Pratique, 1790, by Etteilla p. 58.*

Thus, the spread produces 66 cards, not including the querent card, which is placed in the center of the wheel, as we mentioned before.

The first column on the right, making up 11 cards, from 1 up to and including 11, correspond to the first part of the wheel, cards 34 up to and including 44. These two parts together recall the past.

The 11 cards of the top bar, from 23 up to and including 33, correspond to the 11 cards, that came second in the wheel, from 45 up to and including 55. These two parts together indicate the present.

The 11 cards of the second column, the one on the left, from 12 up to and including 22, correspond to the last 11 cards in the wheel, from 56 up to and including 66. They reveal, together with these latter, the future of the querent.

Let's move on to the operation; after having shuffled the cards mixing upright and reverse, it is given to the querent to open; we draw the first card after the cut and begin the spread, we place successively and in the order of their coming, the first cards in the positions marked 1, 2, 3, 4 etc. of the column on the right. The 11 cards in the marked positions 12, 13, 14, 15 etc. column on the left. The 11 cards in the positions marked 23, 24, 25, 26 etc. of the top bar. From the following 33 cards, we form a three-part wheel consisting of 11 cards each. The first part in the marked positions, from 34 up to and including 44. The second part from 45 up to and including 55. And the third and last part, from 56 up to and including 66. *See fig.*

There will be 11 cards remaining after this operation, however these should not be read.

In all, we thus have; 7x11 cards or 77, plus the one representing the querent, completing the total number of this book of 78.

The third operation is the reading in pairs. The cards of the wheel command those of the columns and the top bar;

but both order themselves by the querent, 1 or 8, depending on the sex.

Cards 34 to 44 command cards 1 to 11, and are thus the repertoire of past events. Cards 45 to 55 command cards 23 to 33, and are the events of the present. The 56 to 66 command cards 12 to 22, these are the events that prepare for the future of the querent.

For convenience sake, we may put in three columns these 66 cards representing the events of the three times in life; *past, present and future*, which will be read successively, one after the other, from right to left, from top to bottom. We will further divide each column into four spaces; A. B. C. D.

Future	Present	Past
D. C. B. A	D. C. B. A	D. C. B. A
. 12 . 56 .	. 23 . 45 .	. 1 . 34 .
. 13 . 57 .	. 24 . 46 .	. 2 . 35 .
. 14 . 58 .	. 25 . 47 .	. 3 . 36 .
. 15 . 59 .	. 26 . 48 .	. 4 . 37 .
. 16 . 60 .	. 27 . 49 .	. 5 . 38 .
. 17 . 61 .	. 28 . 50 .	. 6 . 39 .
. 18 . 62 .	. 29 . 51 .	. 7 . 40 .
. 19 . 63 .	. 30 . 52 .	. 8 . 41 .
. 20 . 64 .	. 31 . 53 .	. 9 . 42 .
. 21 . 65 .	. 32 . 54 .	. 10 . 43 .
. 22 . 66 .	. 33 . 55 .	. 11 . 44.

Space B, will be occupied only by cards from the wheel, space C only by the cards from the columns or from the top bar. The space assigned A, is the normal place of the querent who accidentally moves to D, when the space B is occupied by a card which, in the particular case, controls the card in C, and thus forces the querent card to D.

Example.
For the present in position 46 and 24:

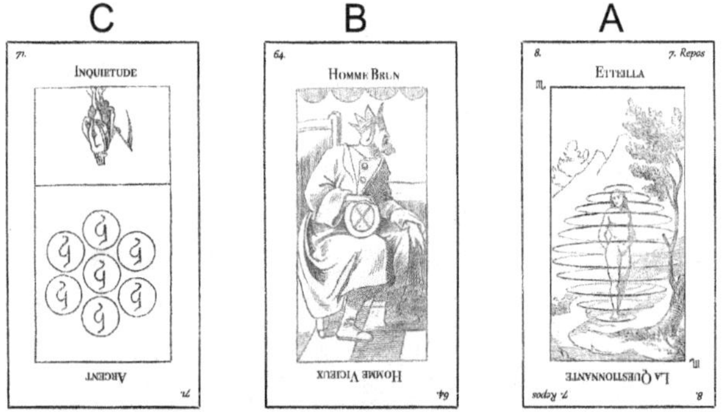

This combination may be read; a female querent dealing with a browned haired man, perhaps a banker, she may owe him money, which causes her a great deal of distress, but she need not worry, this will end, Saturn in the upright.

Example.
For the future in position 59 and 15:

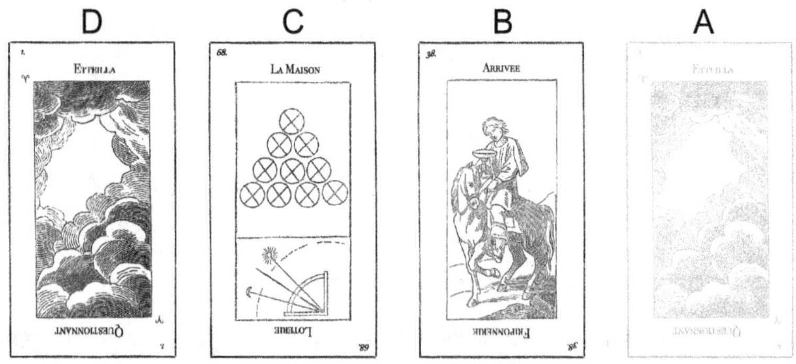

Card no. 38 followed by no. 68 triggers the interpretation; "you will soon be the owner of a property", and opens the space D for the male querent card. This reading may therefore come out as; The male querent is about to become a property owner with proceeds from a speculation.

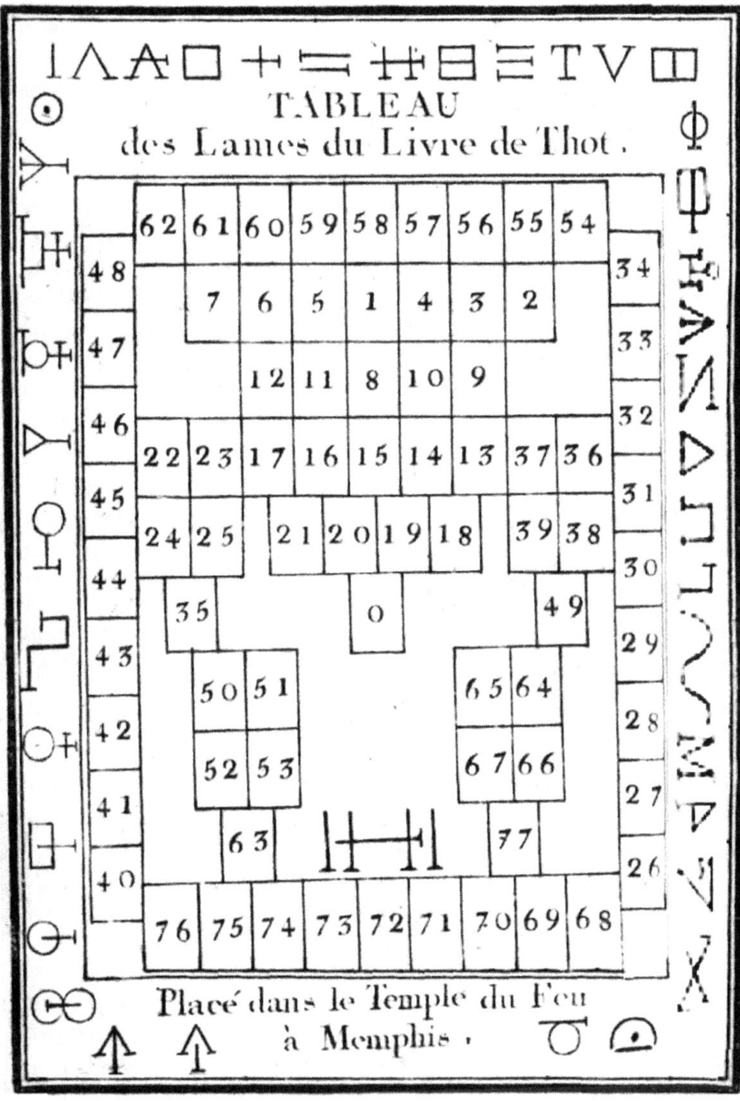

The Table for the cards of the Book of Thoth. From *Science des Signes*, 1806, by M. M. d´Odoucet, pages x and xj.(A replica of Etteilla, from his 4th cahier). Credit: Warburg Institute

APPENDIX

TEMPLE OF FIRE

"The Temple of Fire was dedicated to the eternal, through the hieroglyphs or the symbols of the sun, there to come closer to the minds of the Egyptians, to the Spirit of the purest fire, pervading and animating all the universe."[127]

Man is the most perfect creation of God, although everything, the whole of nature, reflects God´s perfection. This philosophy is written in the book of Thot more intelligibly than in Genesis, whose translators, in creating this text, corrupted the message.

The philosophy in this book is not absurd metaphysics based on assumptions relating to the way of seeing. It relates to God, to man and to nature. The first Magi of Egypt united in the number seventeen under Mercury 3rd of the name[128], in the year 171 of the deluge or the great flood, only put in this book philosophical and scientific truths, that is certain. God, it is said in Genesis, created the world in six days. Recalling that Noah who knew of creation, taught it to his children, Ham, Shem and Japheth; and Moses, who was raised by the Egyptians, and educated by their Sages or Magi, spoke the truth.

Then came the seventh day, which was that of rest. I devised this rest, which the Septuagints[129] and other

---

[127] Translator: *Manière de se récréer avec le jeu de cartes nommées Tarots, by Etteilla, p. 11. (transl.).*

[128] Translator: Athotis, "the king-physician" was one of the first rulers of ancient Egypt and was believed to be a descendant of Mercury.

[129] Translator: Septuagint is the Greek translation of the Old Testament.

interpreters of the Pentateuch[130] did not know how to make.

I explain the gap between the day of rest and the action of man, and all this by the book of Thot or the encyclopedia of the Egyptians under the heavens. In this sublime book, speaking in symbols, gives like the Pentatenque, Esdras, Ecclesiastes, Solomon etc., the road of the work, and does not conflate it, as the philosophers have done, inserting paragraphs on moral, politics and civil histories, etc. If we want to follow the passages of this great work, we must support our theory to the Hieroglyphs; if we make a mistake, the error is easily spotted, because we would no longer have the cards, as they would have been used, and therefore would not be able to be put it in their proper place; as the cards must be taken, from operation to operation, without interruption, in the three operations. At each fertile reading, it is necessary to leave 1, then 2; then 3, even when only 2 are left in front of you. Alas the result is mere vulgar chemistry.

In instructing my student, I made him understand that man is a compound made of three substances: a soul, a mind and a body. From the union of these three substances result life, to exist, to act, etc. and that for each of these substances the Magi profess and exercise a particular medicine; that of the soul through the exercise of worship; that of the mind with the science of symbols, known as the medicine of the mind; that of the body by curing diseases. These three medicines were transmitted, inscribed in hieroglyphic figures, on 78 gold cards by the heads of the most ancient of the peoples of the earth, by the descendants of Ham, who possessed books, of the original sciences and arts, and who already lived in families and in tribes, when the Shemians led their flocks still, and when the Japhethans travelled to go to found the empire of China.

---

[130] Translator: The 5 books of the Torah.

Moving on to the science of symbols, I showed him that among the Egyptians everything was made tangible in the most common and intellectual manner; *rest* was expressed by the *circle*; *movement*, by *clarity*; the *mind*, by the *triangle*; *union*, by the *lines*; the *engine*[131], through the *center*; *animation*, by the *sun* etc. So, they express everything by distinct and natural symbols.

The state was divided into four orders or columns, each of which had its particular chiefs, and all subordinate to a supreme chief. The first order was *agriculture*, producing enough to satisfy the primary needs of man, that of feeding his life. Its distinctive features; the color yellow and the vegetative club.

The second was the *priesthood*: these ancient people considered that after having received life and the means to maintain it, it was essential to give thanks to the divine engine. Its distinctive features were the color of purple and a priestly cup.

The third was the *military*, because after having received life, obtained the means to maintain it and having expressed gratitude, it was necessary to think of preserving the whole by an active surveillance. Its distinctive features were the color velvet red and a plain sword.

The fourth was *commerce*. To be sure it is not enough to exist, to eat and to preserve, it is still necessary to extend one´s connections and one´s relations. They considered this fourth order, the strongest of supports. The foundation of their government from which it was formed, the place the connection and its animation. It´s distinctive features are that of the color blue and a sun, the coin of gold.

Finally, I assigned to this amateur the different points according to which man can devote himself to the science

---

[131] Translator: *Le moteur.*

of symbols, offering him this line; that one can leap from simple amusement to perfect scientific knowledge:

So, in dealing with this science in the first degree, if we encounter truths, we will not have the ability to give a complete interpretation: For example, a trip is announced; but is it prudent to do so? It will be advantageous; but will this advantage not lead to a chain of misfortunes?

The insights of one situation is followed by another. It remains to be understood, whether these successes will be the fruit of perfidy.

At the 2nd degree we discover the results, although science at this point is still being learned, one is usually more reserved than those who have only the first degree.

On the 3rd we proceed confidently and with ease; but it is advisable to master the magic of science as Raphael had the magic of painting.

With mastery of these three degrees and of magic, one is astonished; one throws a bit of administration and one can behave artfully in all the principal events of life.

This course in the science of symbols, which I am publishing today is the repertoire of the various lectures, that I have given to my pupils from the works of Etteilla, made clearer and more within the scope of his teachings; explaining the intelligence and the magic of this science by avoiding the absurdities of charlatans, of illumnites, of demonographers and of the so-called diviners. This brings back the sole consideration of nature; it makes us examine the causes, direct the effects, and it provides the element of foresight and the practice of all moral and social virtue.[132]

---

[132] Translator: This text on the Book of Thoth and the Temple of Fire is a translated excerpt *from Science des Signes, 1806, by M. M. d´Odoucet p.* vij – xjv.

List of books

Manière de se Récréer avec le jeu de cartes nommées Tarots
Pour servir de premier Cahier a cet Ouvrage.
by Jean-Baptiste Alliette (Etteilla)
1 of 4 Cahiers or books published 1783-1786

Cours Théorique et Pratique du livre de Thot
by Jean-Baptiste Alliette (Etteilla)
Published in 1790

Science des Signes, ou Medecine de l'Esprit,
Connue sous le nom d'Art de tirer les Cartes
by M. M. d'Odoucet,
Published around 1806

Le Grand ETTEILLA,
ou l'art de Tirer les Cartes et de dire la Bonne Aventure
by Julia Orsini
Published from 1838

Les Recreations de la Cartomancie ou description pittoresque
De chacune des Cartes du Grand Jeu de l'Oracle des Dames
by Mlle Lemarchand
Published in 1867

Theoretischer und Praktischer Unterricht über das Buch Thot
oder über die höhere Kraft, Natur und Mensch, mit Zuverläßigkeit die
Geheimnisse des Lebens zu enthüllen und Orakel zu ertheilen: nach
der Egyptier wunderbarer Kunst
by Verlag von J. Scheible, Stuttgart
Published in 1857

Le Grand Etteilla,et le Tarot Egyptien
by Collette Sylvestre-Haeberle
Published in 1996

Le grand livre de L'Etteilla tarots égyptiens
by Emmanuel San Emeterio
Published in 1997

Initiation pratique au Tarot Égyptien. Le grand Etteilla
by Claude Darche
Published in 2002

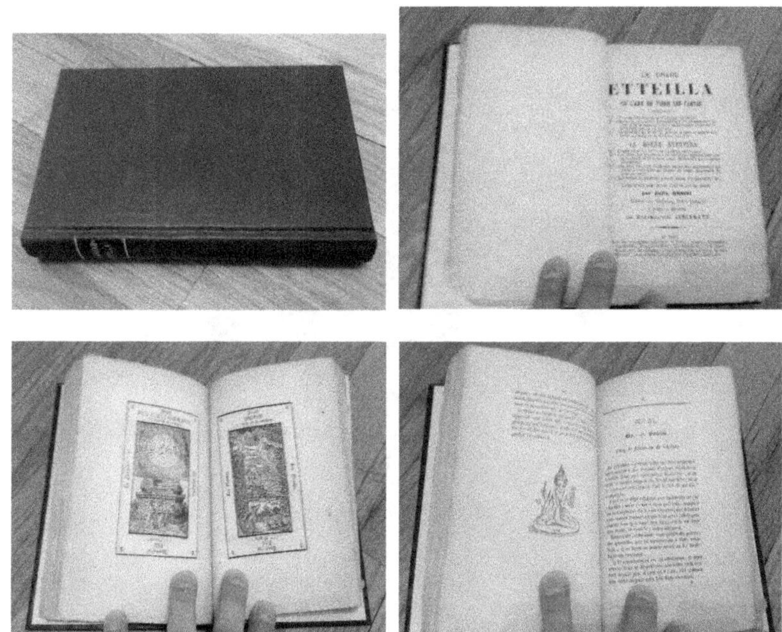

Images from translator´s Julia Orsini booklet.

Images from translator´s Lemarchand booklet.

Other book translations from the same author:

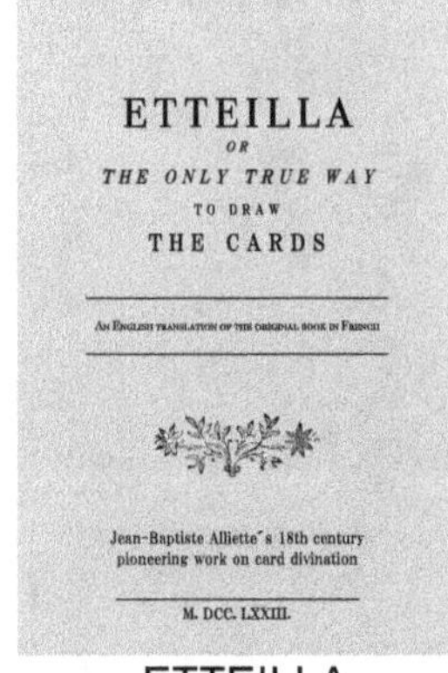

ETTEILLA

Tarot de Marseille
by Paul Marteau

Tarot decks;

The Lemarchand tarot deck

The Z.Lismon tarot deck

9 788826 927064 8